RALLYING

THE 4 WHEEL DRIVE REVOLUTION

A FOULIS Motoring Book

First published 1986
© Palatine Hill

Published by:
Haynes Publishing Group, Sparkford, Near Yeovil,
Somerset BA22 7JJ, England

Haynes Publications Inc.
861 Lawrence Drive, Newbury Park,
California 91320 USA

British Library Cataloguing in Publication Data

Robson, Graham
    Rallying : the 4 wheel drive revolution — 2nd ed.
    (A Foulis motoring book).
    1.   Four-wheel drive cars. Rallying
    I. Title
    796.7'2

ISBN 0-85429-723-5

Library of Congress Catalogue No.
Rallying 4WD 88-81752

Produced by:
Palatine Hill,
Watercombe Studios, Watercombe Park,
Lynx Trading Estate,
Yeovil, Somerset.

Printed in England by: Haynes Publishing Group

ACKNOWLEDGEMENTS

In writing a book like this, memory was useful, but an archive was essential. In that archive were rooms-full of records, some of them-my own, but others derived from books and magazines.

For that reason, therefore, I'd like to acknowledge the invaluable worth of the two principal British rallying annuals:

World Rallying Numbers 1 to 10 - by Martin Holmes.

Rallycourse from 1982/83 to date - edited by Mike Greasley.

- and, of course, I'd have been lost without being able to refer to magazines like *Autosport* and *Motoring News,* which tell us all so much, so often, and in such detail.

I gathered much of the material - the facts, figures, and opinions in the test - over the years for my own use, but I needed help from the teams to get things up to date.

In particular, the team managers, and the British press contacts for Audi, Austin-Rover, Citroen, Ford, Lancia, Mazda, Opel, Peugeot, Porsche, Toyota and Vauxhall all helped considerably.

Many of the black-and-white technical pictures and drawings have been supplied by the factories themselves, and tell a fascinating story, while some of the colour plates also come from the same source.

To name but a few, Juliette Brindley, Paul Buckett, Steve Woolmington, Paul Ormond, Paul Davies, John Evans, Jeremy Snook, Lorraine Parramore, Anne Routledge, David Palmer and Elizabeth Aves all made it a lot easier to provide the full story.

There are, however, three other photographers who have made my job easier:

Hugh Bishop
for some excellent colour action shots

Martin Holmes
for many black-and-white studies

Ralph Hardwick
for filling in the gaps.

Thank you all.

GRAHAM ROBSON

Right

The Mitsubishi Colt Starion was a 4 × 4 'conversion' which the Japanese concern eventually cancelled before it could be homologated.

(Photo: Hugh Bishop)

Far Right

Rob Collinge's Range Rover performed with great distinction in the Safari of the early 1980s. Ideal country for four-wheel-drive!

(Photo: Hugh Bishop)

Below

The massive Dodge Ramcharger made quite an impact when it turned up on the Safari of 1981. This was what 4 × 4 rallying meant at first - but not for long!

(Photo: Hugh Bishop)

CONTENTS

Above
The Audi Quattro was a sensational addition to World rally in 1981, when its four-wheel-drive capabilities were demonstrated. This was Hannu Mikkola's San Remo car -but Michele Mouton won the event in the other Quattro.

Right
Absolute commitment from Stig Blomqvist's A2 Quattro on icy tarmac, near Monte Carlo in 1983. He finished third overall, the best of the Quattros. *(Photo: Hugh Bishop)*

INTRODUCTION

Ten years ago there were no four-wheel drive cars on sale in Europe. Five years ago, Audi's new four-wheel-drive Quattro was just starting to make its mark in World Championship rallying. Today, no competitive rally team can afford to be without a four-wheel-drive car. In a decade, therefore, rallying has undergone a complete revolution.

I intended this book to celebrate the current breed of exciting Group B cars, but now I must make it a valediction instead. The original Quattros were fast enough, but it took just two seasons - 1984 and 1985 - to prove that Group B performance was increasing far too rapidly. Before long, the cars were much too quick for the roads and tracks they were asked to use, and the spectators could no longer relate to them. The horrifying events of 1986 - and the complete turn about of FISA's thinking about rallying which followed them - mean that I now have to tell the complete story of the fastest rally cars the world has ever seen.

What follows is a technical story - of how four-wheel-drive became viable, how various manufacturers adopted it, and used its properties. I could, I suppose, have glorified in the glamour, the speed, the colour, and the spectacle of these Group B cars but, once an engineer, always an engineer - and I found the most fascination in writing about the cars and their equipment, rather than their successes.

At the time of writing, the authorities were trying to reduce the performance of rally cars, and make it reasonable for them to be used on the roads of the world. For a time, no doubt, this will work, but in a few years I would bet that the cars will be as fast as ever they were in 1985 and 1986.

How do I know? The administrators of the sport have persistently tried to slow down the single seater Formula One cars. They always failed, and they will fail again. The same thing, I am sure, will happen to rallying.

No matter. Here; I think for the first time, is the story of four-wheel-drive in rallying, and the Group B cars which were designed to use such systems. I'm glad I was around to see these cars performing at the time. It was a fascinating time, which we may never see again.

Graham Robson

July 1986

Introduction to Second Edition

Even though Group B was killed off at the end of 1986, four-wheel-drive technology flourished. In a very short time a new generation of Group A cars was also developed, and look likely to be dominant into the 1990s and beyond. This, then, is the 'story so far'.

THE PRELUDE TO FOUR-WHEEL-DRIVE

Rallying in the '70s

The first World Championship rally to be won by a four-wheel-drive car was the Swedish, of February 1981, when Hannu Mikkola demonstrated the advantages of Audi Quattro traction on ice and snow. The second, by Michele Mouton in another Quattro, was on the various tarmac or gravel stages of San Remo, in Italy, later in the same year. It was the first proof that Audi's obsession with four-wheel-drive, in rallying, was going to work ...

So, why had this taken so long to happen? There were two reasons - one simple, and one, with hindsight, rather strange. The simple reason was that the use of four-wheel-drive in big-time rallying had been forbidden before 1979, but the rather more surprising one was that until Audi proved otherwise, few were prepared to believe that four-wheel-drive would work!

It is wonderful, now, to be able to look back, after the event, and decide that the rise, to domination, of four-wheel-drive rally cars in the 1980s was inevitable; yet even after the Quattro started winning rallies in 1981 there were still many design engineers, and experienced team managers, who thought it not necessary for *their* new cars.

If rally cars had not become monstrously powerful, perhaps four-wheel-drive would not have been needed, after all. Indeed, for several years in the 1970s, rallycar performance stayed on a plateau, and most drivers and team managers were happy for this situation to persist.

Let's go back more than 20 years, to the early-1960s, to see where, and how, the power race got under way. Until then, the world's best rally cars had been lightly-modified production machines - cars as different as the Sunbeam Rapier and the Mercedes-Benz 220SE, the Triumph TR3A and the Ford Zephyr, the Saab 96 and the Volvo PV544. At which point three new models - the Austin-Healey 3000, the BMC Mini-Cooper S, and the Ford Lotus-Cortina - were developed as 'homologation specials', and the upwards performance spiral began.

It meant an immediate increase, not only in outright power, but in power-to-weight ratio. A Triumph TR3A, for instance, had about 100 bhp and weighed about 2,500 lb., whereas a fully-developed Big Healey had more than 200 bhp, and weighed about 2,600 lb. At the other extreme, by 1967, not only did a Mini-Cooper S have about 120 bhp and a weight of no more than 1,600 lb., but it also had front-wheel-drive stability and response.

The 'homologation' specials started in the U.K., but it wasn't long before the French, and the Italians, joined in as well. To fight the Brits, the French produced the Renault R8 Gordini, while the Italians built the lightweight Lancia Fulvia HF. When those cars were joined by the amazingly simple but effective Escort Twin-Cam,

Top Left
The fastest front-engined 4 × 4 in captivity? Martin Schanche's Ford Escort, with Xtrac transmission, dominated rallycross in 1984.

(*Photo: Hugh Bishop*)

Bottom Left
Private enterprise! The rear-drive RED 4T of 1984 became the four-wheel-drive RED 4 × 4T of 1985, on the basis of the Ford Sierra.

(*Photo: Hugh Bishop*)

The second evolution Sport Quattro S1 was a strange-looking, but very effective, rally car, for all those aerodynamic aids had a genuine job to do. Walter Rohrl astonished everyone by winning this, the 1985 San Remo rally, in great style.

(*Photo: Hugh Bishop*)

the very specialised rear-engined Alpine-Renaults, and the ultra-reliable Porsche 911s, rallying took on an entirely new dimension.

In less than ten years, rallying had changed, from a sport for plucky, well-built, but essentially standard production cars, to one for special cars which had all manner of extra equipment homologated to make them faster and more versatile. But this was only the beginning; all the cars so far mentioned had engines which were already available, and body structures which were essentially standard.

Then came the 1970s, and yet another change of emphasis. Not only were cars allowed to carry sponsorship (which made the sport much more colourful than before, and which helped bring professional marketing, and 'razzmatazz' on to the motoring scene), but a series of new cars were developed which were *only* intended for use in motor sport.

Most of the rallying factories followed the same design path - namely to start from the basis of a series-production machine, to ruthlessly throw out anything they did not find suitable for motor sport, and to substitute special parts in place. Perhaps this was not done on the limited number of so-called 'road cars' which had to be built to satisfy homologation requirements, but it was certainly done by any serious competitor,

and always done by the 'works' teams themselves.

The two perfect examples of this approach were the Ford Escort RS1800, and the Fiat 131 Abarth Rallye. At a casual glance (and at a distance, it must be admitted ....) these cars looked as if they were very close relations of the mass production/meek-and-mild saloons on which they were based which were sold in their hundreds of thousands, but under the skin of the competition cars, there were enormous, and expensive, differences. In the Fiat, for instance, there was a 16-valve twin-cam engine, a unique Collotti transmission, and independent rear suspension, in the Escort there was a Cosworth-designed 16-valve twin-cam engine, a West German five-speed ZF gearbox, and an entirely different back axle and rear suspension layout.

It was really quite pointless for the bar-room pundits to suggest that it was 'cheating' and that 'showroom cars' should be used instead - Group 2 (early 1970s) or Group 4 (late 1970s) rules were quite specific, and there was no doubt that these cars met the rules.

The alternative approach was to design and build a car which was *only* intended for use in motor sport. This was a very ambitious way of going rallying, for it meant that a completely special structure, and chassis items, had to be

Top Left
A quarter of a century ago, rallying was for mass-production cars - Peter Procter and the author (in a Sunbeam Rapier) on the 1962 Monte Carlo rally.

Bottom Left
The Austin Healey 3000 was one of the very first really fast rally cars, and was at its peak in 1965. The Morley wins in the 1965 RAC Rally.

Below
One of the first 'homologation specials' was Ford's Lotus-Cortina - Vic Elford and David Stone in the 1966 Alpine rally.

Above
If there had been deep snow on the 1986 Monte Carlo rally, the second-evolution Sport Quattro S1's 'snow plough' front-end might have been very useful! Walter Rohrl was the driver.

(Photo: Hugh Bishop)

Top Right
BMC's Mini-Cooper S was a tiny, but versatile, rally car, with 1.3 litres, and front-wheel-drive. Rauno Aaltonen won the 1967 Monte Carlo rally in this car.

Opposite
By the mid 1970s rally cars were becoming complex - this being the 2.3 litre 16-valve engine used in Vauxhall's Chevette HS.

developed, and that the legal rigmarole of getting legal (as opposed to sporting) homologation, and later Type Approval, all had to be tackled from scratch.

Ford dabbled seriously with such a design in 1970/71 (the GT70), but abandoned it as more and more of the practical difficulties *and* the costs became apparent, and in the end the only such specially-designed rally car to make it to the market place was Lancia's stupendously successful Stratos. On reflection, such a project was so complex that only an enthusiastic and resourceful company like Lancia could possibly have carried it through to fruition.

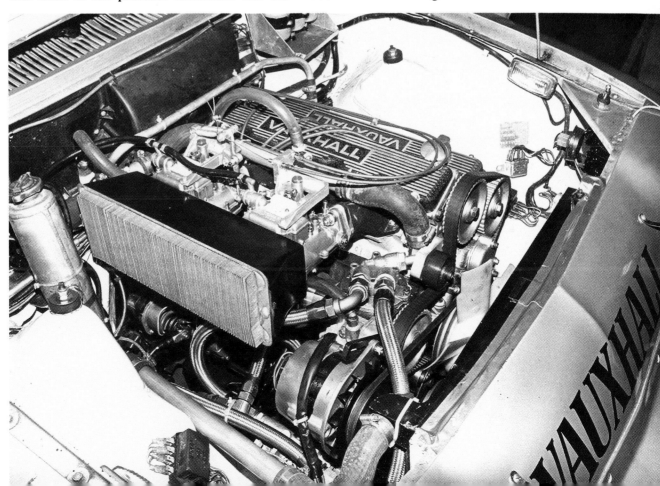

Almost all the competitive late-1970s rally cars were highly-tuned conversions of less specialised machinery - Toyota having their twin-cam-engined Celicas, Datsun their twin-cam Violets, Vauxhall their sixteen-valve slant-engined Chevettes, Renault their mid-engined conversion of the front-engined R5, and Opel their sixteen-valve (Cosworth designed) 2.4-litre version of the Ascona. Saab tried hard with a 16-valve twin-cam version of their 99 model, but eventually withdrew when they saw the costs becoming excessive.

What was technically interesting was that, in spite of the mechanical disparity of all the cars and engines being used by teams hoping to win World Championship rallies, the teams mostly tended to end up with engine sizes between 2.0 and 2.4 litres, power outputs between 230 bhp and 260 bhp, and unladen weights of between 2,000 lb. and 2,400 lb. (900 kg to 1,100 kg). The vast majority of the best cars had front engines and gearboxes, with rear wheel drive, and most even had solid rear axles. By the standard of the mid-1980s, they were relatively simple (though, at the time, we looked on a Stratos or even a

fully-developed 2-litre Ford Escort RS as a sophisticated machine), which meant that a good many private teams could afford to build their own 'works replicas' and win events all round the globe.

For several years, the straight line performance of front-line World Championship rally cars reached something of a plateau. A late-1970s Ford Escort RS could rush up to 100 mph from rest in something like 16 seconds and the Fiat Abarth 131 Rallye was slightly slower than that, whereas the Talbot Sunbeam-Lotus, the Vauxhall Chevette HSR and the Opel Ascona 400 could all get up to the three-figure mark in about 14 seconds. In general, they were all geared to reach about 120 mph in top gear (of a five-speed cluster, usually), which was considered quite enough except for ultra-fast events which used a lot of tarmac surfaced special stages. Only the Stratos, which had handling and reliability to match, and the Triumph TR7 V8, which did not, were noticeably faster than this.

From Point A to Point B, however, these cars definitely got faster and faster in the 1978-1981 period, this being almost entirely due to the development of better and more specialised tyres, to the detailed attention being given to suspension settings and brakes, and to the work which went into making their structures more

Top Left
There is nothing new about 'Yumping' shots! Vauxhall's Chevette HS was their first homologation special, with only 400 cars made.

Bottom Left
Throughout the 1970s, Ford's Escort RS1600 and (here) RS1800 were dominant in the UK, and important in World Championship rallies. Both were strictly conventional, with front engines, and rear-wheel-drive.

Below
Fiat's 131 Abarth saloon was about as far removed from a standard car's specification as you could get in the late 1970s.

and more rugged for use on loose, often rough surfaces.

If the World Championship for Makes had not resulted in a series of astonishingly close-fought contests between Ford, Fiat, and Nissan (Datsun), it would have been easy to suggest that rallying was marooned in a technical backwater. In just the same way, of course, Formula One motor racing had been little more than a glamorous 'Formula Cosworth' for a time in the 1970s.

It was time for an upheaval, and in 1979/80 this duly occurred. Four-wheel-drive was authorised - and the Audi Quattro was launched.

The two great Italian rally cars of the 1970s - the Alitalia-sponsored Lancia Stratos, and the Fiat 131 Abarth.

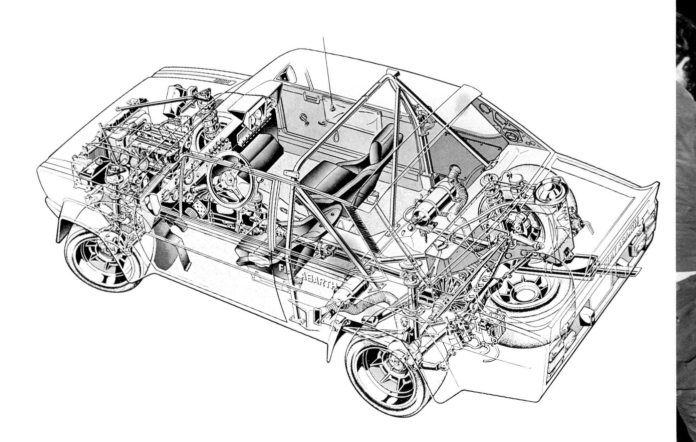

Fiat 131 Abarth saloon with an independent rear suspension graft, a 16-valve twin-cam 2 litre engine, and Colotti five-speed gearbox.

Below
Packed in there somewhere is an engine, transverse transmission, and rear drive - this being the 'business end' of the famous Lancia Stratos.

Before four-wheel-drive rally cars were invented, the Lancia Stratos was the most exciting machine on World Championship events - this being Sandro Munari's car on the Safari.

FOUR WHEEL TRACTION -THE THEORY

-and the practice!

It's not merely the arrival of four-wheel-drive for rally cars which interests me at this point, but the evolution of this type of chassis in private cars as a whole. In the mid-1980s, when there is a real rush of new four-wheel-drive cars, some as exotic as the Mercedes-Benz and BMW saloons, and some as humble as the little Fiat Pandas, it is easy to forget that there was only *one* such car on sale before the 1970s, and that that was the extremely costly Jensen FF.

The technical problem, of arranging to drive wheels at the same time as steering them, was solved many years ago, for there were commercial vehicles with this feature as early as the 1910s in North America, where the Four-Wheel-Drive Auto Co. sold trucks for the unsurfaced roads of the backwoods, and in Europe, where the Latil truck was probably first. Lots of different designs appeared during the First World War, and the layout mushroomed in the 1920s.

It took a lot longer for private cars to follow suit, mainly because they had so little power, and such big wheels, that there was really no need to drive more than two wheels in any case. Way back in 1904, however, there was a Dutch Spyker 4 x 4 racing car, with a vast 8.7-litre six-cylinder engine, although this never went into production, and even Bugatti produced two of the remarkable 4.9-litre straight-eight Type 53 4 x 4 racing cars in 1932.

There were several front-wheel-drive cars in the 1920s and 1930s, most notably the German DKWs and the French *traction avant* Citroens, but no four-wheel-drive machines. During the Second World War this layout received a boost, not only in the shape of the lovable and quite ubiquitous Jeep, but for large and heavy staff cars designed and built by Humber. Then, after the war, the world of motoring went back into its shell.

From 1945 to the mid-1960s, most of the world's cars had a conventional front engine/rear drive layout, though growing numbers of rear engine/rear drive, and front engine/front-wheel-drive models came on the European scene as well. But if you discount the Land-Rover, and its competitors, as a light commercial vehicle, that was that.

It was that erratic genius from Northern Ireland, Harry Ferguson, who picked up the challenge of four-wheel-drive, and began to develop a series of technically intriguing, but very complex, prototypes. Having made his fortune with the Ferguson tractor (and garnered a great deal of money, in damages, from Henry Ford, who decided to copy Ferguson's ideas without paying royalties), he could afford to spend it on such projects. It was to cost him a great deal of money for which - in his lifetime -there was no return.

The original Ferguson schemes were developed by Tony Rolt and that amazing driver/mechanic Freddie Dixon, but it was not until the mid-1950s, and following a move of design and development base to Coventry, that things began to look more serious. From time to time Ferguson tried to sell his ideas, and his patents, to the British motor industry, but as all the top men found him almost impossible to negotiate with, these moves always came to nothing.

However, it was after a visit to a Silverstone race meeting in May 1960 that he decided to build a racing car which incorporated all the Ferguson inventions, and experience gained to date. Unhappily, the tycoon did not live to see this car finished, for he died in October 1960, and the racing car itself, Project 99, a front-engined single-seater (power was provided by the four-cylinder Coventry Climax engine), was not actually unveiled until mid-1961.

P99 and the Novi single-seater race car which Ferguson Research built for the 1964 Indianapolis 500 race, are very important indeed to the story of four-wheel-drive, not only because they demonstrated that four-wheel-drive was feasible, and practical, for use in a competition car, but because they established a general layout which is still used today on a variety of production cars.

On P99, for instance, the engine was front mounted, with the main gearbox behind it, and a transfer gearbox incorporating a centre differential incorporated into that. The general layout of the box pushed the line of the drive several inches to the left side of the chassis, and from the centre differential there were exposed propeller shafts leading forward, alongside the engine sump, to a front differential, and rearwards, to the usual chassis-mounted final drive in the tail. Of equal significance, perhaps, was the fact that the centre and rear differentials incorporated limited-slip mechanisms, while the front diff. was free. It all sounds very familiar to a Ford Sierra XR4×4, or a BMW 325i 4×4 owner, doesn't it?

The principal personality in the design of P99 was Tony Rolt, who was then technical director of Harry Ferguson Research. In later years he was to become managing director of the re-named (FF Developments) concern, and it was under his direction that the modern generation of viscous coupling limited-slip differentials was developed.

Soon after P99 started racing (and it was successful on wet race days, let's never forget), Jensen Motors of West Bromwich signed an agreement with Ferguson to develop a four-wheel-drive layout for a new Jensen model. Work began in 1962, but it was not until the autumn of 1965 that the prototype C-V8 4×4 model was shown. A year later the C-V8 had been rendered obsolete by the impressively-styled Interceptor, and it was a lengthened-wheelbase version of this car, the FF, which became the first-ever British four-wheel-drive car to be put on sale.

The FF was built from 1966 to 1971, and only a few hundred of these expensive cars were ever sold. If nothing else, it proved two things -that at this time four-wheel-drive cars were not only technically feasible, but very safe and pleasant to drive, and that the FF system was extremely finicky to set up, and keep running properly for a long time. The advantages of the FF installation were sometimes masked, to press men, pundits, and customers, by the even greater promise of the crude aircraft-style Dunlop Maxaret anti-lock braking system which was also fitted as standard.

Jensen, like racing car constructors who dabbled with the system a few years later, soon discovered that four-wheel-drive only had some advantages, some of the time. On good hard roads where there was plenty of grip, a conventional rear-drive chassis could cope perfectly well, even with a great deal of torque, as was provided in this case by the massive Chrysler vee-8 engines. Modern tyres were so good that there were only a few cases, and a few moments, where four-wheel-drive was an advantage worth paying for. And an FF installation was extremely expensive at this time ...

Now it is time to get back to the basics of car design, and in particular the function of the tyres. To propel a car along the roads, the torque of the engine has to be translated into the torque of the driving wheels, and this has to be exchanged for a push (rear wheels) or a pull (front wheels) along the road surface by the tyres themselves. In all the excitement of the study of a car's chassis, and its road behaviour, it is altogether too easy to forget that the driver's entire security, and his feel for what is going on, is tied up in four rather small tyre contact patches with the road, each of which may be no larger than the average man's shoe.

Roadholding, grip, and 'balance', therefore, all depend on the tyres, so at this point we ought to summarise what a tyre may be asked to do.

These are its main functions:

(i) To provide contact with the road to transmit torque to propel the car along

(ii) To provide contact with the road to transmit braking forces, to slow the car down

(iii) To provide grip

(iv) To provide a supple cushion between uneven road surfaces and the occupants - to become the first part of the vehicle's suspension.

Nor is that all, for the tyres are expected to perform well on hard and smooth surfaces, on loose gravel and the like, in mud, or snow, or sand where there is reduced grip, or on ice and deep standing water where there may be very little grip indeed. Even as early as the 1920s, tyre designers knew that to keep the tyres working properly, they had to find ways of moving water, dirt, and snow out of the way of the rubber which was seeking to provide grip, and this is how the science (combined with the art) of tread design was pursued so avidly.

However, it is important to remember that a tyre is not possessed of un-natural powers. Within the limits of its construction, which encompass a fabric and/or metal wire based carcase, and rubber, or synthetic rubber-based compounds for the side walls and the tread, it can only do so much. It can drive, or brake, some of the time; it can bend to the will of the driver to create cornering grip some of the time, and it can also be steered, some of the time, to produce changes of the car's direction. Up to a point, a tyre can also be persuaded to carry out all of these functions at the same time, but it is not by any means as easy. The limits of tyre technology, rather than the limits of transmission design, held back the development of a proper four-wheel-drive system for a long time.

For many years (and, in some quarters, even up to the present day), designers and customers agreed that the most sensible way to design a car was for them to have one pair of wheels to do all the driving, and another pair of wheels to do all the steering. The obvious layouts which all produced this condition drove the rear wheels, and steered the fronts. It did not matter whether the engine was at the front of the car, in the tail, or mounted amidships, for the result was the same. It was *not*, however, practical to arrange for the front wheels to be driven and for the rear wheels to be steered; the dynamics were all wrong, as

anyone who has tried to reverse a conventional car at high speeds knows.

This layout worked very well indeed, and especially well on cars which were very powerful, and had tyres with grip limited by the technology of the day. From the 1930s on, however, it became clear that for packaging, and cost-efficiency reasons, there was a case for combining engine, transmission, drive to the wheels, and steering, at the same end of the car - which led to the evolution of front-wheel-drive cars.

This gave the car's four tyres a very different set of tasks. At the rear, now all they had to do was to transmit braking and cornering forces (and to hold the body structure off the ground!): at the front, not only did the tyres have to brake, steer and corner, but they had to transmit driving torque as well. That wasn't too difficult if the car in question was low powered, or had generously-proportioned tyres to match a higher output. By the 1960s and 1970s, however, there were very powerful front-wheel-drive cars like the Citroen SM Coupés, and the Oldsmobile Toronados, which demonstrated that an excess of torque could very easily turn a stable-cornering machine into an under-steering monster.

I can now equate all these problems to the rally cars of the 1960s and 1970s, and show how, and why, the arrival of four-wheel-drive was inevitable, if and when the regulations should permit it to be used. The BMC Mini-Cooper S cars had been amazingly successful, especially in loose surface, and winter-condition, rallies, just so long as they were not 'too powerful for chassis'. Once their lusty 1.3-litre engines began to develop enough power and torque to embarrass the tiny 10 in. wheels they rode upon, their balance was lost. With up to about 100/110 bhp, a Mini-Cooper S was every rally driver's dream car, but with more than about 120 bhp (which was quite easily achievable, even in Group 2 form, by 1968), it proved very difficult to drive to its limits. In later years Saab, with their very powerful turbocharged engines, encountered similar problems, and no modern attempt to develop a competitive front wheel drive car (a BDA-engined Ford Fiesta, for instance) has succeeded.

Cars driving the rear wheels always had much more in reserve, especially as the designers could increase the width of the tyres to absorb all the torque without having to worry

Above
With too much power through the steered front wheels, rally cars tend to understeer (Aaltonen BMC Mini-Cooper S)

Left
.... and with too much through the rears, they tended to go sideways (Monte Carlo rally, on ice).

about the effort required by the driver to steer such fat covers. In any case, the use of excess power only broke traction and pitched the cars sideways into glorious power-oversteering slides, which the spectators loved to watch, and which the skilful drivers could easily control. It was even said that the *real* joy of driving such a car was that it could be steered from the front, or from the rear, at will!

Even so, the 210 bhp developed by an Austin-Healey 3000 was demonstrably too much for the skinny tyres and wheels used in the early 1960s, and the typical 230-260 bhp of a mid-1970s Group 4 car meant that there was a great deal of wheelspin, sideways motoring, and general loss of time, on any but the most grippy of tarmac surfaces. Even the best of the 'works' Lancia Stratos cars, with its engine and much of the weight concentrated close to the driven wheels, had a great deal of trouble in transmitting 290 bhp without wheelspin breaking out.

This, of course, explains why there was no great advance, either of rally car engine power, or of power-to-weight ratios, between about

1973 and 1980. Until, or unless, tyre manufacturers could provide more grip, or limited-slip differentials could be made even more versatile, there was little point in getting more power from an engine if it could not be translated into grip, and acceleration. Not only was the existing power enough to win rallies, but it was all that could be used fully in any case. This was proved, in no uncertain manner, by the Group B Toyota Celica Twincam Turbo, which weighed no more than a Group 4 Ford Escort, Talbot Sunbeam-Lotus, or Fiat 131 Abarth Rallye; yet it also had a 350 bhp engine, a ferocious appetite for tyres, and was only competitive on long endurance events where its strength was, quite literally, its strength.

Throughout this time, of course, the use of four-wheel-drive cars was specifically forbidden in International rallies, although from time to time events like the 'Press on Regardless' rally of North America invoked special rules and allowed cross-country type 4x4s to enter, and rallies like the Scottish usually had a class meant to encourage Land Rover entries from the Services.

Above
The world's best drivers harnessed power-oversteer to give them four steerable wheels, and *at the time* **in the 1970s it was the quickest way round loose corners (Roger Clark, Ford Escort RS 1800).**

Below
Even with the engine and transmission in the rear, two-wheel-drive could not cope with a serious lack of grip on winter events (Jean Ragnotti, Renault 5 Turbo, in testing).

Lancia's mid-engined Rally 037 was the most sophisticated mid-engined/rear-drive rally car, but it still struggled for grip on gravel roads (Miki Biasion, San Remo, 1984).
(Photo: Hugh Bishop)

There is still something of a mystery as to who lobbied FISA and the BPICA so strongly for four-wheel-drive to be authorised, but it can be no coincidence that Audi, who had strong motor sporting aspirations, were already developing a four-wheel-drive sports coupé when it actually happened ....

Whatever, up until the end of 1978, four-wheel-drive cars were not allowed to take part in major events, but from 1979 the authorisation came through. In 1979 and 1980 this made no difference to the competition at top level -though it meant that the Range Rover could start events like the Safari, and Bandama, and stand a chance of finishing with honour, if not actually winning (11th in 1980), while a Subaru 4x4 could compete in the Safari, and take 18th place in 1980. All this, of course, was something of an overture, or a sideshow - the Audi Quattro was coming, and would change the face of World Championship rallying.

Audi (whose series of front-engined rally coupés is described in detail in Chapter 5) were always quite convinced that they had hit on a winning formula for the early 1980s. Although they had quite a heavy car to start with, they were gambling that with a *lot* more power to overcome the power-to-weight problem, and four-wheel-drive to idealise the traction, they could have a winning car, straight out of the box.

This was a view by no means shared by everyone else in, or around, the rallying business. Some pundits thought that the complication of such systems had no place in rallying at that time, where rugged reliability, and the ability of rally cars to be 'fettled', or repaired, in minutes, was thought to be all-important. Others, and I was among them, thought the handling problems would be insuperable.

It is now time to hark back to the late 1960s, and to the brief flurry of four-wheel-drive Formula 1 single seater racing cars which erupted on the scene. There had been very little reaction to the enormously powerful four-wheel-drive Novi's showing at Indianapolis in 1964, where it had qualified fifth fastest, but been eliminated in a multiple pile-up on the second lap, and although BRM also commissioned a 4x4 1½-litre single-seater, it was not until 1967, when the American STP-Paxton gas-turbine car so nearly won at Indy, and 1968, when Lotus built a set of gas-turbine powered Type 56 cars for STP to use in the Indy 500 that the motor racing business sat up and took notice. Once again, Harry Ferguson Research had designed the transmission, which was laid out on conventional (to Ferguson) lines. Colin Chapman's reason for choosing four-wheel-drive was straightforward enough - he thought the turbine

28

engine's power output (of about 550 bhp) but with a monumental 500 lb. ft. of torque!) was too high to be fed through only two driving wheels.

Those fluorescent red cars completely dominated the race - and the headlines - at Indianapolis in 1968 (I was reporting the race for *Autocar,* and remember being electrified by their performance), and led until the very last few laps, when a minor gas turbine engine component broke, and caused both the surviving cars to retire. No matter - they handled well, and looked sensational; it was no wonder that other racing designers began to wonder if Chapman - Chapman the great innovator - knew something that they did not.

sound familiar? The result, in 1969, was that a positive rash of four-wheel-drive 3-litre Formula 1 cars was built. By mid-season a count encompassed Cosworth, Lotus, Matra, and McLaren - and none of these cars ever looked like being a success, or won a major event. The Cosworth, in fact, was tested but never raced - the only complete car ever produced by that famous Northampton-based concern.

Although all followed the same basic principle - that of having the squat Cosworth DFV engine turned round, and driving forward to a central transmission, and transfer gearbox, and having separate propeller shafts linking front and rear differentials, respectively, with those

Ford's first Group B project was a front engine/rear transmission and rear drive conversion of the Mk III Escort body shell. Boreham engineer John Griffiths guarding the test car in Portugal, 1982. *(Photo: Holmes)*

Those who understood his thinking, and could see the way that F1 was progressing, decided to follow suit, and those who didn't understand thought they had better tag along as well. Almost every constructor was using Cosworth DFV engines, these were becoming more powerful every season, and it was thought that the latest F1 tyres could no longer cope with the increased power and torque. Does all that

shafts running along one side of the centre line, in typical Ferguson fashion, none of the cars worked at all well. The rush to build was early in 1969, the short period of glory was in the summer of the same year, but by the end of 1969 it was all over.

What happened? To explain that, I would like to acknowledge Doug Nye's diligent research on the McLaren racing cars (*McLaren,* published by Hazleton Publishing), who summed up the craze as follows:

'Every one of these cars would represent an expensive and time-consuming dead end .... In

29

road racing drivers would find that they could not accustom themselves to the power understeer induced whenever a worthwhile share of engine power was directed through the front wheels. To retrieve some steering feel the only option was to reduce the share of power being fed to the front, and then one ended up simply with a conventional rear-wheel drive car, carrying well over 100 lbs extraneous weight in the complex transfer gearbox, forward propshaft and front final-drive and half-shaft arrangement ....'

When Ford prepared special four-wheel-drive Capris to use on the TV Rallycross circuits, they discovered all the same problems. Because it was possible to play around with the torque splitting arrangement of the centre differential (which could split its torque equally between front and rear, pass only 10 per cent one way and 90 per cent the other, or any intermediate combination of this), all such development tweaks were tried, but it was all in vain. After one season, these cars were abandoned by the factory, their only real advantage being in traction away from the start line, or out of particularly slippery corners.

It was for all these reasons that I wrote a rallying column in *Autocar* in October 1979, which was six months before the new Audi Quattro was unveiled. It was not that I doubted Audi's ability to produce a well-engineered job,

but that: '.... for competition success a lot more than brute power will be needed. The other important factors are, of course, power-to-weight ratio and handling.' One important problem, I thought, would concern transmitting a lot of power through the front wheels, something

The first four-wheel-drive competition car of modern times was the *twin* engined BMC Mini-Cooper S prototype of 1963. It raced once only, but was then abandoned.

For years, four-wheel-drive meant big cross country machines like this Jeep which took part in the 1974 World Cup Rally.

which had already caused problems for Ford and Fiat in developing 150 bhp front-wheel-drive Group 2 Fiestas and Stradas. I thought that: 'After all, sharing 300 bhp equally between two pairs of driving wheels will impose no less of an intractable problem in force vectors and rubber technology on the front wheels than Fiat and Ford have already found - quite literally intractable!

In later years, Audi's PR staff were delighted to wave a copy of these thoughts in my face and wondered if I wanted to recant, but I believe that I was only partly wrong, and that honours are still even. The point I was making was that the equal-torque-split method was not likely to be successful *against more sophisticated opposition,* and this was certainly proved to be the case once cars like the Peugeot 205 Turbo 16, and the Lancia Delta S4 came along. The Audi Quattro won, at first, because it had a better power-to-weight ratio than its principal opposition, and because it was the *only* four-wheel-drive car in world-class rallying.

However, even before the first competitive four-wheel-drive cars appeared in rallying, eminent designers were already making sketches, fingering their calculators, and working out their budgets. It would be fair to say that no other company actually began to design such a beast until they had watched the Quattro in action, assessed its strengths and its weaknesses, and decided on their plan of action. Even though competition cars can be designed, developed, and produced much more rapidly than a mass-production machine, this was still going to give the Quattro a long time on its own - even if it *did* cause a sensation in 1981, no competition was likely to appear before 1983 or even 1984.

Everyone understood why the Audi's 4 x 4 layout was arranged in its own particular manner, for it was perfectly clear that the Quattro was really a conversion of a front-engined, front-wheel-drive car; it might not have been the ideal layout, as far as weight distribution was concerned, but it was *there,* and it could be made to work.

Given a clean sheet of paper, however, no other designer seemed to agree with Audi's choice of a 50%/50% torque split between front and rear wheels, which in their case had been dictated by the design of the centre differential. This, coupled with the front-heavy weight distribution of the Quattro, caused some

eyebrows to be raised. You didn't need more than sixth form mathematics, and a working knowledge of tyre performance, to realise that this almost automatically meant that the front tyres were going to be worked much more severely than the rears, in which case the Quattro promised to be a classic 'power-understeerer' like all the 1960s/early 1970s front-wheel-drive breed had been.

Although it was agreed that there was no single 'best way' to position the important masses in a newly designed chassis - and by 'masses' I include the engine, main transmission, fuel tanks *and* passengers - it seemed that the ideal 4 x 4 rally car should have about the same weight on each wheel while the car was at rest, so that there would be more than 50 per cent of the weight over the driven rear wheels under hard acceleration.

To match this, it was agreed that the transmission ought to be not only designed so that the torque split between front and rear wheels could be changed quickly during an event (by swopping components at the side of the road), but that for most cases something like one third of the torque should go to the front wheels and two thirds to the rear wheels. This, it was thought, would equalise the work the two pairs of tyres would have to do, most of the time.

It also meant that, if the structure, suspension, and transmission was doing a proper job, the car could have neutral, if not even slightly over-steering handling at all times, that it could be cornered a little bit sideways in the traditional manner, and that the steering would not be impossibly heavy, nor insensitive.

Whereas all the signs were that the Quattro type of four-wheel-drive was going to make such a car difficult to drive really fast, the 'idealised' layout described above would still leave the car handling as a rally car should - in other words, in a manner where its attitude could be changed by the driver's actions, and where his amazing skills could be superimposed on the machinery, rather than having to come to terms with it.

That, of course, was just the theory! It would be two or three seasons before it could be proved, or disproved, by practical experience.

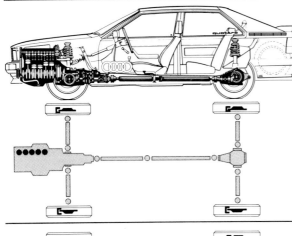

This was the layout of Audi's Quattro coupé, which revolutionised rallying when it started competing in 1980/81. The five-cylinder engine was way out front, and there was a fixed 50/50 front/rear torque split, but for three years it was the sport's dominant car.

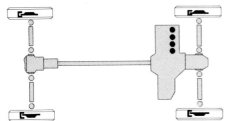

The Audi's transmission system was compromised by a far-forward engine. Later the Citroen BX 4TC would use a similar layout.

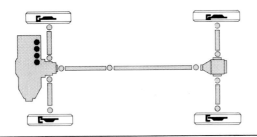

Peugeot were the first to produce a purpose-built four-wheel-drive rally car, and the *only* manufacturer to choose a transverse engine/main transmission installation.

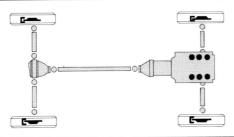

Citroen's Visa 1000 Pistes was really a four-wheel-drive conversion of a transverse engine/front-drive chassis. One of Ford's Escort rallycross variants used the same system in the mid 1980s.

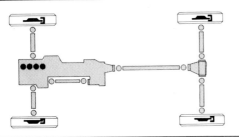

For the MG Metro 6R4, Williams Grand Prix Engineering mounted a vee-6 engine as far back as possible, with the gearbox ahead of it, and the rear final drive alongside the engine sump.

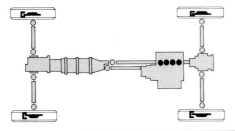

Opel's still-born Kadett 4 x 4 Group S car used an Xtrac transmission, with the front propeller shaft alongside the engine. Similar (but non-Xtrac) systems were used in the Opel Manta 400 4 x 4, the Colt Starion, the Ford Sierra XR4 x 4, and several other four-wheel-drive 'conversions'.

Ford's RS200 installation was unique, with a mid-mounted engine, and a forward transmission/four-wheel-drive casing.

1981-1983-QUATTRO DOMINATION

Traction first, but as for handling...

There was a great deal of talk about four-wheel-drive rally cars, and the Quattro in particular, before it ever made the start line of an event. The project, after all, was already an open secret in 1979, and the car itself was launched in March 1980 - but it was not until October that a rally-prepared example made an appearance, as Course Car, in the Algarve. At this time I can clearly recall talking to world-class drivers who had *not* been invited to join the Audi team, who were not at all convinced that the concept would work.

There was so much scepticism among rival designers of rally cars about four-wheel-drive, at this time, that even after the Quattro had been announced, new and more conventional layouts were initiated. The Ford Escort RS1700T, the Lancia Rally 037, the Nissan 240RS, the Opel Manta 400, and the Toyota Celica Twin-Cam Turbo were all designed in 1980 and 1981. In fairness, however, I should point out that only one of these designs - the mid-engined Lancia Rally 037 - was ever a match for the Quattro, and then only in certain conditions.

Audi, however, had laid their plans as early as 1978, when work on the new Quattro began, and even before the car was ready to be announced they had invited Hannu Mikkola to try a prototype model in simulated rally conditions. Hannu was so impressed that he signed a development and testing contract for 1980, and turned this into a rally driving deal for 1981 and beyond.

The road car received rave notices from the motoring press when they tried it on ice and snow in the spring of 1980, but the first proper evidence of its worth as a rally car came in the Algarve, where Hannu Mikkola, running the Quattro as a Course Car, set fastest time on 24 of the 30 special stages, and would certainly have won (from established drivers like Bernard Beguin, in a Porsche 911, and Antonio Zanini in a Ford Escort RS) if his car had been homologated.

For 1981 there was a full-scale Quattro assault on the World Championship, where the other competitive teams were Rothmans-Ford (Escort RS), Talbot (Sunbeam-Lotus), and Datsun (Violet). Hannu Mikkola and France's first-lady of rallying, Michele Mouton, were to drive the 'works' cars, with a third car also appearing on occasion. It was the best possible season for the Quattro to make a big effort, as Ford, Fiat, and Lancia (the big names of the late 1970s) had all temporarily withdrawn from the scene, so the tempo of competition was reduced.

The records show that in this first year, the Quattro struggled for supremacy, but that by the end of the season it was already the dominant car at World level. There was never any doubt about its pace, right from the start, but it was already quite clear that even the Superstars found it very difficult to drive on the limit, and that on tarmac (where four-wheel-drive traction was not of such critical importance)

it was never going to be the best machine for the job.

In its very first big event (Monte Carlo), Mikkola's car set eight fastest stage times before going off the road due to a driver error - and in its second event (Sweden), Mikkola guided it to an easy victory. After the peak, though, there was a trough, for in Portugal Mikkola's car blew its engine after leading at half distance, in Corsica both cars retired with blown engines, and in the Acropolis all three cars (Wittman drove the third) were disqualified for infringing the technical regulations. On the Acropolis there was also a nasty fire at a service point which put team manager Walter Treser in hospital for a time, and also led to a reshuffle in personnel immediately afterwards.

During the summer the battle between Datsun and Talbot for the Makes Championship, and between Ari Vatanen (Rothmans-Ford Escort) and Guy Frequelin (Talbot Subeam-Lotus) for the Drivers' crown, intensified, and it was not until the Finnish 1000 Lakes event that four-wheel-drive returned to the scene. In this event Hannu Mikkola finished third (behind Vatanen's Escort RS and Alen's Fiat Abarth 131) having led for the first half of the event and having set the majority of the fastest times.

Then, in October, came San Remo, and four-wheel-drive's most emphatic win so far. Mikkola's victory on the snow in Sweden had already been shrugged off as "special conditions suiting a special car", but in Italy, where there was tarmac, gravel, dust, and heat in great abundance, it was a first-class test. Once again it was Hannu Mikkola who set most of the fastest times, but he was always fighting back after a bad engine misfire at the beginning of the event, and it was a remarkably steady drive by Michele Mouton, which led to the Quattro's victory (and, incidentally, the first-ever by a lady driver in a World Championship rally).

Audi didn't bother to go to the Ivory Coast (leaving the tough Japanese Datsuns and Toyotas to fight it out - Datsun won), but on the British Lombard-RAC they once again made no

mistake. Before the last night it was even beginning to look something like a 'steamroller' performance, for Mikkola led from Vatanen's Escort RS, with Ms. Mouton's Quattro always close behind for many hours. The Finn's car even had time to indulge in a quick roll before going on to win the event, but Michele was finally caught out by the ice on a Welsh forest track, and crashed her car.

At the end of the season, several team managers sat down to think deeply about the future, but only one of them - Jean Todt of Peugeot Talbot Sport - got it decisively right at once. The situation at the end of 1981 was that the first-generation rally four-wheel-drive Supercar, the Quattro, had proved itself in no uncertain manner. Except that it could clearly still be beaten on good tarmac surfaces, it had proved its worth in every other rallying condition. Not only that, but a whole generation of rally cars, like the Talbot Sunbeam-Lotus, the Escort RS, and the Vauxhall Chevette HSR, were all about to be rendered obsolete as the Group 4 era came to an end, and a new set of homologation rules, including the 200-off Group B, came in.

Jean Todt, who was already very well established within the PTS hierarchy, never had any doubts. Although he had been involved in the successful Talbot Sunbeam-Lotus effort which had won the 1981 Championship for Makes, he was now sure that such conventional rally cars were obsolete. His colleague at Talbot-Coventry, Des O'Dell, had commissioned Lotus to dabble with a mid-engined/rear-drive Horizon, but this had not come up to expectations. Accordingly, before the end of 1981, Todt made a brave announcement - Peugeot would design and build a brand-new four-wheel-drive Group B car for rallying, and he promised that it would be unveiled in 1983.

The British teams were in a quandary. Ford had already shown their still-undeveloped front-engine/rear-transmission-and-drive Escort RS1700T and proposed to have it ready later in 1982, British Leyland had retired its unwieldy Triumph TR7 V8s, Talbot had been told to co-operate with whatever Jean Todt and Peugeot was planning, and Vauxhall was told that henceforth its commercial partner, Opel, would take over the General Motors rallying effort. BL at least hedged its bets by commissioning a mid-engined four-wheel-drive 'Metro' project from Williams Grand Prix Engineering, but this was

Top Left
Conventional cars like this rear-drive Datsun Violet continued to win endurance rallies in the early 1980s - Shekhar Mehta on his way to winning yet another Safari.

Opposite
Nissan's only Group B design was a normally-aspirated, rear-drive car, the 240RS, which Timo Salonen drove to its very limits - but it was never competitive. The Japanese company never improved on it.

35

to take a long time to develop, even in temporary-engine form.

Elsewhere in Europe, Renault did no more than improve their mid-engined 5 Turbo, Fiat-Lancia finally retired the amazingly successful Fiat 131 Abarth Rallye, and Opel merely rebodied the Ascona 400 saloon, with a Manta coupé body shell, calling the result the Manta 400; the tragedy in this case was that Manta homologation was delayed for a full year, until 1983, by which time it was already technically obsolete.

The Japanese companies in rallying - Nissan-Datsun, Toyota, and Mitsubishi - merely re-shuffled what they had, looked as inscrutable as ever, and seemed to conclude that they did not need to produce a four-wheel-drive car, or that

Top Left
Opel's first Group B car was the Ascona 400, originally homologated into Group 4 in 1980. It combined a front-mounted 2.4 litre engine with rear-drive. Jimmy McRae on the Welsh International rally.

Bottom Left
Opel's Manta 400 was homologated in 1983, far too late to be competitive with the Audis. It was really no more than a rebodied Ascona.

Below
The Opel Manta 400 remained competitive on tarmac into the mid-1980s, helped by excellent handling and driveability. This is a typical Circuit of Ireland stance.

they could win enough events with conventional machinery not to make such expensive efforts worthwhile.

The outstanding new car of the period, however, was the Lancia 037 Rally, which was a beautifully styled mid-engined two-seater, with rear-wheel-drive. It had been evolved with typical Italian *elan:* design had begun in 1980, the first prototypes had been produced in 1981, and the necessary 200 cars to achieve Group B were finished by the end of March 1982. Motor sport director Cesare Fiorio, however, had clearly looked at four-wheel-drive and the Quattro, rejected it as a concept, and opted for the 'road-going racing car' approach, which was really a second-generation Stratos layout.

In 1982, therefore, the Audi team made an all-out, and very expensive, attack on World Championship rallying. They were only resisted by Opel throughout the year, and Lancia from the end of the summer, so it was not surprising that they chalked up most of the victories, and made all the headlines. It was only a stupendously determined, and well-financed, programme by the Opel team (the Rothmans cigarette giant was its paymaster, this sponsorship having already been offered to, and refused by, Audi) which

allowed the lugubrious West German Walter Rohrl to take the Driver's Championship, yet Audi won the Makes series with a late season burst of victories.

This was the season in which the Argentinian Codasur event was cancelled in the aftermath of the Falklands War, but in which Opel contested every event actually to run, while Audi were present everywhere except the Safari. Lancia, who took months to get their 'evolution' cars' specification sorted out, were only really in contention from the middle of the year. To make Opel's, or Audi's commitment, it took several million pounds, not hundreds of thousands, for apart from the pan-European rallies there were qualifying rounds in New Zealand, Kenya, West Africa (Ivory Coast), and Brazil.

Audi certainly intended to go to Kenya for the Safari in due course (when in their typically Teutonic way they would expect to win), but missed it out for 1982, and rallied triumphantly round the world on most other events. Overall, a four-wheel-drive Quattro won seven times - Sweden (snow and ice), Portugal (gravel), Acropolis (gravel), Brasil (gravel), 1000 Lakes (gravel), San Remo (gravel and tarmac), and Lombard-RAC (mainly forestry track gravel) - while the Opel Ascona 400 could only win twice - in Monte Carlo (surprisingly ice-free tarmac), and Ivory Coast (rough roads, on sheer reliabi-

lity). The other three victories went to Nissan-Datsun (Safari - on reliability), Renault (Corsica, on tarmac), and Toyota (New Zealand). Not only that, but three Quattro drivers - Michele Mouton, Hannu Mikkola, and Stig Blomqvist - all shared in the spoils, Mouton so nearly winning the individual Drivers' championship, and Mikkola having an extremely unlucky year by his own exalted standards.

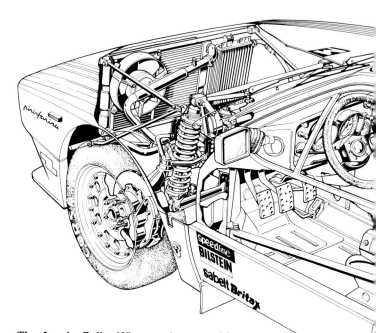
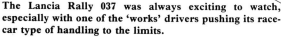

The **Lancia Rally 037** was always exciting to watch, especially with one of the 'works' drivers pushing its race-car type of handling to the limits.

There was growing evidence that the Quattro was beginning to handle better on tarmac events (though it was still too large and heavy to be truly competitive), but there was also every indication that Lancia's 'light and nimble' concept for their rear-drive 037 Rally was also working well. Even in Greece, when still in non-evolution form, Alen's car was as fast as the best Quattros, until its chassis let him down, while

At the end of 1982, there were lots of rumours of four-wheel-drive cars now being designed, but there was still no Quattro competitor actually homologated and in rallying. The Peugeot-Talbot project was forging ahead in great secrecy - all that the media knew was that Des O'Dell was looking after the construction, but not the design, of the prototype, and that the engine would be mid-mounted - and a whole variety of (small) Citroen Visa projects were bubbling away.

Although we did not know it at the time, the Metro 4 x 4 was still only making slow progress,

Lancia's Rally 037 announced in 1981 was a mid-engined, rear-drive 'racing car' for use on rallies. It won the World Championship for Makes in 1983, but was neither as powerful, nor had as much traction, as the Audi Quattro.

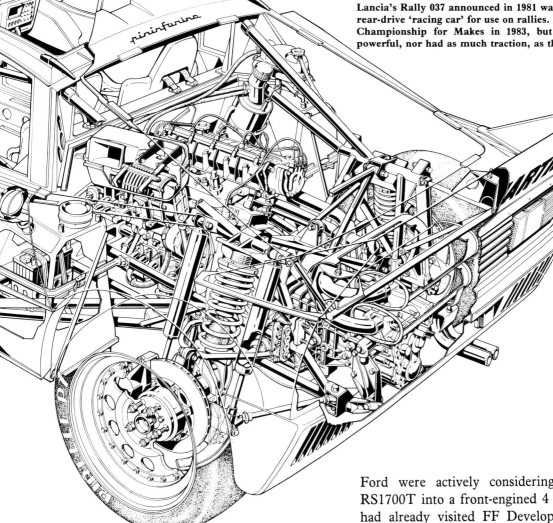

his San Remo stage times were excellent, and his gritty third place overall in the Lombard-RAC rally (behind the Quattros of Hannu Mikkola and Michele Mouton) was a demonstration of sheer determination in most unsuitable conditions. 1983, for sure, looked like being a more competitive season.

Ford were actively considering turning the RS1700T into a front-engined 4 x 4, and Opel had already visited FF Developments with a view to grafting four-wheel-drive under the sleek skin of the Manta 400.

In the meantime, the 1983 season saw a three-cornered battle for World Championship surpremacy, between three entirely different cars - the latest four-wheel-drive Quattros, the old-style front engine/rear drive Opel Ascona and Manta 400s, and the mid-engine/rear drive Lancia Rally 037s - while several of the new four-wheel-drive cars were either shown publically, rallied in prototype form, or merely announced as on-going projects, Audi, if they could bring themselves to admit it, were now living on borrowed time ....

This was a season, however, in which the spoils, and the victory garlands, were still shared around, with Lancia winning the Makes Championship, and Hannu Mikkola (Quattro-mounted) winning the Drivers' series. After a year's absence, the Argentinian event was held once again, though the Brazilian event was no longer a Championship qualifier, so there were 12 events, spread all around the world, to be won and lost.

The season started very badly indeed for the four-wheel-drive cars, as there was virtually no snow on the Monte Carlo rally, and the Lancia 'racing cars' finished first and second, with the best of the Quattros trailing 11 minutes in arrears. However, Hannu Mikkola then won outright in Sweden and Portugal, and the point-for-point scrapping between Audi and Lancia was well and truly joined.

VW used Group A, front-wheel-drive 1.8 litre Golf GTis for a time, but these were not powerful enough to match the Group B competition.

In the end, the four-wheel-drive Quattros won five times (Sweden, Portugal, Argentina, 1000 Lakes, and Lombard-RAC), while Lancia also won five events (Monte Carlo, Corsica, Acropolis, New Zealand, and San Remo) with a late season burst of victories. It was indeed interesting to see that the spoils went to the team with the most suitable car for a particular event; Lancia had refined their Rally 037 as far as they could, with smooth-surface/high-grip handling in mind, while Audi's Quattro was now supreme where high levels of traction, and ultra high performance, was needed.

There was no encouragement of any type, however, for the 'conventional' rally car, unless it was on events where sheer reliability counted for more than modern technology, for although Opel's Ascona won the Safari, and Toyota's Celica won in the Ivory Coast, they were both lucky. The Quattro led the Safari until the last night, and the Ivory Coast until the final hours - while Audi's Hannu Mikkola finished second overall on both events.

Even so, it was a season in which most people were pleased about *something* - Lancia because they won the World Championship for

Makes, Audi because Hannu Mikkola won the Driver's Championship, Opel because at last they got the Manta 400 homolgated *and* beat Audi in the Makes series, and Toyota because their Celica was demonstrably the best 'conventional' car in rallying.

In the meantime, several new four-wheel-drive designs were started, a few were actually announced, and one very important one - the Peugeot 205 Turbo 16 - entered its first competition. The Peugeot was a very significant machine, because it was the first purpose-built 4 x 4 to be seen which looked as if it might beat Audi, once homologated; unveiled in March 1983, tested throughout the year, and test-entered in only one small French event in October, it looked right, and was promised for 200-off homologation in the spring of 1984.

Citroen showed off a fleet of different Visas, one with a front engine, three with mid engines (transverse or longitudinal positions), and one with an engine at *each* end! They also showed two different BX 4 x 4s, both with front engines. One Visa, the 1000 Pistes, it was promised, would be homologated in 1984, and one of the BX designs would be chosen for 1985. It was quite a programme.

In the meantime (and only whispered about, for these projects were supposed to be top secret), Lancia started work on a new 4 x 4 to replace the two-wheel-drive Rally 037, Ford started their mid-engined B200 project (having publically cancelled their Escort RS1700T, when Stuart Turner took over from Karl Ludvigsen), Porsche showed the first of their rear-engined 4 x 4 project cars which would lead to the definitive 959 making its appearance in 1983, Audi showed their new short-wheelbase Sport Quattro, and Mitsubishi started work on a front-engined Starion 4 x 4, half way round the world from the factory, in England.

Phew! While all this was going on, it was easy to ignore the interesting one-off Mazda RX7 4 x 4 of Rod Millen, which rallied exclusively in the USA, the continued development of the MG Metro 6R4 (which was something of an open secret, yet had still not been photographed), and the private-enterprise Ford Escort 4 x 4 project which the Norwegian

One of the Audi Quattro's most controversial appearances in 1981 came in the Acropolis, where the inner headlamps were removed, to allow more cooling air into the engine bay. This was Hannu Mikkola - like his team mates, he was disqualified.
(Photo: Hugh Bishop)

Martin Schanche was refining for use on the European rallycross circuits.

At the end of 1983, therefore, the world of four-wheel-drive rallying entered its second phase. The domination of loose-surface events by Audi was over, and a multi-marque battle for success was about to begin.

Right
In 1982 Hannu Mikkola and Bjorn Waldegard both drove this David Sutton-prepared Quattro to victory in the British Open series. This is a tarmac stage, and notice the odd wheel angles.

Below Bottom
Once the 'works' team had made the Quattro reliable, the cars were used all round the world. John Buffum won dozens of special stage events in the USA.

Below
With the Quattro, it helped if you could get the car sideways going into corners, for it then killed the understeer - M. Cinotto in the Costa Smeralda in an original A1-type.

1984-1986 - THE SECOND GENERATION SUPERCARS

- four-wheel-drive with agility to match

In the early months of the 1984 rallying season, nothing seemed to have changed. Monte Carlo, Sweden and Portugal all fell to the Audis, while Toyota's conventional Celica Twincam Turbo defeated the four-wheel-drive cars in the Safari, and Lancia stormed back to take a 1-2 victory in the Tour de Corse. With typically West German pride, efficiency and organisation, Audi attracted Walter Rohrl to their team, after just one year with Lancia, so they now had four real stars (Hannu Mikkola, Stig Blomqvist and Michele Mouton being the other personalities) to pick for any particular event.

Until the fifth round in the series, indeed, there was no serious four-wheel-drive opposition to Audi. But then, from 1st April 1984, the new Peugeot 205 Turbo 16 was homologated, and the Quattro's limitations were immediately exposed. Not even their own homologation of the short-wheelbase Sport Quattro, in time to compete in the Tour de Corse, could hide that.

The new mid-engined Peugeot was not only a fast, and effective, little Supercar, but it was immediately competitive. The 200 'homologation' cars were lined up for inspection in France, to prove that this was a genuine production car, the necessary 20 evolution cars were completed in the 'works' competitions department at the same time, and within five weeks the cars surprised everyone, by their pace and agility on the Tour de Corse.

Peugeot's team director, Jean Todt, had promised that the car would be ready in 1984 - and it was. He had promised that a top-grade driver would be in the car - and, in the shape of Ari Vatanen, so he was. Since he had already promised a full scale assault on the World Championship in 1985, a number of other teams had cause to worry about their future chances ....

The Peugeot's first event was the Tour de Corse, where nobody expected it to shine. Corsica, after all, was a tight little island where the tarmac stages favoured 'racing' rally cars like the Lancia Rally 037s, and the mid-engined Renault 5 Turbos. Audio were certainly not likely to be competitive, so why should the Peugeot do much better?

It was astonishing. After Bettega's Lancia had led, then shunted in the fog, Vatanen's Peugeot took over the lead, set several fastest times, and held on until two-third distance, when he, too, crashed his car. Although Alen's Lancia won the event, it was Peugeot who impressed everyone, especially as the second team car, driven by Jean-Pierre Nicolas, took fourth place.

The Peugeot was also very fast on the Acropolis event, where the gravel roads suited its four-wheel-drive layout better than the tarmac of Corsica had done. Both team cars, in fact, retired, though not before Vatanen had set 11 fastest stage times, and had led the event for a time.

Then came the Finnish 1000 Lakes,

Audi produced the short wheelbase Sport Quattro (officially, the 'S1'), with much more power, for 1984, but it took
months to get it reliable. Stig Blomqvist trying hard in San
Remo, of that year.   (Photo: Hugh Bishop)

where Ari Vatanen, not only the 'local hero', but
also the right man in the right car, won the event
outright, and finally punctured Audi's reputation as the all-conquering four-wheel-drive
manufacturer. Nor was it a lucky win, for
Vatanen set 31 fastest stage times on a 50-stage
event, and won quite comfortably. It was all the
more impressive because his was the *only* Turbo
16 in the event, and he had to defeat a fleet of
'works' or 'replica' Quattros along the way.

28th August 1984. Mark that date carefully.
Before then, Audi was the undisputed master of
world rallying, but thereafter Peugeot was Top
Dog. Nor was it a gradual change, for Peugeot,
once they had started winning, made a habit of
it!

Four weeks later Peugeot also won the San
Remo event in Italy, a rally which Lancia had
obviously hoped to dominate, with pace notes,
and on their home ground. It was an even more
impressive victory for Peugeot, because Vatanen
set 31 fastest stage times (out of 50), and was
never headed after the early Lancia flourish had
been overcome. The team then decided to ignore
the Ivory Coast event, but completed their hat-
trick of victories on the Lombard-RAC event at
the end of November.

44   It was an astonishing performance, for the

team had notched up three consecutive victories,
in events with very different characters, and
demands on the drivers. This, of course, was
with a car still at the start of its development,
and with 'only' 350 bhp from its 1.8-litre engine.

Because the ousting of Audi by Peugeot, at
the front of events, was so important, it was easy
to forget, or to miss, what was happening just
behind them. Although Audi's Quattros won
seven World Championship rallies, and the
Makes series, with their team driver Stig Blomqvist winning the Drivers' championship from
Hannu Mikkola, they had a more and more difficult time as the season progressed, and only
one of those victories was gained in straight competition with Peugeot.

Their main problem was that the short-
wheelbase Sport Quattro was not as competitive
as it should have been. Though ten inches
shorter than the reliable A2 Quattro, it was
slightly heavier, its 20-valve engine had more
power but was a lot more 'peaky' and not as
reliable, and the handling was even more difficult. The drivers embarrassed their team by
queueing up not to drive the car ....

It was not until Blomqvist won the Ivory
Coast (with Hannu Mikkola, in his re-prepared
practice A2 type behind him), against negligible
opposition, that the Sport Quattro achieved its
first major success. Clearly, with other second-
generation cars coming along, Audi had a great
deal of thinking to do. Although they steadfastly

denied that a mid-engined rally prototype was being developed for the future, sneak pictures proved otherwise; that car has never appeared in public.

In 1984, too, Lancia were struggling to stay competitive with the latest evolution version of their Rally 037s, even though these cars had performed so well in 1983. In the whole World Championship year they won only once - in the tarmac-racing conditions of the Tour de Corse, but it says a lot for the team's aggressive enthusiasm that they also took four second places (three of them with Markku Alen at the wheel), in venues as far apart as Finland, Portugal, and New Zealand. It was a year in which development of the car stopped, and work on the new four-wheel-drive car proceeded apace.

And what of 'the rest'? Toyota, having homologated their turbocharged rear-drive Celica Twincam Turbo in July 1983, made a very effective old-style rally car of it. Not only did Bjorn Waldegard win the Safari outright (leading the event most of the way, and never letting the Quattros get the better of him), but the team also took a valiant third place in the Lombard-RAC, and were 'placed' in Portugal, New Zealand, and the 1000 Lakes. Even so, on loose-surfaced stages it was easy to watch the spumes of gravel being thrown up by their rear wheels, which were trying to transmit 350 bhp with no help from the fronts, and realise why four-wheel-drive was taking over so rapidly.

Opel, having lost their Rothmans sponsorship (to Porsche, who made even less of it...), were no better placed than Toyota, for their normally-aspirated engine was stuck at 275 bhp, and their best performance was second place on the Safari (Rauno Aaltonen was the driver, notching up his umpteenth 'second' in this rally that he so dearly wants to win).

Although it was never remotely in the running for outright victories, I must also mention the four-wheel-drive Citroen Visa 1000 Pistes, which was homologated, as promised, on 1st March 1984. Looking almost exactly like the front-wheel-drive Visas which Citroen had previously used, this car had a transversely-mounted front-engine position, and a very simple four-wheel-drive 'conversion', but with a mere 145 bhp from its 1.4-litre engine it could

The Audi Quattro Sport S1 seemed to have a longer nose than the original car, and was a lot quicker in a straight line. Michel Mouton struggled with it in the 1984 Lombard-RAC rally though.
(Photo: Hugh Bishop)

not be expected to match the Audis and Peugeots. Very bravely they chose to start by entering the Safari, where they won their capacity class, but both cars broke their transmission in the 1000 Lakes, and all retired in San Remo with a variety of problems.

In the meantime, various new designs were revealed, and it was obvious that Audi's success

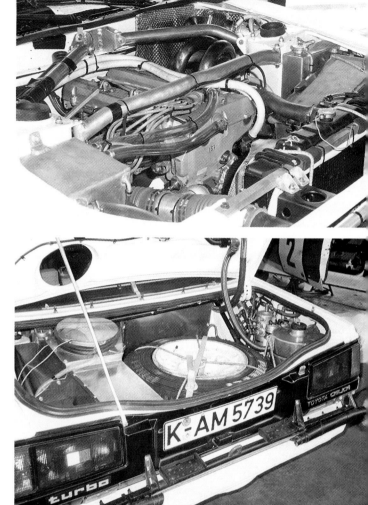

Top Left
Walter Rohrl was determined to make the best of the unweildy Audi Sport Quattro, and when using pace notes was the fastest of all Audi's drivers.

Bottom Left
The lack of four-wheel-drive badly hindered the progress of the Nissan 240RS on gravel stages, and it was too heavy to win on tarmac - Timo Salonen took fourth place in New Zealand in 1984.

Top Right
The Toyota Celica Twincam Turbo's engine was submerged under stiffening tubes in the engine bay ....
(Photo: Holmes)

Middle Right
.... while the boot was full of petrol tank, oil tank, spare wheel and fuel pumps. *(Photo: Holmes)*

Below
The best of the old-style conventional rally cars was the very powerful Toyota Celica Twincam Turbo, which won the Safari in 1985 and (here) 1986. *(Photo: Holmes)*

had inspired many other designers to try to improve. Mitsubishi showed the four-wheel-drive Starion, which rallied once, but was soon cancelled when it became clear that its front-engined layout was not going to be competitive, while the one-off Mazda RX7 4 x 4 carried on winning in North America, but showed no signs of being produced in numbers, or therefore becoming homologated.

Without a doubt, the four most important new cars of the year were Lancia's Delta S4, Ford's RS200, Porsche's 959 (now committed to production) and Austin-Rover's MG Metro 6R4. These cars all had very different interpretations of the engine layout/transmission/structural theme, but three of them (not the Porsche) were being developed with World Championship honours in mind. Lancia forecast homologation in time for the 1985 1000 Lakes, and the British manufacturers for the 'end of 1985'.

Before the 1985 season began, the battle lines had already been drawn. Audi prepared to carry on, convinced that their short-Quattro could be made to work, and ready to prove it with an unchanged team of drivers. Peugeot not only believed that they could win the World Championship, but had the financial backing to prove it, allied to the signing of ex-Nissan driver Timo Salonen to support Ari Vatanen in his quest for the title. Lancia realised that their Rally 037 was obsolete, but looked eagerly ahead to the début of their Delta S4.

Those were the main four-wheel-drive championship contenders, but in the meantime Renault had produced a more powerful mid-engined 5 Turbo (the Maxi), Nissan struggled on with the out-dated 240RS, Toyota improved the Celica Twincam Turbo even more, Ford and MG prototypes would appear from time to time, and Opel beavered away, behind closed doors, at a new car which the world still knew nothing about. It was going to be quite a year.

To turn the 1985 season into a series of headlines, I would have to write : Rally cars much faster than ever. Peugeot (and Salonen) win the World Championships. Lancia's Delta wins first-time-out. Audi produce a successful second-evolution Quattro. Then, as sub-headings, I would also write: Aerodynamics arrives in rallying. Metro 6R4 homologated. Ford RS200 delayed. Porsche 959 delayed. Opel Kadett 4 x 4 revealed. New four-wheel-drive

Citroen announced. Toyota win both African events. Ari Vatanen gravely injured. Truly, the pot was coming to the boil - and, tragically, in 1986, it would all boil over.

In 1985, though, there was no doubt that Peugeot dominated the World Championship scene. Not only did a team of 'works' cars appear on every event except the Ivory Coast (where only Audi and Toyota turned up), win seven round, finish second three times, and win the Makes *and* the Driver's series, but they were quite obviously the standard by which every other team was measured. The second-evolution 205 Turbo 16 was homologated on 1st April, a car which, with 430 bhp instead of 350 bhp, and the very effective use of aerodynamic features, moved rallying one clear step up the ladder towards F1 racing.

However, everything did not go as planned. Peugeot had always looked on the Finn, Ari Vatanen, as their Number One driver, and it was hoped (planned, even) that he would be the main contender for honours. The season started well for Ari, when he won Monte Carlo, and Sweden, but then everything began to go wrong. Mechanical failures in Portugal, Safari, and Greece were compounded by a crash in Corsica.

Team-mate Salonen beat him in New Zealand - and then came Argentina. On only the second special stage Vatanen's Peugeot crashed, rolling end over end at high speed, and seriously injured the Finn. It was only the prompt action of the team's helicopter, in getting him to hospital, that saved his life, and for days his condition was critical. With serious damage to his legs, the unlucky Vatanen was not expected to rally again.

After this horrifying misfortune, Timo Salonen went on to win the Drivers' series, with five outright victories, and a second place, no-one else coming close. The real surprise, however, was that this was not the lethargic, laid-back driver of old, who had done his best with out-dated Nissans but never looked too disappointed if they had let him down. The 'new' Salonen was a gritty professional who fought for every point, and impressed the rally-watchers.

After four years at the top, Audi should have been due for a bad year, and the miracle was that they remained so competitive. It was true that the Sport Quattro was still not right, and old-style 'long' Quattros were out-paced by 1985

Above
Jimmy McRae won several tarmac rallies in Britain and Europe with the 275 bhp rear-drive Opel Manta 400.

Top
Opel fought a stubborn rearguard action with their Manta 400s, which are still winning, all round the world. This is Andrew Wood in one of Russell Brookes' cars in a 1986 National series event.

(even though they continued to win all over Europe, Scandinavia, North America, South Africa, and the U.K., where few people could afford to buy the ultra-expensive 'customer' Peugeot 205 Turbo 16s which might have beat them), so much so that the drivers were not even placed on season-long contracts at first, in case management decided to withdraw altogether.

Audi worked very hard to improve the original 'short' Sport Quattro, so successfully that the car finished second overall in Monte Carlo, Sweden and Greece, plus third place in Portugal; each time the cars were respectably close to the winning Peugeots, and in Monte Carlo and Portugal the extremely determined Walter Röhrl actually led for at least half of the event.

Then, in mid-season, Audi surprised everyone by producing the second-evolution 49

The shape of modern rallying in the mid 1980s! Henri Toivonen's Lancia Delta S4 on its way to winning the 1986 Monte Carlo rally. Second rally, second victory.

(Photo: Holmes)

Quattro Sport (which is often quite wrongly called 'S1' by journalists - *all* Sport Quattros are S1s, according to the homologation form ....), homologated it in July, and immediately showed how much better it was. The 'E2' Sport Quattro not only had much better weight distribution than before (due to having components like the water, oil and transmission coolers in the tail), but it also used advanced aerodynamics to help produce downforce. The E2 derivative, like the E2 Peugeot, was very obviously 'using the wind' to hold it on the ground.

There was no doubt that it all worked, for in the first few months Blomqvist used it to finish second to Salonen's Peugeot in the 1000 Lakes (where he lost by just 48 seconds), and Walter Rohrl won the San Remo event very convincingly indeed. *Vorsprung durch Technik*, perhaps, was a justified advertising slogan.

Although Lancia pluckily turned up with their old-style Rally 037s, from time to time (Biaison's second place in Portugal was their best showing), they could offer no real opposition to Peugeot and Audi until the new Delta S4 was homologated. Like every other manufacturer of four-drive homologation 'specials', they found that building the cars was often more difficult than designing and developing them, so a promised début in the 1000 Lakes had to be cancelled, and so did a San Remo date.

However, to make up for it all, two 450 bhp evolution cars, which like the other front-runners had various aerodynamic appendages, started the Lombard-RAC rally - and they finished first and second overall! It was no fluke either, for the Lancias were always right up with the leaders, even though all the 'works' Audis and Peugeots dropped out of the event before half distance.

The significance of the Lancia showing was that it proved just how much they had learned merely by watching, how high they had set their targets from the beginning of the programme, and how effective the Torinese team was, even when under pressure on a début appearance.

It was on the Lombard-RAC rally, too, that the newly-homologated MG Metro 6R4 started its first international event, and Austin-Rover's British fans were delighted to see that Tony Pond kept his car going, to take third place overall behind the two Lancia Deltas. The Metro, in fact, had been around for some time, for the chopped-Rover engined cars had been used in British events during 1984 and 1985, with the various aerodynamic wings, skirts, and add-ons being developed during that time, while the new four-cam 'homologation car' had been launched in May 1985, and had already won at Na-

Austin-Rover produced the four-wheel-drive MG Metro 6R4, which was really anything *but* a Metro. Tony Pond finished third in the 1985 Lombard-RAC rally, in the car's début after homologation. This was Malcolm Wilson's sister car.

tional level. It was generally agreed that it looked awful, and that its choice of a normally-aspirated 3-litre vee-6 engine layout was controversial, but without exception everyone wished it well for a full assault on World Championship events in 1986.

Austin-Rover, at least, achieved their homologation target, whereas Ford missed theirs twice. Not only could they not take part in the Lombard-RAC, but they also had to miss the 1986 Monte Carlo rally as well. A prototype car won a British national event in September (the Lindisfarne), and tested competitively on various well-known stages, but there was little other evidence that it was going to be competitive. What *was* interesting, however, was that the RS200 seemed to need no aerodynamic aids to achieve stability, for there was built-in

down force in the body as styled by Ghia.

Also in 1985, Porsche 959 production did not even begin, though prototype cars failed in the Paris-Dakar 'raid' at the beginning of the year, and won the Pharaohs event later on, Opel unveiled their idea of what a four-wheel-drive machine should look like, but preferred to work towards Group S in 1988, rather than Group B in 1986; their choice of a front-engined 'conversion' of the Kadett made several other designers raise their eyebrows though a study of the weight distribution showed this to be more favourable than - say - the second-evolution Sport Quattro.

In October 1985, too, another front-engined 4 x 4 was finally launched - the bulky-looking Citroen BX 4TC. This, in many ways, looked to be something of a rallying dinosaur, for it had been conceived way back in 1982/83 when the Quattro was still dominant, and it copied that car's layout, with a big and heavy in-line engine up front, ahead of the front wheels. With a five- 51

The Peugeot 205 Turbo 16 won its first World Championship event, the 1000 Lakes of 1984, and has been the pacesetter ever since. *(Photo: Holmes)*

The Peugeot also handled magnificently in Italy, as well as Finland, with Ari Vatanen taking outright victory in 1984. *(Photo: Hugh Bishop)*

door body shell, 'only' 380 bhp when the average top-class car was already using 430-450 bhp (and 550 bhp being spoken of for some 1986 evolution cars), and theoretical disadvantages in weight distribution and handling, it seemed to be carrying its own difficulties, without encountering others. Nevertheless, homologation was promised (and achieved) at the beginning of 1986, and the cars were to start the new season with high hopes.

The other event of major importance which occurred in 1985 was that FISA, and the 'constructors trade union', the BPICA, agreed that the costs of tooling up for, building, and then attempting to sell, 200 very specialised Group B cars, was excessive. Accordingly, with 1988 in mind, it was suggested that a new, and still un-

The second evolution Peugeot 205 Turbo 16 was not only 100 bhp more powerful than before, but had aerodynamic aids to help it 'fly' better. Timo Salonen in the 1986 Monte Carlo rally. *(Photo: Holmes)*

finalised, Group S, should be introduced in place of Group B. The whole point of Group S was that only *ten* cars of any particular type would have to be built, though serious restrictions on engine size, and power output, were proposed at the same time.

This meant that the Ford RS200 was likely to be the last of the 200-off Group B projectiles to be homologated, while several manufacturers (Opel and Toyota being the perfect examples) held back from building 200-off Group B cars, and started to think seriously of ten-off Group S cars instead. Even so, it was a proposal which was likely to result in freak cars being built, for even at the start it was suggested that Lancia would 'borrow' Ferrari F1 engines for their cars, Ford the new Ford-Cosworth Vee-6, and that BMW would come into Group S events with their own four-cylinder F1 engine. Stuart Turner of Ford, in particular, was very scathing about the whole thing.

And so we came to 1986, the most traumatic which the sport has ever seen. For sure, the morons who only wanted to see ultra-fast cars and their brave drivers engaged in gladiatorial duels were delighted to see so many monstrously fast rally cars finally matched against each other, but those who had warned of the dangers of such machines being used on public roads, and between 'barriers' of spectators, finally saw their predictions come horrifyingly true.

The season lined up as follows: Lancia's Delta S4, and Peugeot's 205 Turbo 16 (second-evolution model) were favourites to win most events, not only because they were committed to competing in all of them, but because they were also spending most on drivers, extensive back up in terms of light aircraft surveillance, masseurs and other specialist medical services, along with a great deal of testing and on-going development.

Even though Audi's programme was set to be much more restricted than in the past, and the basic Quattro layout was starting its sixth rally season, the Audi Sport Quattro (second evolution) was expected to put up a good show in the events for which it was entered. Ford's RS200, it was said, would be competitive right away, especially as the team had signed the 1984 World Champion, Stig Blomqvist, as its leader, although there was still no clear plan to build an evolution car, and the 200-off machine was known to be quite heavy.

Most controversy surrounded the MG

53

Metro 6R4s and the big Citroens. The Metro's normally-aspirated engine was not only unproven, but was already on the 3-litre limit, and seemed to be incapable of further development if a second-evolution car became necessary. Nevertheless, the team planned a full European assault on World Championship events, and there seemed to be no lack of finance to back the programme. The Citroen team not only faced 1986 with a 1983-design, front-engine, fixed torque-split and all, but their team was lacking in top-level current rallying experience, with only Jean-Claude Andruet having any sort of previous success record.

Right at the start of the season, the signs were ominous, for the cars were clearly a lot faster than before, and the drivers complaining of too many spectators, and a complete lack of crowd control, on the Monte Carlo rally. A year earlier, Ari Vatanen's Peugeot had slid off the ice-bound roads at one point, bowling over a spectator, but fortunately not hurting him much, and with so much enthusiastic interest in the new breed of four-wheel-drive projectiles, and so many people wanting to watch them, the problem was obviously much worse.

The best point at which to summarise the disturbing events of the 1986 season is at the half-way point, after the Acropolis rally, for all the steam had been knocked out of the competition between makes by that time. No-one who is at all interested in World Championship rallying needs to be reminded that in that half season, in Portugal a car plunged off the road into the crowd on the side of a stage, killing three people, in the Tour de Corse Henri Toivonen and his co-driver Sergio Cresto were killed when their Lancia Delta S4 left the road and exploded, and that as a result the world of rallying was thrown into turmoil by instantly-formulated proposals, and counter-proposals, to reduce car performance, and bring the sport back to sanity, and safety.

The first half of the season comprised the usual six events - two on snow and ice (Monte Carlo and Sweden), two gravel events (Portugal and Acropolis), one on tarmac (Corsica), and of course the entirely special Safari. Except that all the works cars were withdrawn after the accident on the Sintra stage in Portugal, the results were almost exactly as expected, with Peugeot winning three events, Lancia just one - and the rugged, front-engine/rear-drive Toyota Celica Twin-

cam Turbos winning the Safari, just as they had done in 1984 and 1985. Before the holocaust which took his life in Corsica, poor Henri Toivonen's Lancia had been leading the event at half distance.

Audi's 1986 effort was workmanlike, but limited, and almost bound to fail. Although Hannu Mukkola's Sport Quattro S1 finished third in Monte Carlo, he was seven minutes off the winning pace at the end, and there were no more successes before the whole team was disbanded in the days following the Corsica tragedy.

Opposite
Ford's RS200 was homologated in 1986, and plunged straight into winter rallying. Mark Lovell gave the car its first International British outing in the National Breakdown rally, and finished fifth. *(Photo: Ralph Hardwick)*
Below
By mid-1986, the Ford RS200 was a potential winner, especially on gravel. Mark Lovell took second place in the Scottish rally, in spite of rolling on a late stage.
(Photo: Ralph Hardwick)

Ford had little chance to prove their new mid-engined RS200, for although Blomqvist was quite capable of leading every event he started, his car's engine blew in Sweden when he was making his push, he naturally withdrew from the Portugese event, and in the Acropolis he actually went off the road while leading. A third place in Sweden was the team's best actual result, but a 1-2 position in Greece before both cars retired was encouraging, to say the least. However, with international event wins all over Europe, by 'private' owners, and encouraging performances in the U.K., it was clear that the car had great potential.

Of Citroen's BX 4TC, and Austin-Rover's Metro 6R4, what can one say? The Citroens never looked remotely competitive, and were always fragile - both had retired after six Monte Carlo stages, Andruet's car finished sixth, and 24 minutes off the pace in Sweden, they did not start the Safari or Corsica because management admitted they were not fast enough, and in the Acropolis it was all over after three stages. There was no chance that they could win anything at this level.

The Metros, at least, looked fast while they were going, but every single car which started a World Championship event either crashed, or retired with mechanical breakdowns; the engines, in particular, had given a lot of problems, as had the transmission. Suspension breakages in testing before the Acropolis led to the entries being scratched. In the U.K., however, the cars were successful in home-based International events, but even here the mechanical problems re-occurred. The fact that the team's designer left abruptly before mid-season may tell its own story.

For the many Porsche fans in the world, the disappointment was that the 959's production run was put back again, and yet again. Even though there was already an evolution version (the 961) which raced with honour in the Le Mans 24 Hours event, Porsche had already announced that they had no plans to use the car in top-class rallying. The Rothmans-sponsored team, based at Silverstone in the U.K., had started up in 1984 with conventional rear-engined rear-drive 911s, and had originally attracted Henri Toivonen to drive for them because the four-wheel-drive 959 was in prospect, but because they now had no proper programme to look forward to in 1986, they switched to building a home-based MG Metro 6R4 for Jimmy McRae to use, instead.

By mid-year it was clear that World Championship rallying would never be the same again, that rally car performance would have to be reduced, and that the era of the four-wheel-drive Supercars was almost at an end. In a mere six years, the typical Supercar had changed from being a 300 bhp model, based on a quantity-production car, to a purpose-built 500 bhp device, built in strictly limited quantities and using space-age materials, and expensively-developed aerodynamic aids. Along the way their handling and roadholding qualities had been transformed, but they were still extremely hard work to drive flat-out, and their acceleration had become quite phenomenal.

The Formula-car type of construction, the four-wheel-drive traction and balance, and the agile handling had all helped to make this kind of rallying safer, but it was the massive increase in straight-line performance which had served to make them potentially lethal. Light-hearted (or should I say cynical?) drivers used to say that a spectator could run faster than a Group 4 rally car - but that was certainly no longer true by 1986.

In 1979 the typical Group 4 car could sprint to 60 mph in about 5 seconds, and 100 mph in about 14 seconds, but by 1986 those figures had dropped to 3 seconds and eight seconds respectively. Not only that, perhaps, but it was the modern Group B cars's ability to dig deep for traction out of gravel corners, and rocket - say - from 60 mph to 100 mph in about five seconds, which made them so mind-bogglingly fast.

It all seems to be light years away from 70 bhp front-wheel-drive Saabs winning the RAC rallies, or even from 260 bhp front-engine/rear-drive Escorts winning the 1979 World Championship. The rallying revolution, therefore, is complete. Will we ever see cars like this again?

AUDI QUATTRO AND SPORT S1

In the period covered by this book, Audi were first at every important juncture - first to get involved with a competitive four-wheel-drive car, first to win a World Championship event, *and* first to withdraw completely from rallying after the horrifying events of 1986 caused such an upheaval in the sport. As a marketing exercise, their six-year involvement in rallying must have paid enormous dividends, for their Quattros won events all over the world. If any one series of events had been calculated to convince the world that Audi and four-wheel-drive was synonymous, this was it!

In six years, there were four distinctly different types of Quattro in World Championship rallying - the original 'long wheelbase' Quattro, the 'A2' development of that car, the short wheelbase Quattro Sport S1, and the second evolution 'winged wonder' which was developed from it. Because the Quattro Sport S1 types did not come into use until the Peugeot 205 Turbo 16 was also ready, they did not have as much success as the original cars. Nevertheless, the Quattros, of whatever size, or whatever configuration, were always competitive, and at World Championship level their team always included top-class drivers.

After a long lay-off, from the 1950s, Audi came into rallying in 1978, and for the first three seasons they used front-wheel-drive 80s, with limited success. Right from the start, however, they had four-wheel-drive, and the

Quattro, in mind, for their future.

During the 1970s, Audi (which was, and is, a part of the huge VW group of companies) had developed a range of front-wheel-drive family cars, one of which (the 80) was also sold, in modified form, as the VW Passat. Most had four-cylinder engines, but from 1976 there was also the new Audi 100, which had a 2.2-litre *five*-cylinder engine, developed by the simple expedient of adding one cylinder to the basic configuration of the 1.6-litre 'four'. In every case, Audi's cars had in-line engines, mounted ahead of the line of the transmission and final drive. In the case of the straight five-cylinder engine, this meant that there was considerable front overhang, and a rather forward-biased weight distribution.

At the same time, Audi also were designing a new light-weight four-wheel-drive vehicle, aimed at winning a large contract from the West German military authorities, to replace the ageing DKW Munga. This machine, when it finally appeared, would be badged as a VW, and called the Iltis. The basic layout was that of the Audi 80/VW Passat passenger car, in that the same front engine and transmission layout was used at the front of the car. The important difference, however, was that the engineers devised a very simple gearbox conversion to allow a shaft to be taken to the back, to drive the rear wheels. This machine was finally put on sale to the general public in February 1979,

On the San Remo rally of 1985, Walter Rohrl astonished everyone with the pace of the second-evolution Audi Quatro S1.

by which time large military orders had, in fact, been secured.

The Quattro project began, unofficially, at Ingolstadt, in 1977, when one of the company's project managers, Walter Treser, produced an 'unofficial' four-wheel-drive prototype, which combined the general layout of an Audi 80 saloon, with modified versions of the 4 x 4 Iltis transmission. I use the word 'unofficial', because there was a very rigid product planning system at Audi-VW which, theoretically, did not allow 'private-enterprise' projects to take shape at all, and the planners had not yet thought of a four-wheel-drive car for themselves.

A new generation of front-wheel-drive Audis was already being planned for launch in 1979 and 1980, there being four-door saloons which were expected to sell in large quantities, and coupés which would appeal to a more sporty-minded clientèle. The decision was made to bring together the new coupé body style, the refined and productionised four-wheel-drive transmission, and the most powerful possible version of the five-cylinder engine, to produce a completely new type of Supercar. This car, to be called the Quattro, was launched in the spring of 1980, and Audi were already developing rally car

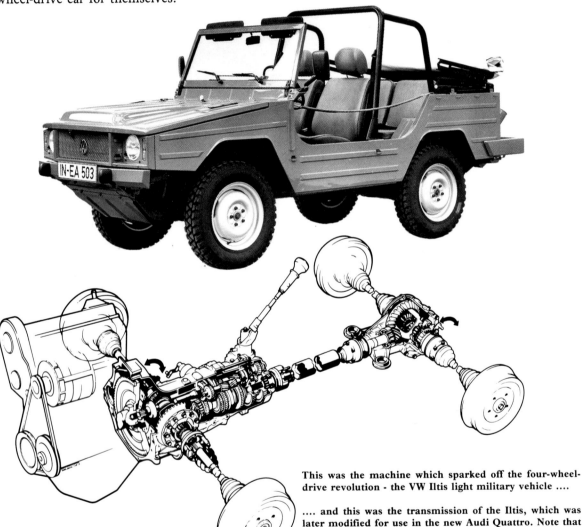

This was the machine which sparked off the four-wheel-drive revolution - the VW Iltis light military vehicle ....

.... and this was the transmission of the Iltis, which was later modified for use in the new Audi Quattro. Note that there was no centre differential in the Iltis design.

The happy ending to this story was that Treser demonstrated his prototype to Audi management, who were soon convinced of its merit, and speedily took it on board as an official project. It was from these early days that the Audi philosophy of 'four-wheel-drive with everything' was developed.

parts for it at the time.

Because the Quattro was not only developed from the Coupé, by using a new floor pan and modified mechanical components under a slightly-modified superstructure, and because it was meant to be made at the rate of at least 10 cars a day, it was a fully refined, civilised, but

Above
The short-wheelbase Audi Quattro Sport was supposed to make the rally car more nimble and lighter for 1984. It failed completely on both counts!

Top
Audi's Quattro road car was a handsome, if rather angular, style, based on that of the *front*-drive Audi Coupé.

rather big and heavy four-seater car. It was only because the engine could be supertuned, and because it was the *first* four-wheel-drive car to be properly developed, that it was made immediately competitive.

The basic statistics of the Quattro road car show that this was no homologation special, for the 8ft. 3.4in. wheelbase was matched by an overall length of 14ft. 5.4in., and the unladen weight was about 2,840 lb. Nor was the weight distribution ideal for four-wheel-drive rallying,

for no less than 61.3 per cent of the weight was concentrated over the front wheels, and only 38.7 per cent over the rears. The fact that there was a bulky iron-blocked engine up front meant that the car would tend to be directionally stable, and this was also not ideal for rallying, where a driver sometimes needs to alter the attitude of his car, in an instant, when he encounters unexpected conditions, or hazards.

The structure of the car used a newly-designed steel floorpan, welded to a slightly-modified Audi GT coupé superstructure; there were two passenger doors, and a close-coupled four-seater layout. Even though, by its style, the car looked as if it should be a hatchback, the rear window was actually fixed in place, and there was a conventional boot lid below it.

61

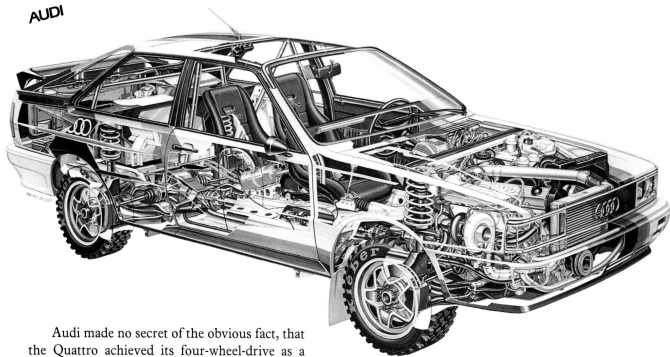

The rally-prepared Quattro, in original 'A1' guise of 1981, showing just how much of the heavy machinery was concentrated at the front of the car.

Audi made no secret of the obvious fact, that the Quattro achieved its four-wheel-drive as a conversion of the GT's front-wheel-drive layout. The engine was completely ahead of the line of the front wheels, with the final drive on the line, and with the five-speed gearbox behind that. (The engine was so lengthy that there was no space for the cooling radiator ahead of it - that vital component actually being positioned alongside the engine, to the left of it). Drive to the rear wheels was taken out of the back of the gearbox, and was permanently engaged, though there was a tiny grapefruit-sized centre differential between the gearbox and the propeller shaft itself; no such device had been fitted into the Iltis military-vehicle's transmission. There was no limited-slip mechanism in any of the three differentials on the road car, though front and rear diffs could be locked up, by operating cockpit controls, if necessary. The chassis-mounted rear final drive was a modified Iltis-type unit.

Because of the simple transmission layout, the engine torque was always split evenly - 50%/50% - between front and rear wheels. Most engineers, and tyre designers, agreed that such a split was not ideal -generally speaking, it is thought that about one third (33%) of the torque should go through the front, steered, wheels, and two thirds should go to the rears. Even though the very sophisticated FF Developments viscous couplings were already available, the Audi layout was neither of the right type, nor was there sufficient space behind the main gearbox, for such a limited-slip mechanism to be used, even as an expensive homologated extra. The tiny centre differential was always the weak

spot in the super-tuned rally car's transmission and on most occasions it was removed completely so that there was a direct, shaft, connection between front and rear differentials.

The engine itself was a much-developed version of the corporate five-cylinder 2,144 cc single-overhead-camshaft unit, which was installed in the engine bay with the block leaning over 20 degrees towards the right side of the engine bay. The 170 bhp turbocharged version used in the 200 saloon, was further developed with the aid of an intercooler, and produced 200 bhp at 5,500 rpm. The engine, the turbocharger, the intercooler, and the water radiator itself all helped produce a *very* full engine bay. The miracle of it all was that in fully-modified rally-car guise, it was still possible to keep engine-bay temperatures within bounds.

Whereas the Audi Coupé, a front-wheel-drive car, had 'dead axle' rear suspension, the Quattro featured Audi 200-style MacPherson struts at front and rear, allied to independent suspension all round; at the rear, incidentally, much of the Audi 200's *front* end componentry was used, in a very neat, and elegant, installation. There was power-assisted rack and pinion steering, something which was by no means common in World Championship rally cars at this stage. To keep the whole thing in check

Quattros under preparation at David Sutton's workshops in West London.

there were four-wheel disc brakes (ventilated at the front), and the chunky, broad-shouldered, styling was set off by the use of cast alloy road wheels.

The Finnish Superstar, Hannu Mikkola, had already test-driven an Audi 80-based development 'chassis' in September 1979, so when the Quattro was officially unveiled in March 1980 the company was able to announce that he had signed a testing and development contract for the rest of the year, and that a full-scale 'works' competition programme was planned for 1981. Group 4 homologation was originally planned for 1st August 1980, but there were delays in building the first 400 cars, so it was actually achieved on 1st January 1981. By that time, Audi had already announced their 1981 team, with Mikkola being joined by the French girl, Michele Mouton.

Audi spent a great deal of money, and neglected nothing, in their effort to make the Group 4 car competitive right from the start. Not only did they carry out a great deal of testing in 1980 (which included that phenomenal 'Course Car' performance by Mikkola in the Algarve in October 1980), but they homologated a mass of extra equipment. The engines were tuned to provide at least 310 bhp for the very first event, but by the end of 1981 the best engines produced about 330 bhp at 6,500 rpm. Naturally there were alternative gear ratios, axle ratios, brakes, engine dry sump kits, suspension items, fuel tanks, and body items. If there was to be an homologation 'race', Audi were going to be among the leaders - a measure of their seriousness was the use of space-flight materials such as Kevlar for competition wings, and the sump/transmission guards.

The Quattro's first season was really a fight for reliability, and - at one stage - credibility. Teething troubles were inevitable, as were engine blow-ups, and it soon became clear that even for drivers like Mikkola, Ms. Mouton, and Franz Wittman the Quattro was a difficult car to drive very fast. There was never any doubt about

63

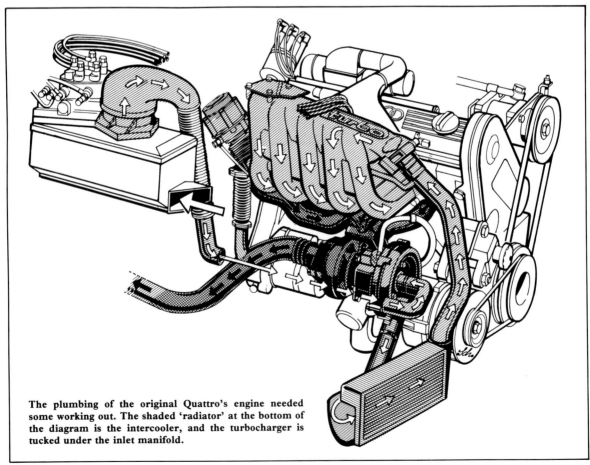

The plumbing of the original Quattro's engine needed some working out. The shaded 'radiator' at the bottom of the diagram is the intercooler, and the turbocharger is tucked under the inlet manifold.

Top Left

This Quattro A1 engine layout shows the five-cylinder engine, slanted over towards the right of the engine bay, and the water radiator tucked in alongside it, on the left of

Michele Mouton was always one of the unluckiest Quattro 'works' drivers, and she never really came to terms with the ill-handling Sport Quattro S1, Lombard-RAC rally of

the traction of the Quattro, or about its straight line performance, but the front-heavy weight distribution meant that the Quattro could 'bite back' if provoked; it was rather too easy to get the car into an under-steering situation on corners, from which there was no easy escape. Drivers who could analyse their instinctive approach to rallying at flat-out speeds finally decid-

ed that the Quattro had to be driven like an ultra-powerful front-wheel-drive car which also happened to have power going through the rear wheels as well!

In that first year the problems centred on transmission reliability, and on engine difficulties. On several occasions the cars broke one or other transmission components while well away from service - but sometimes they carried on with front-wheel-drive only, or sometimes with rear-drive only. Engines either blew up, or got themselves very hot, and it was in an attempt to control these temperatures that the team was

Top
The Quattro's front skid-shield was a huge Kevlar device, which is wearing through on this well-used example!

Above
'The office' of a works Quattro, which was a bit different from the plush layout of the road car, Note that there was only one transmission lever, the gear lever, and no chance of making mode changes.

Top Right
Well-up off the ground over a hump, this Quattro A1 is bellowing its way to another success - the event is the Scottish rally, and this is another of David Sutton's cars.

Bottom Right
The Quattro A2's distinguishing features included the moulded depressions in the rear wheel arch extensions, which could be opened up to feed fresh air to the rear brakes. This was Hannu Mikkola, on his way to winning the Scottish rally.

Above
Audi's neat way of increasing the oil cooler capacity on the A1 Quattro was to squeeze a large radiator under the tail spoiler.

This was the car which started the rallying revolution - Audi's original long-wheelbase Quattro. This is the 1982-model A1 model, as rallied in the U.K. by Hannu Mikkola and Bjorn Waldegard.

68

All the excitement of modern rallying, with an A1 Quattro
(Hannu Mikkola driving) reaching the finish of the Mintex
rally of 1982.

involved in controversy in the Acropolis rally. The inner headlamps were removed, and flexible flaps fitted in their place; these were forced open as forward speeds rose, and more fresh air found its way into the engine bay. Neither this, nor the extra battery put inside the passenger compartment to aid engine re-starts in very hot conditions, impressed the organisers, who promptly disqualified them all.

There was also a particularly nasty fire at a re-fuelling halt, which put team manager Walter Treser in hospital, but this did not deter Audi management, who promptly removed him from his position, in favour of Reinhard Rode. Thereafter the 'works' Quattro team was a bit less flamboyant, and the cars became progressively more reliable. Treser, incidentally, soon left Audi completely, and went on to develop a thriving customising and conversions business centred around Audi products.

Before the end of the year a new bonnet/nose assembly had been homologated (which effectively made the revised under-bonnet arrangements official and road-legal ....), and - equally important - so had a new oil cooler arrangement, where the massive radiator itself was

Above
A partly-built short-wheelbase Sport Quattro, showing the engine, radiator, and front end layouts. Note that the alternator is in front of the radiator block. *(Photo: Holmes)*

Top
All neat and tidy, with new HB cigarette company sponsorship, is a Quattro A2, liveried up for Stig Blomqvist to drive it. By this time the 'works' cars had abandoned Kleber tyres in favour of Michelins.

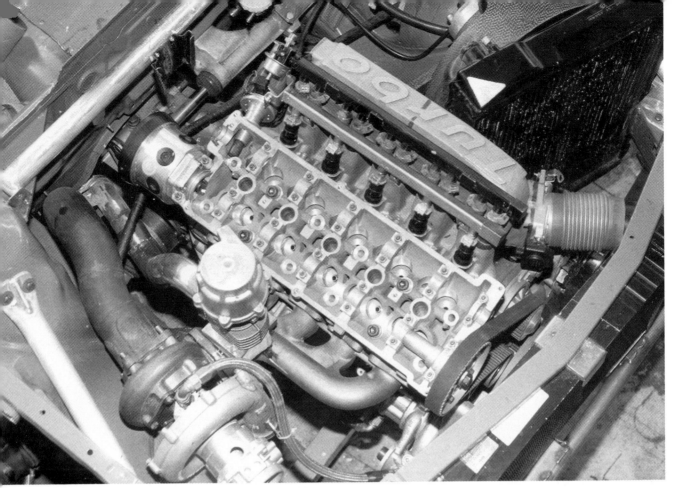

tucked away under a raised rear spoiler.

The cars, however, were always competitive, with Mikkola winning easily on the snow and ice of Sweden in February, Ms. Mouton fourth in Portugal, and Mikkola third in the 1000 Lakes. Then came San Remo, and Michele's resounding victory against all the odds, and Mikkola's easy victory in the Lombard-RAC rally. There were many Quattro successes in other countries, but world-wide domination was yet to come.

After this, it seems, several other teams became convinced that they had to produce a four-wheel-drive car, to remain competitive, but Audi were comfortably aware that none of these projected cars could possibly be ready until 1983 or 1984. In 1982, too, the new generation of regulations came into force (although old-style Group 4 cars could still be used, or have their homologation transferred into the new régime), so the second Quattro season was bound to be something of an interim year.

The most important change however, already homolgated on 1st December 1981, was that the Quattro could now use a light-alloy cylinder block, which saved 22kg/48lb, while the more widespread use of Kevlar panels brought the total saving up to 100kg/220lb. and the weight distribution of the rally cars was

The Sport Quattro's engine had four-valves-per-cylinder heads, and twin overhead camshafts, which helps to explain the complexity of this view. *(Photo: Holmes)*

significantly improved. For the next four seasons, indeed, Audi consistently tried, but only partially succeeded, to shift Quattro weight rearwards, to improve the natural handling balance of what was still quite a heavy car.

This was also the year in which David Sutton prepared, and ran, a Quattro for Hannu Mikkola (and, once, Bjorn Waldegard) to drive in the British series, which the car dominated, and in which John Buffum started his domination of North American rallying with his works-built car. There would be many such 'private' programmes in other countries - notably South Africa - in the years to come.

This, too, was the season in which Audi had no modern competition until the new mid-engined, rear-drive, Lancia Rally 037 arrived, and that car was not really competitive until the evolution version was homologated, and reliability was achieved towards the end of the year. Unless events were held on tarmac surfaces, where more conventional cars could benefit from a great deal of diligent practice, a 'works' Quattro was *always* likely to win; it was almost inevitable that a truly massive effort, which included sending cars all the way to New

71

Above

J-C. Andruet's Citroen Visa 1000 Pistes in the 1985 Monte Carlo Rally. This was the lowest-priced of all Group B 4 x 4s - but plagued by transmission problems.

(Photo: Hugh Bishop)

Top Left

Audi's way of up-grading their original Quattro for rallying was to produce the 20-valve, short-wheelbase, Sport Quattro S1 of 1984 - Stig Blomqvist on his way towards the Driver's World Championship of that year.

(Photo: Hugh Bishop)

Left

Understeer! This is the evolution version of the front-engined Citroen BX 4TC, in the 1986 Swedish rally.

(Photo: Hugh Bishop)

Zealand (in vain) and Brazil (where Michele Mouton won outright), should result in the Quattro winning the World Championship for makes. The Mikkola-Mouton 1-2 in the Lombard-RAC rally was a fitting end to the 1982 season.

Surprisingly, neither team driver had a lucky, or consistent year, so their rival Walter Rohrl, driving an obsolete Opel Ascona 400, won the Driver's series. Even more interesting was the showing of Stig Blomqvist who, in a 'private' Quattro, might have won the 1000 Lakes event if team orders had not required him to finish second behind Mikkola, and who actually *did* win the San Remo event a few weeks later.

For 1983, there were new rules, which required all existing rally cars to be rehom-

Right

Deep water, snow in the background, and a Sport Quattro make this an atmospheric shot of rallying in 1985 ....

Below

The first UK appearance for a short-wheelbase Sport Quattro was by Walter Rohrl, in the Ulster rally of 1984. Rohrl came to terms with this car's strange behaviour more readily than any other 'works' driver.

ologated from group 4 to the new Group B, and there was the prospect for Audi of determined opposition from Lancia, whose car had finally begun to win important events. The existing Quattro was re-homologated from 1st January 1983 but a most important derivative, universally known as the A2 model (which meant that the original became retrospecively known as the A1), was homologated from 1st May 1983.

At a casual glance, there was little to distinguish an A2 from an A1, but more detailed scrutiny showed that enlarged wheelarch flares had been adopted (this allowed wider-section racing tyres to be used for tarmac events), and that there was a moulded scoop arrangement on the new rear arches, which could be opened out to feed more cool air to the rear brakes.

Under the skin, which featured even more Kevlar than before, there was a minor change to the engine, which had a 79.3 mm bore instead of 79.5 mm, and whose capacity was 2,135 cc instead of 2,144 cc. This made absolutely no difference to the performance potential, although other development changes had allowed peak power to be increased to about 340 bhp at 6,000 rpm, but because of the fact that FISA regulations imposed a 1.4:1 conversion factor on the capacity of a turbocharged engine, it allowed the A2 to fall neatly inside the 3-litre class limit, at 2,989 cc instead of 3,003 cc. This allowed the car to run at a lower minimum weight limit - if Audi should ever be able to build a Quattro down to that!

1983, as I have already recounted in an earlier chapter, was the year in which Audi had to fight extremely hard against Lancia. In spite of the team mounting a mighty effort, with multi-car teams being sent to the Safari, New Zealand, Argentina and the Ivory Coast, as well as all the usual venues, this was the season in which Lancia won the Makes championship, but in which Hannu Mikkola actually won the Driver's crown that he had deserved for so long. Those extremely expensive forays, incidentally, were only partially successful, for although Hannu Mikkola won in Argentina, he had to settle for second place in Kenya and in the Ivory

Walter Rohrl's Sport Quattro scrabbling around a gravel hairpin in the San Remo rally of 1984. The second evolution version of this car won San Remo a year later.

(Photo: Hugh Bishop)

Ford's RS200 looked right, and well-balanced, in this Swedish rallying shot. There was no evolution version of the car, though one had been planned for late 1986.

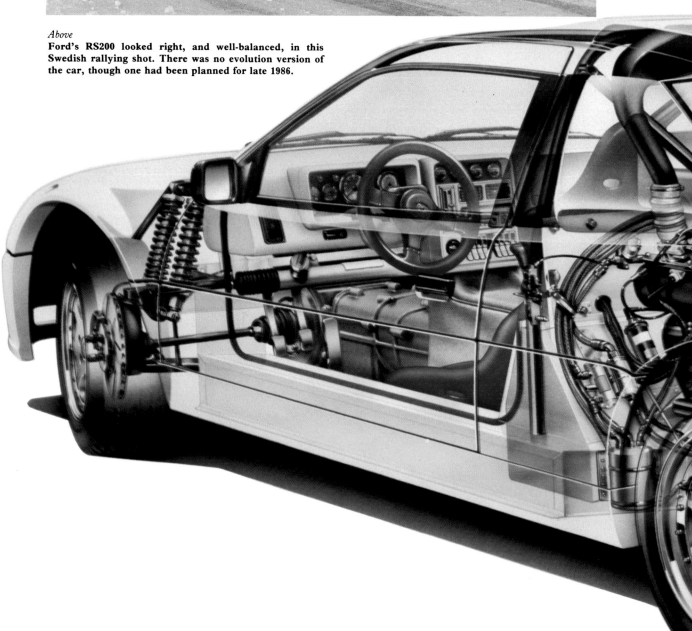

Ford's RS200 of 1984-86 was the *only* completely special Group B car to be rallied. It bore no visual resemblance to any other Ford car.

Stig Blomqvist (Ford RS200) on the Acropolis rally of 1986.
He was leading the event when he put the car off the road

Coast, while none of the cars even finished in New Zealand.

This was the year in which Roland Gumpert became the dominant management figure at Ingolstadt, in which the team switched from Kleber to Michelin tyres, in which Stig Blomqvist became a regular team member - and it was also the year in which Audi realised that the long-wheelbase Quattro was already at its peak and might soon to be caught, and even be beaten, by a new generation of four-wheel-drive cars.

The engineers, however, had not been idle, and by the middle of 1983 rather blurred sneak pictures showed that another new model was on the way. This car, previewed at the Frankfurt motor show of September 1983, and homologated (with 200 cars completed) on 1st May 1984, was the stubby, but much more specialised, Sport Quattro. This car, incidentally, was called 'Sport Quattro S1' on the homologation papers, and the car which the *media* now calls the 'S1' is merely the second-evolution derivative of that model. Clear now?

The easy, but misleading, way to describe this model was to call it a short-wheelbase Quattro, but there was more involved than just chopping 32cm/12.6 inches out of the wheelbase of a standard Quattro. In terms of the basic pressed steel structure, this is precisely what had been done, with the 'spare' material being taken out of the structure behind the driver's seat, and ahead of the rear wheels, for the basic shape was much as before, there was now some very cramped '+2' rear seat accomodation, and the problem of a front-heavy four-wheel-drive car had actually been exacerbated, not reduced. When *Autocar* tested one of the 200-off 'homologation cars' in August 1985, they found that the weight distribution was slightly more nose-heavy than before, with 62.1 per cent of the weight being carried over the front wheels. Nor was the car noticeably lighter than before, for it turned the scales at around 2,800 lb., in spite of the 200-off homologation cars all having Kevlar wings, roof and apron, as there was full trim, instrumentation, glass windows, and creature comforts.

The most important change, for the new car, was to its engine, which had a completely new cylinder head, with four valves per cylinder, and cross-flow breathing for the first time on a Quattro. With 1.2 Bar/17.4 psi of turbocharger boost, the 2,135 cc engine produced a remarkable 306

bhp at 6,700 rpm in standard form, and when fully tuned for rallying there was no less than 400 to 450 bhp at 7,500 rpm on tap! The standard car had the usual Audi five-speed transmission, but for rallying an alternative six-speed transmission was also homologated, and this was necessary in some cases, for the rally-tuned 20-valve unit was very 'peaky' indeed. As with earlier Quattros, the centre differential was usually omitted from fully-prepared rally Quattros (this was tantamount to admitting that the standard 50%/50% torque split was not ideal for ten-tenth's motoring), though as the 1984 and (later) 1985 seasons progressed, the Audi engineers became more and more reluctant to give out information to the press, and at times seemed deliberately to give false information to confuse everyone, not least their rivals.

It is only fair to say that the Sport Quattro was not at all as successful as the well-proven A2 model, and that for some time the regular

Below
By the end of 1985 the second evolution Sport Quattro S1 was homologated, and had won the San Remo rally. Hannu Mikkola drove this car in the 1985 Lombard-RAC rally, but was forced to retire.

drivers tried very hard *not* to have to use it in World Championship events. It was much faster in a straight line (even the standard car did 0-60 mph in 4.8 sec., and reached 154 mph - and that was with 'only' 306 bhp!), but its engine was much less reliable at first, and it was visibly more difficult to drive to the limit. Another noted rally-watcher has described the original

Sport Quattro as showing 'fire-belching, erratic progress', and as giving 'an impression of a complete dynamic mismatch', which is a vivid way of summarising the car's lurchy, bucking, barking way through stages. Audi, however, were

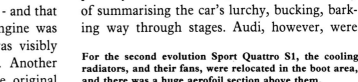

For the second evolution Sport Quattro S1, the cooling radiators, and their fans, were relocated in the boot area, and there was a huge aerofoil section above them.
(Photo: Holmes)

The second evolution Sport Quattro S1 (which most people merely call the 'S1') had radically new aerodynamic aids at the front of the car, complete with rubberised 'fences' along the peak of the wheel arches. *(Photo: Holmes)*

committed to making this car work properly ('face' is just as important to the West Germans, it seems, as it is to the Japanese ....), and persevered with it.

Old-style A2 Quattros were taken to New Zealand and Argentina in 1984 (they won both events, convincingly), while on the 1000 Lakes the team was comprehensively defeated by the sensational new Peugeot 205 Turbo 16. There was more disappointment on the San Remo, when Rohrl crashed his Sport Quattro, and Stig Blomqvist's car blew its engine, so by the time the team went to the Ivory Coast they were in despair.

There wasn't much competition in Africa (and Mikkola's A2 Quattro was Blomqvist's rebuilt practice car), but there was still great relief when the Sport Quattro notched up its first victory. Even so, it was noticeable that Mikkola's Lombard-RAC rally mount was an A2 derivative ....

Things improved in 1985, after Audi sold off all their old-type long-wheelbase Quattros, though it was clear that the new car was no longer a match for the Peugeot. Walter Rohrl's car was astonishingly competitive on the Monte Carlo rally (and finished second to Vatanen's Peugeot), while Stig Blomqvist was a close second to Ari in Sweden. Then came Portugal, where Walter Rohrl's car looked set to win until a late stage, when the five-speed gearbox broke. The cars (henceforth fitted with six-speed transmissions) failed in the Safari and Corsica, but Blomqvist's car was again second in the Acropolis, and Rohrl's third in New Zealand, once again only headed by the flying Peugeots.

Then, in mid-season, Audi suddenly produced, and homologated, the 20-off second-evolution version of the short-wheelbase car, the model usually called 'S1' in magazine reports. Roland Gumpert claims that development of the 'E2' variant only started in March 1985, and that homologation was originally targetted for the 1000 Lakes in August, but as it happened the first 'E2' appeared in a non-championship rally

in the USA (Olympus) in July, and its World Championship début was in Argentina four weeks later.

For the 'E2' model, the two principal aims were to improve the weight distribution, and to make better use of aerodynamics. The original second-evolution type not only moved *all* the cooling systems (water, oil, and transmission) into the boot compartment, with twin electrically driven cooling fans pulling air through the radiator blocks, and exhausting it through the rear panel, but also placed the hydraulically-driven alternator there as well; on the official 'homologation cars', the alternator returned to its place on the engine. The result was not only to improve the weight distribution, to a much more manageable 51 per cent front/49 per cent rear, but it also gave the ultra-powerful five-cylinder engine much more space 'to breathe' in the front compartment as well.

All the aerodynamic improvements were obvious - *very* obvious. At the front of the car there was a large 'cow-catcher' front spoiler, while at the rear there was a large aerofoil, mounted on pylons attached to the boot (or, should I now say, cooling compartment!) lid. Ahead of the rear wheels were large scoops to direct fresh air into that cooling compartment, there were skirts along the side of the shell, and wider-than-ever front wheel arch extensions were topped by rubberised 'fences' to direct the air in the required directions.

The system certainly worked, for tests showed the car to be 'flying' better than before, and settling down sooner; at high speeds up to 1,100lb/500 kg of downforce was generated. Stig Blomqvist soon discovered the proof in the Argentine event, for after a shunt had wiped off the front spoiler he found that the car was understeering considerably.

Engine changes were concentrated on moving the mass of the torque curve down the rev range and making the unit more 'driveable', for peak power stayed at 440 bhp, and while the six-speed transmission was standardised, work began on refining a semi-automatic Porsche transmission (which was actually used in Rohrl's car in the Lombard-RAC rally).

By this stage Audi were very guarded indeed about giving information to the press on the development work they were doing on the transmission, but it soon became clear that some form of central slip-limiter was taking over from

---

Top Colour
Ford's Kalle Grundell took the RS200 to third place in Sweden in 1986, and was leading the Acropolis before a service problem put him out of the running.

Opposite Colour
Markku Alen's Lancia Delta S4, Corsica 1986. This rally was very demanding of such 450 bhp 4 x 4s.

(Photo: Hugh Bishop)

An evocative shot of the final version of the Quattro, short wheelbase, aerodynamic aids and all, as driven by Walter Rohrl into fourth place on the 1986 Monte Carlo rally. Notice the driven wheel tracks from all four wheels ....
(Photo: Holmes)

the solid drive of the earlier cars. First used in the 1000 Lakes event, this was fitted behind the main gearbox, and seemed to work rather like ABS braking, but in the opposite way, and required its own electronic black box to sense changes in drive shaft speeds.

In conjunction with viscous couplings on the front and rear differentials, this certainly transformed the Quattro's traction and handling balance, and finally got it away from a fixed 50/50 split of torque delivery when conditions demanded it. It looked, and apparently felt, a much easier car to drive, and was once again 'on the pace'.

The début in the non-championship Olympus rally was promising enough (for Hannu Mikkola won the event comfortably), but an even more encouraging performance came in the Finnish 1000 Lakes, where Blomqvist's car not only finished second to Salonen's Peugeot, but was only 48 seconds behind, and set 16 fastest stage times. Then came San Remo, where Walter Rohrl dominated proceedings, in spite of moaning publicly about the car's handling problems beforehand, and won easily.

But the rest of the season was disappointment. Not only was there the scandal of the Ivory Coast rally, where Michele Mouton's original-type Sport Quattro was accused of having been swopped, in mid-rally, with a chase car, but on the Lombard-RAC rally Rohrl's E2

model crashed when well placed, and Mikkola's E2 car retired with electronic problems.

The Ivory Coast drama was never properly resolved, but there must have been substance in it all, as team chief Roland Gumpert was removed from his job shortly afterwards.

However, even though the Sport Quattro 'E2' was a demonstrably better car than any of its predecessors had been, the Audi team definitely faced a crisis in 1986. Not only was the Peugeot still around but the new Lancia was obviously its equal, while Ford's RS200 and Austin-Rover's Metro 6R4 were all coming on strong.

In the first six World Championship events of the year, the best Quattro result was Mikkola's third place in the Monte Carlo rally. Rohrl was falsely accused of being the ringleader behind the 'drivers' strike' in Portugal, and after the Lancia crash which killed Henri Toivonen in Corsica, Audi management was so sickened that they immediately withdrew from rallying at all levels. Not only the World Championship team, but such notable 'private' teams as the British effort (where Hannu Mikkola had started the 1986 season so successfully in an original-type Sport Quattro), and John Buffum's USA team, also withdrew.

If and when rallying returned to sanity, Audi bosses implied, they might consider coming back to the sport, but it would be with a Group A, saloon-based, car. In that respect, at least, they would be well placed, as there is a four-wheel-drive version of every car in their range.

CITROEN VISA 1000 PISTES

and a hatchback, and rather narrow, sit-up-and-beg styling.

Perhaps the sweet little Visa 1000 Pistes, which Citroen homologated on lst March 1984, and used spasmodically at World Championship level for the next two seasons, was the *only* four-wheel-drive Group B car which made any sense to the average private owner. It was, after all, the only such machine which did not set out to wrest outright victory from its rivals, and the only one which could be purchased, and actually rallied, without massive financial support from a sponsor.

Citroen's rallying activities had been very restrained in the 1970s, and their last major victory (in the 1974 UDT World Cup Rally) had been achieved by a private team from Australia, but in 1980/81 a new policy saw ex-team driver Guy Verrier installed in a revived competitions department, with the brief of livening up Citroen's rather stodgy image.

Right from the start, the team chose to concentrate on the front-wheel-drive Visa, and it was developments of this car which finally led to the 1000 Pistes car of 1984. The original Visa had been launched in 1978, a front-wheel-drive car with the floor pan and suspensions of the existing Peugeot 104, but a choice of engine/transmission packs - one being the transversely-mounted 1.1-litre four-cylinder Peugeot 104 unit, the other being a Citroen 2CV-style air-cooled flat-twin engine of 652 cc, with longitudinal transmission. All mass-production Visas had four passenger doors

In the first two years the team developed larger-engined, more-powerful, front-wheel-drive Peugeot-engined Visas, starting with the 1.3-litre Visa Super X, and then for 1982 they produced the 200-off Visa Trophee Group B car, which had a 100bhp/1,219cc engine, and was a good class-winning proposition.

But there was more. At the 1000 Pistes rally of 1981, Citroen entered a prototype Visa, which had a 210bhp 2-litre CX Reflex engine (as originally seen in the Peugeot 505) transversely mounted behind the seats, and driving the rear wheels through a five-speed transaxle. During 1982 and 1983, more and more variations on a Visa theme were produced, and even occasionally used in events where homologation was not required; it would be fair to say that every possible avenue, and design layout, was assessed, not merely on paper, but in running prototypes.

Specifically, there was a larger-engined front-wheel-drive car built as an evolution of the Group B Trophee, there were mid-engined/rear-drive cars with in-line and transverse engine locations - and then there were no fewer than five four-wheel-drive testbeds. Three of these (with Peugeot-Talbot Tagora V6, 2.2-litre Matra-modified four-cylinder, and 2.4-litre Citroen CX units, respectively) had mid-mounted engines, one phenomenal machine had twin Visa engine/transmission

Left
Before Citroen settled on a front-engined four-wheel-drive car, they also produced a twin-engined prototype, here seen being built in Paris, in 1983. *(Photo: Holmes)*

Bottom Left
The Visa 1000 Pistes had a transversely-mounted front engine, laid well back towards the passengers' knees. The transmission is all hidden underneath this. *(Photo: Holmes)*

Right
The simple rear end of the Visa 1000 Pistes included a differential bolted up to the floor of the body shell, and trailing arm suspension. *(Photo: Holmes)*

Below
There was very little to choose between the appearance of a front-wheel-drive Visa Trophee, and a four-wheel-drive Visa 1000 Pistes. Work this one out for yourselves ....

packs, one at the front, and one at the rear, while the fifth had a transversely-mounted 1.55-litre four-cylinder Peugeot/Visa type of engine at the front, in the normal production-car location.

Most of these cars were rally tested in the 1000 Pistes of 1983, but only one of them - the front-Visa-engined 4WD car - made it to the finish. As this also looked likely to be the simplest, and cheapest, car of all to build, Citroen announced that they would therefore put it into production, and that its name would be '1000 Pistes'.

When the Visa 1000 Pistes finally went on sale it was not at all easy to tell it apart from the Visa Trophee/Chrono from which it had been developed, as the same basic five-door body style, front end treatment, and small tail-gate spoiler, were all used. However, whereas the Trophee had used standard Visa rectangular headlamps, the 1000 Pistes model used four circular headlamps instead, there were wheel arch extensions, and a different decorative scheme along the flanks.

Compared with the 100 bhp Trophee model, the 1000 Pistes had a wheelbase longer by one centimetre/0.4 in., the front track remained unchanged, while the rear wheel track had been increased by four cm/1.6 in.

Because the four-cylinder Visa models all used one or other variation of the transverse-engined Peugeot 104-style engine installation (the same as was later adopted for the Peugeot 205 model), it made a conversion to four-wheel-drive relatively simple. As viewed from the side of the normal mass-production front-wheel-drive Visa model, the light-alloy four-cylinder engine was above the 'gearbox-in-sump' transmission, and inclined backwards at the astonishing angle of 72 degrees (in other words, it was nearly flat!), with the spur-gear final drive and front differential behind the transmission, but effectively hidden away *under* the engine.

To produce a four-wheel-drive conversion,

it was only necessary to 'tap' the rear of this spur gear final drive with a transfer gearbox, take a propeller shaft to the rear, hang up a rear differential/final drive unit behind the back seat, and feed drive shafts out to a modified trailing arm type of rear suspension. The only important body shell modifications needed were to the floor, to accommodate the run of the propeller shaft, and to accept the rear differential which, incidentally, included a limited-slip mechanism.

It was, in other words, a very cheap-to-build rally car, with little sophisticated engineering. Because of the transmission layout (there was no centre differential), the torque split was a straight 50 per cent/50 per cent, and because there was more front end than rear end weight, the handling tended towards understeer. However, apart from having better traction, the 1000 Pistes was a better handling car than the Trophee had been, purely because of the torque split and the four-wheel-drive. The ultimate-tune Chrono, which had a 1,434 cc engine, had had to feed 135 bhp through the steered front wheels, thus giving it Mini-Cooper S handling, though with the benefit of larger diameter road wheels; the 1000 Pistes was sold as an 'homologation car' with 112 bhp, but in fully-tuned evolution form in 1984 the same engine had 145 bhp *split equally between front and rear wheels,* and this gave the front tyres an easier job.

The transverse Peugeot-designed engine was a neatly detailed unit, made as light as possible with die-cast cylinder block and head components, wet cylinder liners, and a sturdy five-bearing crankshaft. There was a single overhead camshaft in the cross-flow cylinder head, and because of the way in which the engine was installed in every car which used it, the exhaust ports were behind/underneath the head as fitted, with the inlet manifold and carburettors at the front/on top. The 1000 Pistes, therefore, had two twin-choke Weber 45DCOE carburettors whose bodies, and the air filter feeding air into them, quite dominated the crowded engine bay.

Like the Mini, this engine installation featured a three spur gear transfer of torque from the crankshaft, to the gearbox below it. For the 1000 Pistes this was a five-speed all-synchromesh assembly (with the same parts, and internal ratios, as the front-wheel-drive Trophee/Chrono), though the final drive ratios of the homologation car were slightly lower-geared (4.067:1 instead of 3.87:1). As with the Audi Quattros of the period, there was no way of varying the torque split from front to rear wheels, though at least the car could carry on in front-wheel-drive if the rear-drive part of the installation became deranged for a time!

The fully-prepared 1000 Pistes had 145 bhp, and weighed about 770kg/1,700 lb. It was, in

other words, a light and efficient little package - but naturally there was no way that it could be competitive in straight-line performance, particularly up-hill, or in heavy going. In good old-fashioned Imperial terms, the 1000 Pistes had a power/weight ratio of 191 bhp/ton unladen, which compared rather badly with the Sport Quattro's 360bhp/ton and (in 1985) the Peugeot 205 Turbo 16's 480bhp/ton unladen. In addition, of course, the lightweight Visa suffered relatively more than the heavier cars when two occupants and a load of fuel was taken on board.

However, not even Citroen expected it to be a winning car. They merely expected it to uphold the Citroen name with honour, as an interim machine between the obsolete front-drive Trophees and Chronos, and the much bigger and faster BX 4TC which they were already starting to develop. The existence of the 1000 Pistes was announced during 1983, production began in the winter of 1983, and the necessary 200 Group B homologation cars, with 1,360 cc engines and 112 bhp, were completed by 1st March 1984.

Right away, an extra 20 'evolution' cars were built, and homologated from 1st April 1984 (and, no, that date was *not* significant!), the principle changes being the use of over-bored, 1,434 cc, engines with 145 bhp, and lightweight body skin panels. Because the car was sold for such a reasonable price, Citroen had no problem in 'moving the metal' - the factory took most of the evolution cars, with the balance going to lady drivers competing in a French regional promotional championship. The object, in all cases, was to have a sure-fire class winner, which might just be useful in the Group B category of rallies not entered by the Supercar hotshots. Naturally the 1000 Pistes was expected to be more useful on gravel rallies, than on tarmac.

There was no doubt that, compared with the previous front-drive generation of small Citroens, this was a great advance - in 1984 the British 1000 Pistes car run by Chris Sclater for Citroen UK was reckoned to be between three and four seconds per mile quicker than the Chrono which had been used in the previous year.

But what an event to choose for the World Championship début! Citroen did not take the safe way out, by entering a known European event, or even by blooding them in a minor rally which would not be well reported - instead they took the very brave step of entering no fewer than three cars for the Safari.

Because the event was run in the second half of April, Citroen hoped that the rains would have arrived, and produced the sort of wet conditions which would be kind to their little cars. As it happened, the rally tracks were as dry, hard, and ruthless, as ever ....

Nevertheless the cars amazed everyone, for two of the three cars finished - and one of them, driven by Chomat, won its capacity class. It was a good beginning, helped along in this country when Mark Lovell used Citroen UK's car to take ninth place overall in the Welsh International rally. Lovell's showing was exactly what Citroen wanted to prove - for every car finishing ahead of it had a larger engine, and all would have been considerably more expensive to buy and run.

Unfortunately, the start of the season was also the high point for the teams. In the U.K., the car broke its transmission after only 15 stages, while in Ulster it broke its distributor at a point where Lovell had urged it up into the top ten. In the World Championship, Citroen scored no points at all with their cars, for they experienced continuous transmission problems. and the team effort had to be abandoned. On the 1000 Lakes event, for instance, where the jumping puts a great strain on the drive line, Wambergue's car lasted for a mere four stages, and Chomat's car nine; both cars went further at San Remo, but both, equally, disappeared before the end.

If the 1000 Pistes had been more competitive, and *if* the team had not got the prospect of the much faster BX 4TC ahead of them, then Citroen might have persevered with the car, but in the end it was quietly dropped, and the team were rarely present on the World Championship scene in 1985. Not that their wait was worthwhile, for the BX 4TC, as we shall see, was just as troublesome.

CITROEN BX 4TC

There is really no diplomatic way of saying this, but - in one combine, how could Peugeot get their Group B Rally car project so right in 1982/83, yet a couple of years later Citroen could get it so wrong? Citroen, after all, is owned by Peugeot, so was there really no way that Citroen's Guy Verrier could consult, and take advice from Peugeot's Jean Todt, before settling on the design of the disastrously unsuccessful BX 4TC model?

Perhaps marque pride, and a sense of Citroen tradition, had a lot to do with this, for in times gone by the 'works' team had enjoyed real success. But those times were years back. The great days of the Citroen team were under team manager René Cotton in the 1950s and 1960s, when the over-weight, but front-wheel-drive, DS19 and DS21 saloons worked wonders on rough going. Dogged determination, brave drivers, and the team manager's cunning, counted for a lot. By the 1970s, however, Citroen had been left far behind by the various Group 4 'homologation specials', and the team's rebirth only began in the 1980s with cars based on the front-wheel-drive Visas, and the four-wheel-drive versions already described.

Although the BX 4TC was a long time a-coming, its design was not actually frozen until 1983/84, by which time the shortcomings of the Quattro's mechanical layout had become obvious, and the potential of the new Peugeot 205 Turbo 16 had also become apparent.

Even while Citroen was evolving the Visa Mille Pistes from the Visa Trophee, the team was also dabbling with the design of a larger car, to be based on the BX model, which had been launched in 1982. In its mass-production form, the BX was a transverse-engined front-wheel-drive car, with Bertone styling and a five-door layout, and there was no obvious competition potential.

Team manager Guy Verrier, however, thought there was, and in 1983 three prototype cars were eventually produced, all of which had front engines, mounted in line, not transversely like the production car. Two different factory cars were built around the Peugeot 505 Turbo engine (which had evolved from the old Chrysler 180/2-litre design of the 1970s), one with front-wheel-drive, the other with four-wheel-drive, while outside the factory the specialist firm of Polytechnic produced a 4×4 powered by a 2.4-litre 'ROC' engine. There was no horse-power shortage for any of these prototypes, for the Peugeot unit was already known to be capable of at least 400 bhp.

Before the end of 1983 it was known that the four-wheel-drive Peugeot-engined car had been chosen, and it was hoped to have it ready for 1985. As Ford, Austin-Rover and Lancia all discovered as well, Citroen found it difficult to keep up with ambitious build targets, and although a prototype was on display at the Paris Salon of October 1984, the definitive BX 4TC machine was not launched until October 1985, and homologation was achieved on 1st December 1985.

The key to the design, it seems, was that Citroen were either obliged, or had chosen, to use many more production-car parts than the Peugeot 205 Turbo 16 had done, and a brief study shows how this made the car the way it was. It is easy, of course, to say that Citroen should never have chosen a front-engined layout in the first place, especially with the iron-blocked engine sitting so far out ahead of the front wheels, but once it had been decided to use an existing in-line gearbox/transaxle to mate with it, there was really no other choice. Guy Verrier, in any case, told the press that he preferred that layout, anyway.

The basis of the BX 4TC (4 = four-wheel-drive, and TC = Turbocharged, incidentally), therefore, was a remarkably standard BX five-door body shell, with front and rear wheel arch extensions, and a spoiler on the hatchback lid. Standard Citroen-type self-levelling hydro-

pneumatic suspension units, all-independent suspension with some CX components, and full-power rack and pinion steering also featured, as did four wheel ventilated discs, those at the front being CX GTi parts.

Below
Developing the first four-wheel-drive Citroen BX 4TC, at the Paris workshops. The Peugeot-Talbot four-cylinder engine is ready to be offered up to the monocoque structure. *(Photo: Holmes)*

Above
In the Citroen BX 4TC the turbocharged four cylinder engine was mounted a long way forward, rather like that of the Audi. Like the Audi, it was an understeering car, with a very crude four-wheel-drive installation. *(Photo: Holmes)*

The engine was mounted well forward, and was a modified version of that used already in the Peugeot 505 Turbo, which is to say that it had a light-alloy, single-overhead-camshaft, two-valves per cylinder, construction. So that the rally car would fall neatly into the 3-litre class, the Peugeot engine was reduced from 2,156 cc to 2,141 cc by the simple expedient of reducing the cylinder bore - this gave an equivalent capacity of 2,997 cc when the 1.4:1 factor of comparison was applied. Maximum boost on the 200-off 'road' car was limited so that only 200 bhp was produced at 5,250 rpm; on the evolution cars, the engine was rated at a more ambitious 380 bhp at 7,000 rpm, with the aid of a larger KKK turbocharger. An interesting detail was that Citroen also placed a big electrically-driven fan

in the induction plumbing, to boost the turbocharger's effect at low rpm - this indicating that the problem of boost, and response, had by no means been solved.

The engine was bolted up to a slightly-modified version of what is still called the Citroen SM five-speed gearbox/final drive assembly, though I should point out that this invaluable component is also used in the Peugeot 205 Turbo 16 (but transversely mounted), and in the Lotus Esprit/Esprit Turbo sports car. For the SM installation, the gearbox was ahead of the line of the final drive, but in the BX 4TC's application it was turned round through 180

Right
The Citroen BX 4TC somehow looked a lot larger than the mass-production car from which it was evolved. If only the performance had matched the 'Macho' looks ....
(Photo: Holmes)

Below
This was the evolution version of the Citroen BX 4TC, as revealed in the Autumn of 1985. It was a bulky car, with four passenger doors, and the far-forward engine position is obvious from the car's styling. Note the big aerofoil section above the tailgate.
(Photo: Holmes)

degrees, to be positioned Lotus Esprit-style, with the gearbox immediately behind the line of the driven wheels.

Because the SM transaxle is a two-shaft transmission, with the output shaft below the line of the primary input shaft, it was simple enough to 'tap' the rear of that output shaft in order to take power to the rear wheels. This was done through a one-to-one transfer gear set bolted to the rear of the standard casing, which takes power up once again to primary input shaft height, before it was led aft, by a two-piece propeller shaft, to a Peugeot 505 rear differential.

The only sophistication was that the transfer drive also included a dog clutch which allowed drive to the rear wheels to be disconnected altogether if conditions seemed to justify it. There was, however, no centre differential (so the tyres had to deal with any front-to-rear wind up as best they could), and the torque split, front to rear, was therefore rigidly set at 50 per cent/50 per cent.

Perhaps this would never have been critical if the car's weight distribution had also been idealised, but according to Citroen's published figures, 56 per cent of the evolution car's weight was over the front wheels. All in all, the car looked set to handle in much the same way as an early-type Quattro had done, and with an even less sophisticated transmission system. Not only that, but the weight of the 'road' car was given as 1,280kg/2,822lb, and even the much-modified evolution model, complete with big rear wing and Kevlar panels, weighed in at nearly 1,150kg/2,535lb, which was a great deal more than the class limit for a '3-litre' Group B car. As Michael Scarlett wrote, in his technical appraisal of the car in *Autocar:*

'... there remains a question over the simplification of the drive system, which lacks even a centre differential, deemed necessary by most other 4WD proponents. Its makers obviously believe that this is unnecessary - and *if* Citroen is right, there are going to be some awfully red faces.'

Prices, ex-factory in Paris, but before any taxes were applied, were 245,000 Francs (about £21,500) for the road car, and a more frightening 800,000 Francs (£70,000) for the fully-prepared rally car.

For 1986, however, Citroen said they would tackle most of the World Championship rallies -their leading driver being the French veteran Jean-Claude Andruet, who would be backed up by Phillipe Wambergue in the second car. The ambitious, and hopeful, programme would open in the full glare of French media publicity, in the Monte Carlo rally.

That first outing, unhappily, was a real fiasco for Citroen. Wambergue's car suffered engine failure on the second special stage after a water pipe had broken, while Andruet's car needed a push out of the Aix-les-Bains *parc ferme*, and went off the road immediately afterwards. Would Sweden be better?

It was, but only marginally so. The same two 380 bhp 'works' cars turned up, and got much further round the course this time. Wambergue's car broke its engine after 24 stages, while Andruet gritted his teeth and kept the BX 4TC going, to finish sixth, no less than 24 minutes behind the winning Peugeot. On a 10 minute stage he tended to lose about 40 to 50 seconds to the Peugeots, Quattros, or RS200s -the predictions, that the Citroen was simply not going to be fast enough, were rapidly being justified.

The team was immediately in crisis. Entries for Portugal were withdrawn before the start, so that more pre-Safari testing could be completed, but next the cars were withdrawn from the Kenyan event as well. Next, it was said, just one car would be entered for the French World Cham-

Because the big Citroens retired so early on all their early outings, it was difficult for photographers even to catch them in action! This was J-C Andruet's car in the Acropolis rally, understeering hard, as usual. *(Photo: Holmes)*

pionship qualifier, the Tour de Corse. In the end, Andruet did not make it to Corsica, either, so the team then took a deep breath, looked for an event where the traditional Citroen strength and riding qualities would count more than the performance, and promised to send three cars to the Acropolis at the end of May.

Certainly a lot of development work had been done in the three month layoff, for the three brand new cars which started in Greece (Maurice Chomat was the new driver) were 50kg/110 lb. lighter than before, and the engine power was being quoted at 400 bhp instead of 380 bhp. The ride height was way up on standard, and the team was cheerful, if not exactly confident.

But there was no good news for the French. Two of the three cars actually retired on the first special stage - Chomat's with collapsed suspension, and Wambergue's when his car lost a wheel - while Andruet's car also broke a wheel on the third stage and he had to abandon his car there and then.

By mid-1986, therefore, it began to look as if the BX 4TC was never going to be a winner, and Citroen's top management pulled out completely before too much money had been thrown away. Because of FISA's proposals regarding Group B cars, in any case, the 4TC could not be used in rallying after the end of 1986.

The Ford RS200 was styled by Ghia, with a very few Sierra components (glass, and door outlines), but was otherwise completely special. Note the minimum front and rear overhang, and the considerable ground clearance.

FORD RS200

At the end of the 1979 season the factory had temporarily retired from rallying, to get on with the development of a new car - and by 1983 that car was neither ready, nor competitive. After a management upheaval, early in 1983, it took almost three years to conceive, design, develop, and homologate, a new four-wheel-drive car. The long wait, however, was worth it, for the RS200 was the first 'no compromise' four-wheel-drive rally car to be built.

In three short years, Ford's rallying reputation had sagged alarmingly. In 1979 the company had used a fleet of conventional Escort RS saloons to win the World Rally Championship for Makes, but by mid 1982 its strategy was in disarray.

Ford of Britain had become a major force in rallying during the 1960s, and its rugged and versatile Escorts had been competitive from 1968, until the early 1980s. From 1970, when the Cosworth-designed 16-valve BDA engine became available, the Escorts were always as powerful, and accelerative, as any of their rivals. By the end of that decade, however, the rear-wheel-drive Escort era was drawing to a close. for a new, front-wheel-drive, Escort Mk 3 was on the way, and would be launched in the autumn of 1980.

When the company settled down to develop a new rally car in 1980, there were two constrictions on its layout. One was that, for company 'image' reasons, it had to be based on the basic style and structure of an existing model. The other was that although it was known that new homologation rules were to be enforced, their detail had not so-far been settled.

Two basic layouts were considered - one being to evolve a mid-engined, rear-drive car, the other to evolve a front-engined, rear-drive car. Although a mid-engined Fiesta was schemed out, that project was soon cancelled. A front-engine/rear-drive Fiesta was then built as a quick 'look-see' prototype, but from the autumn of

The fat rear tyres of the Escort RS1700T give the game away - this was a rear-drive car based on the body of the front-wheel-drive Escort Mk III. These cars later rallied in South Africa, with mixed success.

Ford's first Group B Project was this front engine/rear transmission and drive conversion of the Escort Mk III, the RS1700T. Unveiled in 1981 when still not complete, it was cancelled early in 1983.

1980 the design centred on the use of a much-modified Escort Mk 3 hatchback shell. This would have a turbocharged version of the Cosworth BDA engine (which became known as BDT), and torque tube transmission to a rear-mounted transmission/final drive unit.

The new car, coded 'Columbia', was eventually given the name of Escort RS1700T, was shown to the press in July 1981, and was forecast to be homologated by mid-1982. In the meantime, the four-wheel-drive Audi Quattro had been announced, was already rallying, and looked likely to become dominant.

In the next two years, the RS1700T project's fortunes slumped. Not only did the production of the 200 cars necessary to achieve Group B homologation have to be put back to the spring of 1983, but it gradually became clear that the rear-drive concept had been rendered obsolete, even before the cars could be put on sale.

In February 1983 Stuart Turner returned from the Public Relations division, to become Ford's Director of European Motorsports, replacing Karl Ludvigsen. In the next few days he not only cancelled the RS1700T model completely, but he determined to get on with the design of a new four-wheel-drive model. Out of the ashes of the RS1700T project, therefore, the new B200 model was born. The original plan, soon seen to be over-ambitious, was for 200 cars to be built, and homologated, by January 1985.

Right from the start, the B200 was a 'no compromise' project, which meant that it did not necessarily have to look like any other Ford car; as Ford later explained, the company operated all round the world, with different looking cars, styled locally, so it was even better for their purposes if the new car merely had a Ford 'flavour' about it, rather than being a look-alike of a European mass-production model. Nor were there any pre-conceived ideas about the layout it should have. Four different designers were asked to suggest new schemes, in what was a straightforward design competition. Except that it was fairly clear that the best engine for the job was the turbocharged BDT unit (which the Escort 1700T was to have used -and for which car 200 engines had already been made), they had a complete free hand.

The chosen design was an amalgam of a scheme from the Boreham team, led by John Wheeler, and a platform-chassis structure proposed by racing car designer Tony Southgate. Detail work began in the summer of 1983, construction began in the autumn, and the first prototype was finished in March 1984. A major redesign of the chassis (to make it easier to change components in a hurry at road-side service points) then followed, but when the car was unveiled in November 1984 as the RS200, four complete cars were running.

A few components from the Sierra model were used in the RS200 - the windscreen, the steering column, and the cut-down profile of the doors, side windows, and mechanisms - but everything else was special. Even the doors were built of an advanced composite material, rather than the steel of the Sierra. Because Ford's own Ghia subsidiary had produced the style, it had a distinct family likeness to other modern Fords, but was quite unmistakeable on its own account.

There was a rugged structure (Ford now admit that it was perhaps over-engineered, and that some weight could have been saved - but this, at least, helped the car to survive high-speed crashes without collapsing completely), which was really a platform chassis in aluminium honeycomb and carbon-fibre composites, with pressed steel front and rear extensions, to which a complete roll cage, a passenger compartment structure in GRP, tubular front and rear chassis braces, and large hinged front and rear body sections were all bolted up.

Although the RS200 was an attractively styled car (smoother, even than the Peugeot, and a completely different proposition from the ugly MG Metro 6R4), its packaging was completely subservient to the engine/drive line/transmission installation. Along with the Lancia Delta S4, the RS200 was one of the first four-wheel-drive rally cars not to have to make allowances for a constricting body envelope.

It was easy enough for Ford to decide that the ideal place for the engine (in weight distribution, and heat dissipation, terms) was in the classic racing mid-ships position, behind the seats, and ahead of the line of the back wheels, but it then had to make two important decisions about the transmission.

Both for simplicity's sake, and to idealise the weight distribution of the running gear, the main gearbox and four-wheel-drive mechanism was separated from the engine/clutch assembly. In addition, the engine was considerably offset from the centre line of the chassis to allow the propeller shafts to use that centre line, and to allow equal length drive shafts to be used on each side of the car.

The light alloy engine, in fact, was turned round from a conventional stance, and drove *forward* through the clutch and primary stage reduction gears. It had its crankshaft centre line placed five inches to the left of centre, and tilted slightly down towards the front of the car, by 1.5 degrees. To equalise the weight on each side of the car, as much as possible, the engine was tilted over to the right at an angle of 23 degrees. The reduction gears (whose ratios could be

changed easily at scheduled service points, at the side of the road by service crews, to affect a speedy modification in overall gearing) then aligned with a primary propeller shaft which took the drive forward to the complete transmission casing, which was between the passenger footwells.

FF Developments both designed, and manufactured, that five-section casing, which included the centre differential, the main five-speed gearbox, the final drive, and an ingenious two-wheel-drive/four-wheel-drive 'cuff joint' control. Drive to the front wheels was taken

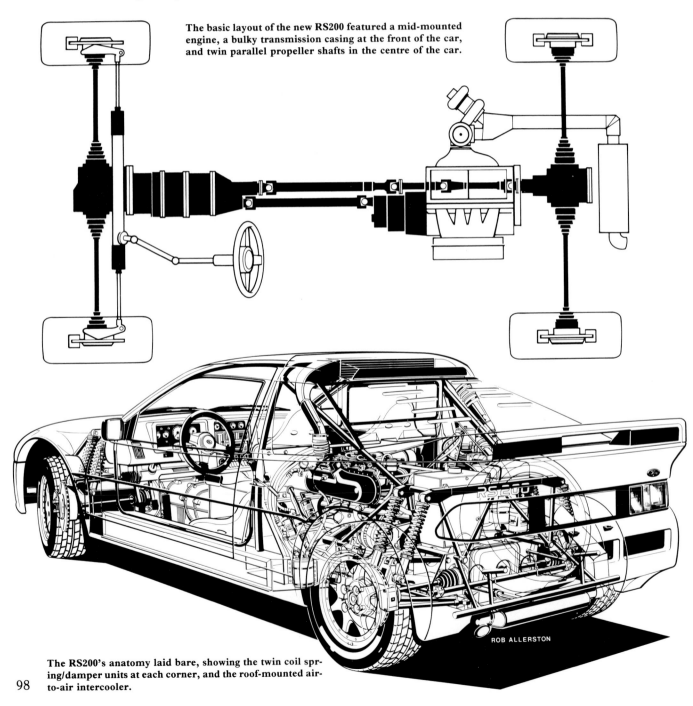

The basic layout of the new RS200 featured a mid-mounted engine, a bulky transmission casing at the front of the car, and twin parallel propeller shafts in the centre of the car.

ROB ALLERSTON

The RS200's anatomy laid bare, showing the twin coil spring/damper units at each corner, and the roof-mounted air-to-air intercooler.

directly, from exposed drive shafts at either side of the casing, while a second, two-piece, propeller shaft led back alongside the engine itself, to a separate rear final drive, and - via exposed drive shafts - to the wheels.

The transmission had every kind of alternative drive system built into it, for the drivers to play with. Not only did FF Developments provide viscous-coupling limited-slip mechanisms for all three differentials - front, centre and rear - but the use of one of these units in the centre allowed engine torque normally to be split

This workshop shot, effectively taken from the 'front' of the car, shows the transmission, the two parallel propeller shafts, and the mid/rear mounting of the engine/clutch/transfer gear assembly.

37 per cent to the front wheels, and 63 per cent to the rears. There was a secondary 'mode-change' transmission lever, mounted alongside the main gearbox lever, which allowed a three-way choice between 'normal' four-wheel-drive transmission, four-wheel-drive with a locked centre differential (which, by definition, split the torque 50 per cent/50 per cent, front to rear), and the ability to divert drive to the rear wheels only.

(After the design had been frozen, and test driving had begun, development work, in fact, showed that there was really no case in which rear-drive only was better than four-wheel-drive, and although this provision was built into every RS200 transmission ever built, it was not expected to be much used in road, or rallying, conditions).

In spite of its complexity, the whole assembly was designed with quick changes in mind. Subsequent experience showed that the bulky transaxle assembly (which had magnesium casings), and the clutch/transfer gear assembly, could be swopped at service points in a matter of minutes, by dropping them downwards out of the flat-bottomed chassis.

Fortunately for Ford, a great deal of experience, in development and in motor sport, had already been built up around the turbocharged BDT engine before it was decided to use another version of it in the RS200. Fully-tuned normally-aspirated versions, known as BDG by Cosworth Engineering, had been used in old style Group 4 Escort RSs for some years, but the turbocharged types had also been raced successfully by Zakspeed in the 'silhouette' Capris, in rallycross by famous personalities like Martin Schanche, and were being developed for use in Group C World Endurance Championship sports cars. A normally-aspirated 2.0-litre BDG could produce up to 270bhp, in rally tune a 1.8-litre version for the Escort RS1700T produced an easy 350bhp, and for the Capri 'sprint' cars anything up to 550bhp was extracted from 1.75-litre units.

When the RS200 car took shape, first thoughts were to use a cylinder capacity slightly under 1,786cc limit which allowed a turbocharged car to compete with normally-aspirated 2.5-litre cars (and which would also allow the car to run to a lower minimum weight limit), but it was soon realised that this would place a limit on the engine's potential for future evolution cars. Accordingly, when the design was settled, the definitive RS200 engine measured 1,803cc

99

100

Triple world-champion Jackie Stewart assessed the RS200 on several occasions. Here he discusses a problem with the car's designer, John Wheeler. There is only one rear spring, but twin dampers, on this development car.

(equal to 2,525cc when the 1.4:1 'factor of comparison' was applied), and the car ran in the 3-litre category. In theory this meant that the RS200 would have to carry excess weight, but in practice this was never an important factor, as the car was always well above the lower limit that a 2.5-litre class regulation would have allowed. At this time, in 1984, the intention was that a future evolution car (which has never been used, due to FISA's rule changes, which became effective in mid-1986) would have an enlarged engine of 2.1-litres (equivalent to the full 3-litres after the comparison factor was applied). Work carried out on this engine by Brian Hart's company in 1985/86 saw it produce 550bhp, and the phenomenal peak torque of 400 lb.ft.!

The technology and knowledge surrounding turbocharged engines was improving all the time in the early 1980s, and peak power figures quoted for the BDT engine prove this point. In 1982/83, as finalised for the Escort RS1700T the 200-off 'homologation cars' would have had about 200bhp, and the 'works' team cars about 350bhp. When the RS200 was announced, in prototype form, in November 1984, these figures had risen to 230bhp and 380bhp, respectively. By the time the 200 Group B 'production' cars were built in the winter of 1985/86, and the 'works' team had started using RS200s, road cars had an easy 250bhp available, and the 'works' competition cars had 420/430bhp.

By comparison with the running gear, the steering and suspension looked positively conventional, but even here there were interesting little differences of detail. There was independent suspension by coil springs and wishbones at front and rear, but with twin coil spring/damper units being used at each 'corner', and adjustment for ride height not only in the spring pans, but in the actual wishbone chassis mountings. There was also a separate toe-in control link in the rear suspension, and although the production cars had manual steering, the fully-prepared rally cars had power-assistance. Ventilated disc brakes were fitted at front and rear, with a separate handbrake caliper on the rears.

The design had always featured a turbocharger on the right side of the engine bay, and the engine's inlet manifold was on the left side. The pressurised air from the turbo was swept up and over the engine bay, by tubes, to cross sides, and there was a long, slim, intercooler across the rear edge of the roof, hidden by a cowl perched on top of the hinged engine bay cover. The RS200 seemed to have an insatiable appetite for fresh air into the rear end, so when serious rally development proved that more was needed, an extra pair of 'ears' was added, one at each side of the intercooler's letter-box' slot.

It took quite a lot longer to develop, and produce, the RS200, than its sponsors had wished. No sooner had detail design begun than the 'January 1985' deadline was dropped, but as soon as the car was announced to the world in November 1984 it was stated that homologation should be achieved by the autumn of 1985 (and it was always clear that this meant the return of the 'works' team to rallying at the Lombard-RAC rally in November).

Rather than attempt to produce such a limited number of special cars at a Ford factory, the company had all but the first few prototypes assembled at a redundant Reliant factory at Shenstone, north of Birmingham, and as part of its philosophy the company also put the car through the rigorous National Type Approval programme which every other Ford car had to meet. The production car was also given a six-year anti-corrosion warranty! The details, and the extra work involved, in meeting such targets meant that assembly dates slipped somewhat, and in the event the first cars were not actually built until October/November 1985, but the 200th and last was finished before the end of January 1986. The car was therefore homologated on 1st February 1986, and started its first event as a World Championship contender - the Swedish - just a few days later.

Ford's director of European Motorsports, Stuart Turner, stated publically, more than once, that although he personally disagreed with the whole idea of special 200-off Group B cars, he was determined that Ford should be competitive if they wanted to go rallying again. However, not only did he not like the idea of Group B, but he positively hated the idea of ultra-expensive, and extra-special evolution cars (which in his view might make the *original* 200 cars somewhat uncompetitive against the 'works' team. Accordingly, he refused even to consider the building of a 20-off evolution car at first, and all of Ford's 1986 team cars were modified from the basic production run.

Apart from the fact that they were a touch heavy, perhaps, the RS200s were never hampered by this decision, as they had been

101

'designed up', rather than 'designed down', with this philosophy in mind. In particular, the body had been shaped to provide positive down-force at all times, and needed no extra ugly hang-ons (cow-catchers, spoilers, or aerofoil sections) to allow it to 'fly' well over the bumps, there was all manner of adjustment built into the suspension geometry (and space for the whole range of allowable wheel rim diameters and widths to be used), while the engine (and, in particular the turbocharger itself) was dimensioned with 400/450 bhp in mind, rather than with the 250 bhp of the road cars as the primary consideration.

Other team managers have scoffed at Ford's insistence on having a genuine 'road legal' car, and pointed out that various compromises meant that it was a less competitive rally car. Some

Left
The fully-trimmed RS200 'road' car, showing the fully-equipped facia, and the two transmission levers. The smaller lever controls the transmission mode selection.

Below
The RS200's first outing was in a British national event, the Lindisfarne, in September 1985, when Malcolm Wilson won outright. Almost immediately after this, Wilson 'defected' to Austin-Rover, and the MG Metro 6R4.

details, indeed, bring a smile to the totally committed rally fanatic's face - such as the extra sets of tail lamps inside the lift-up engine cover, the provision of three-point rather than full harness safety belts as standard, the preparation of a detailed Workshop Manual, and even the provision of space to instal a radio/cassette receiver!

Although the RS200 was officially announced 15 months before it competed in its first World Championship rally, there was time for quite a lot of testing, but Ford did not enter prototypes in many minor events during 1985. Test sessions on stages recently used in the Portugal rally (with Malcolm Wilson driving the car) proved that the car was already on terms with the Peugeots, but the chance to complete in the 1000 Pistes rally was ignored.

It was not until September 1985 that the car started its first event, the Lindisfarne national rally in the U.K., where Malcolm Wilson battled with the MG Metro 6R4, which was also competing as a prototype. The Metro incurred road penalties after a service hold up, and slipped back, but in spite of going off the road in front of cameramen, Wilson kept the RS200 going to record a victory, first time out.

Soon after this Ford's competition manager, Peter Ashcroft, achieved a real coup, by persuading the 1984 World Rally Champion, Stig Blomqvist, to leave Audi, and sign a long-term contract with Ford. Malcolm Wilson, offered a Ford contract for 1986, chose to move to Austin-Rover instead (where he has had a truly miserable time with unreliable cars, breakages, and high-speed accidents), so as Ford's second driver Ashcroft also signed up the Swede, Kalle Grundel, who had won the 1985 German rally championship for Peugeot in a Turbo 16, and had finished fifth in the 1000 Lakes in one of those cars.

Blomqvist celebrated his new contract by taking Wilson's ex-Lindisfarne car out on a pre-Lombard-RAC rally test session and outpacing all the homologated cars, then taking the *original* 'old nail' to Norway to finish second in the Norway rally, but these were merely minor talking points, pre-homologation, when everything got serious.

In 1986 the RS200, like the MG Metro 6R4, and other newly-homologated cars, did not have a real chance to settle down before the whole future of Group B was placed in doubt after the events of March and May. Strictly speaking, the

Above
Two 'works' RS200s started the Swedish rally of February 1986, and Kalle Grundel's car finished third overall. All the 'works' cars had '200' registration numbers....

Top Right
Kalle Grundel used his 'Sweden' car on the Circuit of Ireland; his team mate, Mark Lovell took fourth place after a spate of transmission problems. *(Photo: Ralph Hardwick)*

Below Right
By mid-season Mark Lovell had learned all about the RS200 handling, and might even have won the Scottish rally if it had not been for a brief roll-over. He finished second overall. *(Photo: Ralph Hardwick)*

results show that the RS200 had not gained a World Championship victory by mid-year, but on the other hand it had led one major event (the Acropolis), been competitive on another (Sweden), and the 'works' and Ford national team cars *had* won international events, outright, all round Europe.

The encouraging sign, for Ford, was that the cars were soon seen to be winning rallies on snow, on tarmac, or in the loose, winning rallycross events, and also winning hillclimbs in the Swedish championship. In a two month period (March and April 1986), RS200s won outright the Rally of Ardennes, Portugese Centro, Tulip, Helendoorn (Holland), Rota do Sol (Portugal), and Haspengouw (Belgium).

The car's first World Championship outing was in the Swedish rally, where the team's two Swedes, Blomqvist and Grundel, were in their

element (or, as a rather naive TV skiing commentator once said: 'On their home snow' ...). It was a very important occasion for Ford, as this was the first full-house factory entry since the Lombard-RAC rally of November 1979 - the lay-off had been no less than 5 years and 3 months.

After ten stages (about one third distance), Blomqvist's car was in fourth place behind Kankkunen's Peugeot 205 Turbo 16 and Markku Alen's and Henri Toivonen's Lancia Delta S4s, but almost immediately the engine failed, as did Toivonen's Lancia unit, and eventually the third spot was inherited by Kalle Grundel in the other RS200. It was an encouraging start for the team, especially as Blomqvist

later announced that he had not been driving flat out, and that he was just about to start going faster when the engine's timing belt came off ....

For Portugal the same two cars were used, about 30 kg lighter, and with full 420 bhp engines, but for Ford the tragedy was that Joaquim Santos was in the brand new 'customer' RS200 which plunged off the road on the very first special stage (to avoid spectators in the middle of the road), striking and killing a woman and two children who could not get out of the way. The rally, as a sporting contest, disintegrated from that point, and all the factory cars were withdrawn.

Santos's car was only lightly damaged in this horrifying incident, and it is a matter of record that it was quickly repaired, and won another Portugese event just a couple of weeks later.

Although Ford dabbled with the idea of competing in the Tour de Corse, where one of the drivers *might* have been the Grand Prix driver Marc Surer, who was about to start using an RS200 of his own in other European events, they decided to give this speciality-tarmac event a miss, and prepare two new cars for the Acropolis instead.

The records show that neither car finished the event, which was won by Kankkunen's Peugeot, for both Fords were out of the event after 18 stages (or one third distance), but they also show that Grundel's car led from the start, that both he and Blomqvist had spells in the lead, and that the cars were actually in a 1-2 placing when misfortune overtook them. Of all things, Grundel's car needed an emergency hub change after a mechanic forgot to spray-lubricate the wheel studs after a wheel change - which meant that the studs broke when being torqued up - and ran out of time, while Blomqvist actually put his car off the road shortly afterwards, where there were no spectators to help retrieve it.

Following the FISA death sentence on Group B cars, the 'works' team then withdrew from World Championship rallying to start designing Sierras for the 1988 Group A season. Although engines were boosted to 450bhp a final

Look carefully and you might recognise Sierra tail lights on the RS200, but almost everything else is special. The 'ears' on each side of the intercooler scoop were to feed more air into the engine bay. Scottish Rally, June 1986.

(Photo Ralph Hardwick)

Ready to start the Acropolis rally, the 'works' RS200 looks purposeful. The two team cars were first and second in the event when both had to retire. *(Photo: Holmes)*

outing on the Lombard-RAC rally was unsuccessful, with Kalle Grundel's car fifth overall and three other cars retiring.

Several RS200s won National Championships in Europe during 1986 - Mark Lovell taking the RAC Open Series in a car prepared by the Mike Little team (but without actually winning an event), Stig Andervang winning the West Euro Cup, and sharing the Nordic (Scandinavian) Championship with Kankkunen's Peugeot, Robert Droogmans winning the Belgian, and Andervang the Dutch series.

Before long Ford realised that the evolution car *was* going to be necessary to beat Lancia and Peugeot, and work was put in hand on a '100 by 100' project (100bhp more, and 100kg lighter). This featured a 40bhp 2.1-litre version of the engine, designed and developed by Brian Hart, with extensive lightening of the structure, incorporating light alloy instead of steel sub-frames,

and more carbon fibre and Kevlar in place of the steel and light-alloy tub. 25 engines were built, but the high-tech structure was abandoned.

Most 'works-spec' RS200s were sold off to the rallycross fraternity for 1987, and with 600bhp versions of the 2.1-litre engine became 200 'E' types, where they proved to be outstandingly successful. Martin Schanche won three European championship events, Mark Rennison's dominated the British scene, while Mikael Nordstrom's car won the British Rallycross GP at Brands Hatch in December.

LANCIA DELTA S4

This section should not only cover the design of one type of car but it should also salute the record of its manufacturer. The reason quite simply, is that in the last twenty years Lancia has been the most consistently successful marque in world-class rallying. In that time the company produced several amazingly competitive cars, and has rarely had to go rallying as an underdog. In the 1970s and 1980s Lancia has won more World Championship rallies than anyone else. First there was the Fulvia HF, next the fabulous Stratos, after that the graceful Rally 037, and finally the four-wheel-drive Delta S4. At the time of writing too, Lancia is the only company to have designed, homologated *and* won with two entirely different types of Group B car.

In the 1970s Lancia broke new ground, by becoming the first manufacturer to design a new car specifically to go rallying. The famous Ferrari-engined Stratos was a completely purpose-built homologation special, for which no sales or marketing compromises were made. The rules, at the time, said that 500 cars had to be built - so that is precisely what Lancia, in collaboration with Ferrari, and their body-builders Bertone, set out to do. Designed in 1971 and unveiled at the end of that year, the Stratos started rallying in 1972, achieved homologation in 1974, and was the world's best rally car for the next four or five years. It was an object lesson of how to go rallying at World level, if the money was available - and Lancia repeated the exercise twice more in the 1980s.

Their first Group B car was the Rally 037, which was at its peak in 1983 and 1984. Design began in the spring of 1980, at the same time as the Quattro was publicly launched, but motor sport *supremo* Cesare Fiorio was not convinced that four-wheel-drive was necessary. The car which Abarth developed for him was a classic 1970s-layout Italian racing sports car, for it had a mid-mounted engine (evolved from the Fiat 131 Abarth saloon's unit), rear-wheel-drive, multi-tubular chassis construction around the basis of a Lancia Monte Carlo two-seater pressed-steel passenger compartment, all-independent suspension, and a sleek two-seater coupé body style. The only surprising feature was that the two-litre 16-valve engine was not turbocharged, as expected, but supercharged instead.

The Rally 037 was launched in December 1981, homologated on 1st April 1982 (but this was no April Fool's joke, believe me, as 200 cars genuinely seem to have been built by that date ....), won its first event (the British Audi National) in October 1982, and won its first World Championship round (Monte Carlo) in January 1983. With a driving team which included Markku Alen and Walter Rohrl, the Martini-sponsored Lancia team battled head-to-head against Audi throughout the year,

won five World Championship rounds, and finally took the World Championship for makes as well.

Even then, of course, the Rally 037's two principal problems were clear. In spite of its performance on tarmac events, it was already clear that it ought to have had four-wheel-drive to make it truly competitive on all types of event, and the choice of a positive-displacement supercharger meant that the 2-litre engine power was limited to about 310 bhp. For 1984, however, Lancia's only recourse was to produce a second evolution model, which had modified rear bodywork, and an enlarged (2,111 c.c.) engine which produced up to 325 bhp. It was not enough to keep the 037 abreast of Audi, but heroic driving by Alen and Attilio Bettega saw the car win once (on tarmac, in Corsica), take second place four times (Portugal, New Zealand, 1000 Lakes and San Remo), and third once (Acropolis). At the end of the year Lancia were second to Audi in the Makes series, while Markku Alen was also third in the Drivers' championship. 'Customer cars', in the meantime, were cleaning up all round Europe, where Biaison's car won the European Rally Championship in 1983, and Carlo Capone repeated the dose in 1984.

To their lasting credit, Lancia did not persist with the 037 after it was clear that they had miscalculated in 1980. Early in 1983 they began the design of a new rally car which would take over from it, and this one *would* have four-wheel-drive. The experienced design team in Turin realised that they could not possibly get the new car homologated before mid-1985, so they effectively conceded the 1985 season to their competitors; in that year the Rally 037 put up several plucky performances, especially with Alen behind the wheel, but it was outclassed, especially by the new Peugeot 205 Turbo 16 model.

The new project began to take shape, at Abarth in Turin, under the project code of 038. Like its predecessor, although it was effectively a completely new design, it paid lip-service to the

Top Left

One of the Lancia's earlier successful rally cars was the pretty little front-wheel-drive Fulvia 1.6HF, which Sandro Munari drove so well.

Left

The most charismatic Lancia of the 1970s, naturally, was the Ferrari-engined Stratos, which was affectionately known as the 'plastic pig'. Behind that Nomex mask is Tony Carello, about to start the Giro d'Italia.

Lancia sales force by looking superficially like one of their series-production models. There was a major shift in emphasis, however. Whereas the Rally 037 had looked a little like the Monte Carlo coupé, the new 038 was arranged to look rather like the Delta hatchback. Under the skin, of course, there was absolutely no engineering in common, for the Delta was a front-wheel-drive car with a transversely-positioned engine in the nose (all evolved from the rather more humble Fiat Ritmo/Strada hatchback layout), and a conventional pressed-steel body/chassis unit, whereas the new 038 was to be a four-wheel-drive car with the engine behind the seats, and was to have a sturdy multi-tube chassis/roll cage structure! The only actual Delta production-car parts used in the Delta S4 were the windscreen, lights, grille, and steering column stalks.

This time, too, the designers at Abarth were not obliged to use any existing Fiat/Lancia running gear, and naturally they also chose to use a completely new 'chassis'. The basis of the new car, which was christened Delta S4 in time for the public launch in December 1984, was a steel and aluminium multi-tube frame, to which all the glass-fibre, Kevlar and other exotic-material body skin panels were attached. The coil spring and double wishbone independent suspensions, at front and rear, were inherited from the Rally 037, where they had all done a very good and efficient job, and of course there was rack and pinion steering. Naturally there were massive ventilated outboard disc brakes all round, and the car was intended to run on 16 in. wheels at first, though other diameters were already being considered, to optimise the car for all types of going.

The whole design, however, centred around the newly-designed four-cylinder engine, main gearbox, and four-wheel-drive systems, which had absolutely nothing in common with the Rally 037 which the Delta S4 replaced, or with any other components used in any Fiat or Lancia production car of the period.

Press men who went to Turin for a new Lancia rally car announcement were always ready for a surprise, and in this case they certainly got it. Not only was the engine *entirely* new - two years after the launch of the Delta S4, there is still no sign of this unit, de-tuned or not, being used in any other Fiat-Lancia product - but it was turbocharged *and* supercharged at one and the same time!

Fiorio was convinced that his engineers   111

In 1980 and 1981, Lancia developed their first Group B car, the mid-engined, rear-drive, Rally 037, which had Pininfarina styling. It won many events until 1984, by which time it had been outclassed by Audi and Peugeot.

could not only produce a strong *and* light four-wheel-drive rally car, but he was also sure that a '2.5-litre' engine would produce perfectly competitive horsepower. Accordingly, it was decided to produce a new machine inside the 2.5-litre limit. So, remembering the 1.4:1 'factor of comparison' which applied to engines with forced induction, Abarth therefore designed and developed a 1,759 c.c. four-cylinder unit, which used conventional four-valves-per-cylinder combustion chambers, all-alloy construction, and Weber-Marelli fuel injection. The real innovation, however, was that the engineers had provided a Volumex lobe-type supercharger (mechanically driven by a chain of gears from the engine's crankshaft), operating *in series* with an exhaust-driven KKK turbocharger. In the lower rev range below about 5,000 rpm - the supercharger provided most of the pressurised air to the turbocharger (and hence to the engine),

and helped to reduce turbo lag, while as revs built up the turbocharger took over its conventional duties, there being a complex system of manifolding to make sure that the supercharger did not then 'choke' the turbo unit of its ration of air. In any case, there was an air volume-sensitive by-pass valve control system to maintain an effective 'short-circuit' of the mechanical 'blower' at high revs when the turbocharger was working at its peak.

Because Abarth and Fiat/Lancia had so much experience of high-performance engines (and could also consult their industrial partners, Ferrari, if they wanted to know more!), there was never any problem in producing enough peak power. Right from the start, Abarth claimed 440 bhp at 8,000 rpm for the fully-tuned evolution competition car, which when linked to an unladen weight of about 990kg/2,185 lb meant that the Delta S4 was sure to be shooting for outright victory as soon as it was homologated.

When the car was unveiled, at the end of

On their very first World Championship rally, the
Lombard-RAC of 1985, Lancia's Delta S4s took first and
second positions overall. Sutton Park water-splash on the
first day.

The Delta S4, as launched, carried Martini sponsorship, and a near standard Delta look at the front end. The aerodynamics would change, however.

1984, Lancia were by no means happy with the response of the engine, and during 1985 a lot of work went into matching the characteristics of the two types of 'blower'. The cars which were homologated, and used in competition from November 1985, had different turbochargers *and* different superchargers from those shown in December 1984. The ever-thorough development engineers, led by the experienced Giorgio Pianta (who was, himself, no mean driver too - it always helps if your drivers have complaints about the car's behaviour which you can prove, or disprove, personally!), not only perfected the Weber injection system, but also tried a rival Bosch installation instead.

By mid-1985, as assembly of the homologation cars began, the response had been considerably improved over the original, though in the first few rallies the sudden arrival of a lot of

turbocharger-inspired torque made fast driving on gravel something which had to be learned all over again.

By comparison with the engine, therefore, the Delta S4's four-wheel-drive transmission layout was almost conventional - conventional, that is, by modern Group B rally car standards. As with the Ford RS200, and the MG Metro 6R4, the Delta's engine was 'turned round' in the chassis, so that the nose of the crankshaft (from which camshaft, and Volumex supercharger, drives were taken) was towards the rear of the car, and the clutch face was towards the front of the car.

The main five-speed transmission was immediately ahead of the engine, in chassis terms, actually being placed between and below the two seats, and was an all-indirect layout, with a spur gear central differential drive being taken off the secondary shaft. Open propeller shafts then took drive to separately-mounted front and rear final drive units, the rear prop being to the left side of the cylinder block, the engine being slightly off-set to the right to make this alignment possible. At launch, the torque split, front to rear, was said to be 'variable', between 40 per cent front/60 per cent rear, and 20/80 - but it was also

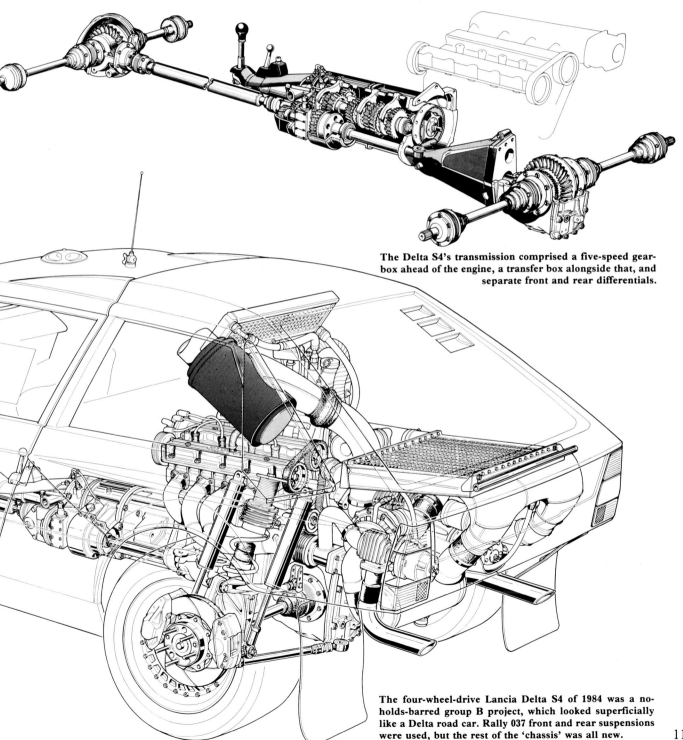

The Delta S4's transmission comprised a five-speed gearbox ahead of the engine, a transfer box alongside that, and separate front and rear differentials.

The four-wheel-drive Lancia Delta S4 of 1984 was a no-holds-barred group B project, which looked superficially like a Delta road car. Rally 037 front and rear suspensions were used, but the rest of the 'chassis' was all new.

Lancia's four-wheel-drive Delta S4 was typical of that successful rallying company, practical with flair, *very* fast, and always capable of winning.

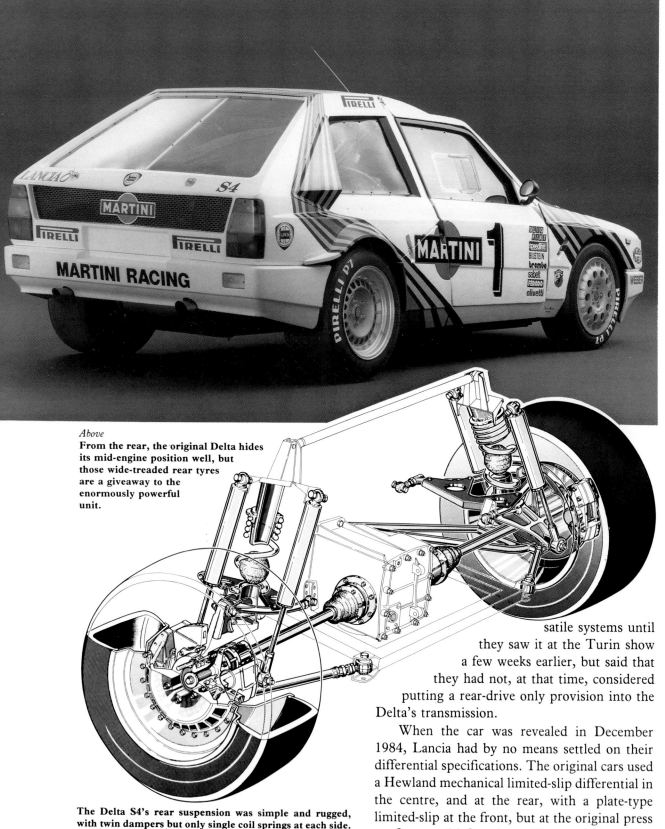

Above
From the rear, the original Delta hides its mid-engine position well, but those wide-treaded rear tyres are a giveaway to the enormously powerful unit.

The Delta S4's rear suspension was simple and rugged, with twin dampers but only single coil springs at each side.

admitted that no firm decisions had then been made. There was also a secondary transmission lever in the cockpit, alongside the main gear lever, which allowed the centre diff. to be locked up, and the torque split to become 50 per cent/50 per cent, as on existing Audis and all first-generation four-wheel-drive systems. Lancia had not known about the Ford RS200's ver-

satile systems until they saw it at the Turin show a few weeks earlier, but said that they had not, at that time, considered putting a rear-drive only provision into the Delta's transmission.

When the car was revealed in December 1984, Lancia had by no means settled on their differential specifications. The original cars used a Hewland mechanical limited-slip differential in the centre, and at the rear, with a plate-type limited-slip at the front, but at the original press conference chief engineer Pianta admitted that FF Developments viscous couplings would shortly be tested.

The launch of the Delta S4 was handled with great panache - it included what we first thought was a video of a prototype being demonstrated on the airfield some distance from the workshops, but this showing ended with the same car actually being driven through a door,

For the Delta S4, Abarth produced a brand new 1.75-litre engine, which featured turbocharging *and* supercharging. This has always worked very well indeed.

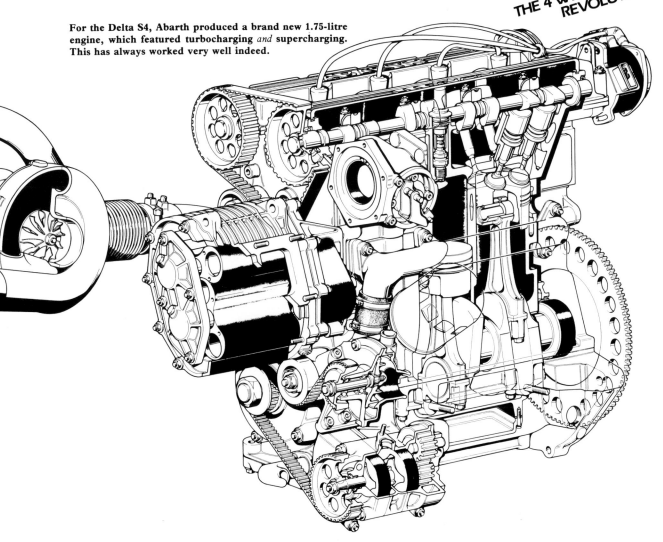

and up on to a plinth, in the press conference hall itself! However the car shown was a fully-prepared evolution version of the basic design, which was not ready to be demonstrated to the press until September 1985, when the production run was well advanced.

The 200-off production car, which was assembled at Lancia's own San Paulo factory near Turin, was a much more civilised machine than the Martini-liveried competition car, and although there was a rather stronger resemblance to the Delta series-production car there was little chance of the two types ever being confused.

For one thing, all the normal Delta road cars had five-door body shells, with four-seater accommodation, and a hatchback, while even the 'basic' 200-off Delta S4 had two passenger doors, two-seats, large ear-like air-scoops at the side of the cabin to direct air into the mid-ships engine bay, and a spoiler on the roof immediately ahead of the top of the rear 'hatchback' window. The whole of the front bodywork was ar-

ranged to hinge forward from the nose to give access to the front end, and front differential, while the rear bodywork, like the Peugeot's, and that of the RS200, was arranged to hinge at roof level, behind the line of the seats, giving access to *everything*.

Compared with the series-production Delta, too, all the basic dimensions were slightly different (which, if nothing else, proved that the body stylists had done a great job in preserving the same identity and proportions). The Delta S4 four-wheel-drive car had a 1.1 in. shorter wheelbase, but a 4.3 in. greater overall length. There was a hump in the rally car's roof behind the seats, and the wheel tracks were 10 to 12 cm (4.0 to 4.7 inches) wider. There was a sturdy roll cage built in as part of the multi-tube chassis

Overleaf Colour
The Lancia Delta S4 was not only very fast indeed, but it also handled well in all conditions .... Lombard-RAC rally, 1985.
(Photo: Hugh Bishop)

Above

Henri Toivonen (left) and Markku Alen were the star drivers in the Delta S4s during 1985 and 1986. It was the tragic crash in Corsica which killed Henri Toivonen, and caused all further development of Group B cars to be banned.

Below Right

The Delta S4 had a sturdy multi-tube chassis frame. The complicated plumbing, the location of intercoolers, and air filters, is obvious in this study of the rear end of the car.

structure, and most of the unstressed skin panels were glass fibre. The drag coefficient was quoted at 0.467, which sounds pretty awful by modern mass-production standards - but this was nevertheless 12 per cent better than the Rally 037 had ever achieved. In any case it is stability, rather than slippery aerodynamics, which matters most for a Group B rally car, where acceleration from - say - 60 mph to 120 mph was more important than a high maximum speed.

Power output had been set at 250 bhp at 6,750 rpm (very close indeed to the level chosen for the other contemporary 4 x 4s, the Ford RS200 and the MG Metro 6R4), while the changeover point where turbocharger boost became more important than supercharger supplies was set at about 4,000 rpm. The claimed weight of this, the 'road' car was a surprisingly heavy 1,200kg/2,645 lb., with 43.8 per cent of that weight over the front wheels. (The evolution rally car, of course, was more than 200kg/440lb lighter.)

For the 200-off 'road' cars the five-speed gearbox had synchromesh, and there was a 30 per cent front/70 per cent rear torque split, provided by a central FF-type viscous coupling differential. The rear final drive had a mechanical limited slip, provided with '25 per cent' settings, while there was no limited-slip at the front of the

car. Wheel and tyre equipment featured 205/55VR16 in. Pirelli P7s, on eight in. rims, while there was power assistance to the rack and pinion steering, not by the usual hydraulics and an engine-driven pump, but by a pneumatic cylinder working off engine vacuum and a storage reservoir.

When the car was first seen, Lancia predicted that the 200 cars would be finished, and homologation achieved, by 1st August 1985, in which case the car would make its début on the Finnish 1000 Lakes rally. The very strong driving team comprised Markku Alken, Attilio Bettega, and Henri Toivonen - the only problem being that Henri had not only badly injured his back in a 1984 rallying accident, but was in the middle of a contract dispute between Lancia and one of his previous teams, Rothmans-Porsche.

Things began to go wrong in the first few months of 1985, when the development cars experienced handling problems, and a great deal of work on the torque-split, the various differentials, and their settings, was needed before Pianta and his top drivers pronounced themselves satisfied. There was personal tragedy for the team in Corsica, when Attilio Bettega was killed in a Rally 037 accident. Later, the production run struck trouble because of the difficulty in getting supplies - Ford and MG also had their problems, and any other manufacturer who states that building 200 special cars is a straightforward business is quite simply not telling the truth! The result was that the car was not homologated in time to start the 1000 Lakes (which displeased Markku Alen considerably), but worse still, it also missed the Italian San Remo event, a rally in which Toivonen and Alen drove their hearts out to take third and fourth places in old-style Rally 037s.

In the meantime the cars appeared as 'course cars' on various events, including Costa Smeralda, where a good deal of rallying experience was gained, while Markku Alen's Delta S4 was the only starter in the 'prototype' category of the 1000 Pistes rally, held in the South of France. On that event the car broke its turbo on the first day, but ran quickly, and without fuss, on the second day. The only other development hang up was that the intercooler proved to be too small.

Nevertheless, the team's morale was in need of a boost by the time that homologation was achieved on 1st November 1985. By special dispensation from FISA the car was allowed to run in the Algarve rally - which started on 31st October - where Markku Alen's evolution car broke its rear transmission, but the Lombard-RAC rally which started on 24th November was its first big test.

Since the 1000 Pistes rally appearance the Delta S4 evolution car had been modified yet again, for the authorities would not approve the roof-mounted wing which was fixed to the top corner of the rear body panel. A much smaller roof spoiler was fitted in its place, and at the

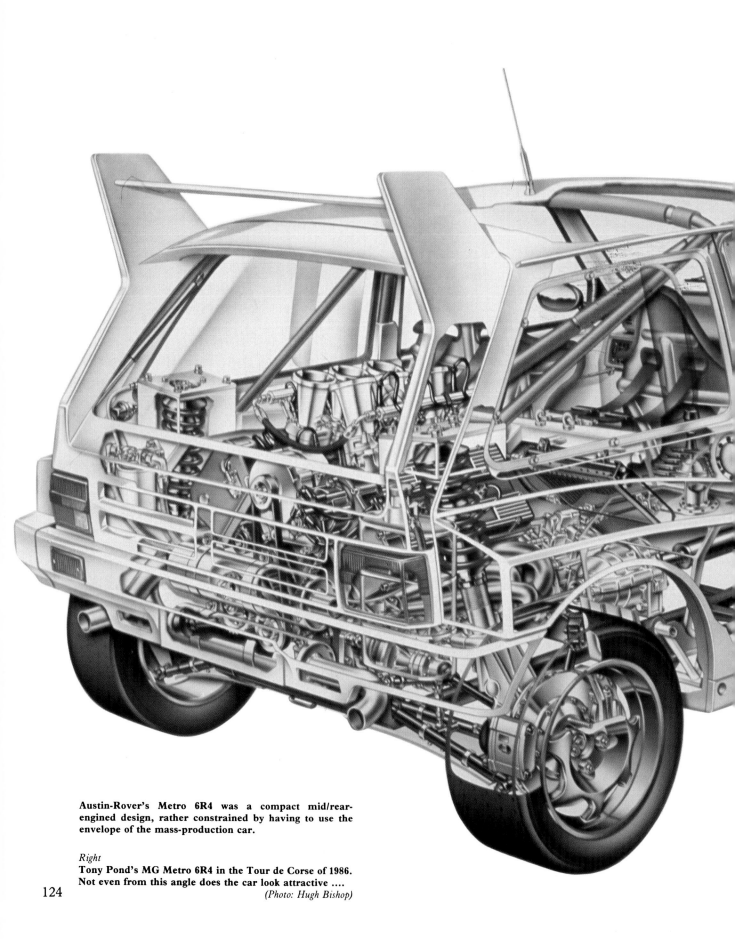

Austin-Rover's Metro 6R4 was a compact mid/rear-engined design, rather constrained by having to use the envelope of the mass-production car.

Right
**Tony Pond's MG Metro 6R4 in the Tour de Corse of 1986.
Not even from this angle does the car look attractive ....**
(Photo: Hugh Bishop)

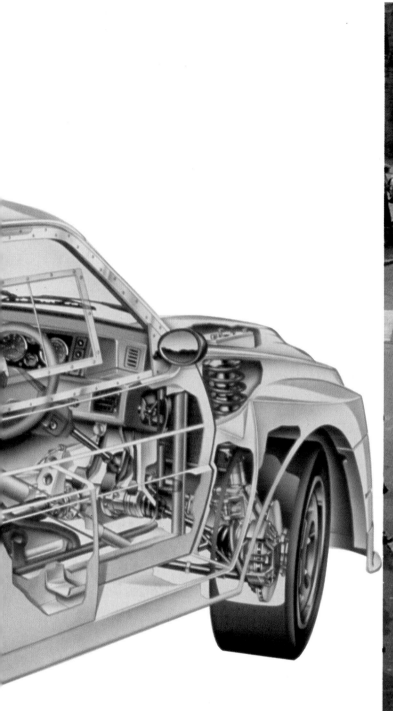

front of the car there was an under-nose 'snow-shovel' type of spoiler to trim the handling some more. There were FF Developments VC differentials at front, centre and rear, the first rally engines developed about 430 bhp (and Alen was already saying that he needed 500 bhp in 1986 to be competitive!), but the turbo torque still arrived in a rush in mid-range.

Those who were ready to write off the Delta's chances in the Lombard-RAC should have remembered how often Cesare Fiorio's team ever produce a poor rally car - never! Right from the start, against the latest Peugeot 205 Turbo 16s, the second evolution Audi Quattro S1s, and the much-publicised MG Metro 6R4s on *their* first international event, the Delta S4s were immediately competitive. Markku Alen's car was fastest on five of the first seven stages, and when the cars returned to Nottingham for the first rest halt, he was leading the event from Tony Pond's Metro 6R4, and Henri Toivonen's Delta S4. The challenge of the Audis and the Peugeots had already faded.

In the second half of the event, Lancia were

Above

The Delta S4, still not homologated, was brought out on the 1000 Pistes rally of 1985, where Markku Alen did his best to break the chassis. Note the 'interim' aerodynamic shape of the front end.

in first and second places at one point, but then Alen went off the road for a time, Toivonen indulged in roll in front of video cameras, and at the end of an enthralling 65 stage rally it was Toivonen who won, with Alen less than a

Above
The Delta S4's first World Championship rally was the Lombard-RAC of 1985. At a service point on that event, the front end was being removed completely, for mechanics to reach the front suspension. *(Photo: Holmes)*

Left
Compare this front end shot of the Delta S4 car, as homologated, with the car's original style. There was a much larger spoiler under the headlamps, which also acted as a splashguard to the lamps. *(Photo: Holmes)*

Bottom Left
The Delta S4 evolution model had an engine bay and rear end full of kit. This was the 1984 'launch' specification - some components were shifted around before rallying actually began a year later. *(Photo: Holmes)*

Below
You could still get a Delta S4 sideways, in spite of its efficient four-wheel-drive - but, then, this was a flat out pre-rally test session in Scotland, before the Lombard-RAC rally. Those huge 'ears' are to channel air into the engine bay.

Austin Rover's MG Metro 6R4 looked superficially like the Metro production car, but had a mid-mounted vee-6 engine, and four-wheel-drive.

The Metro 6R4 'jumped' straight and level - helped considerably by its special aerodynamic aids. This was Malcolm Wilson's car in the 1986 Scottish rally.

(Photo: Hugh Bishop)

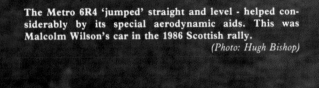

Two Delta S4s started their first World Championship rally and finished first and second overall! This was Alen's car, which was second, while Henri Toivonen won the event.

minute behind in second place. The stage summary told it all - for Alen had been fastest 27 times, and Toivonen 16 times, with no other car even coming close.

The Lancia team then mounted an all-out assault on the 1986 World Rally Championship, with a strong three-car team of drivers - Markku Alen, Henri Toivonen and European Champion 'Miki' Biasion. For the Monte Carlo event, three brand-new cars appeared, the normal peak engine output had risen closer to 450 bhp, and the cars were set up with a 25/75 torque split, well biased to the rear end. In an event where the team even indulged in a mid-stage 'pit stop' to change from racing slick to studded tyres, Henri Toivonen's car was once again the fastest overall, winning in spite of having a head-on accident on the open road with a spectator's car.

There were no important changes for Sweden, except that the chosen torque split was 30/70 this time. Biasion didn't enter, but the two other drivers revelled in the conditions until Toivonen's engine blew, and Alen's engine suffered mysterious boost problems for a time, so the 'Italian Finn' had to settle for second place at

the end of the event.

The Deltas were withdrawn from the Portugal rally, like all the other top teams, even though no Lancia had been involved in the spectator problems, and for the Safari Cesare Fiorio chose to run the ancient rear-drive 037s for one last time (and finished third).

Then came the Tour de Corse, for which Lancia had prepared so assiduously. Three cars started - all, this time, using ZF differentials and a 25/75 torque split, along with full 450 bhp engines. After the first stages Henri Toivonen's car was leading, with Biasion third, and Alen fifth - two of the latest Renault Maxi 5 Turbos getting in the way. In the next few hours Henri - acknowledged, by this time, to be *the* fastest of all World-class rally drivers, extended his lead, until on the 18th stage - it happened.

For no reason that anyone can work out, the Delta S4 crashed over the edge of a typically-twisty piece of Corsican road, somersaulted into the trees, exploded into flames, and was com-

Henri Toivonen, well on the way to his biggest victory of all, with the Lancia Delta S4 in the Monte Carlo rally of 1986.

pletely burnt out. There were no spectators nearby, but tragically the two poor occupants were already beyond human help. Both driver and co-driver (Sergio Cresto) were killed in the accident. The only thing that Cesare Fiorio could do was immediately to withdraw his other cars from the event, and return to Italy.

It was this tragedy, added to Joaquim Santos's crash in Portugal, which brought about an immediate upheaval in rallying. For Lancia, and all their friends, of course, there was the loss of two fine sportsmen (it was a blow made doubly hard to take for Lancia, as they had lost another team driver on the same event in 1985), but for the whole of rallying it was the end of an era.

It was not Lancia's fault, but the accident brought the whole question of high-performance Group B rally cars into question. FISA, in immediate emergency session, declared that this sort of car would be banned after the end of the 1986 season.

It was a measure of Lancia's character, and the resolve of its principal characters, that the team could bounce back from tragedy, turn up in Greece for the Acropolis, and expect to beat the rest of the world. Everyone in the business, indeed, was disappointed that they did not do so.

In the Acropolis the battle was between Lancia, Ford and Peugeot, and was resolved by the RS200s both retiring, and by Alen's car suffer-

ing an engine failure. Peugeot won the event, but Biasion's Delta S4 finished close behind.

Although there were victories to follow, the rest of this sombre season did not go Lancia's way. The team went on to win in Argentina (Biasion from Markku Alen), San Remo (Alen, Cerrato and Biasion) and the USA (Olympus-Alen), but were beaten by Peugeot in New Zealand, the 1000 Lakes, and the Lombard-RAC rally.

Along the way, too, there was scandal, for Peugeot's team was disqualified from San Remo on spurious grounds, to give Lancia a walkover. At the end of the year FISA annulled the San Remo results, which meant that Alen's Drivers' World Championship success lasted for only 12 days!

Delta S4s never achieved success in private hands (the cars were too costly and expensive to run for that), though Fabrizio Tabaton's works-prepared example won the European Rally Championship, as did Dario Cerrato's car in the Italian series. By the end of the season the Delta engine could produce up to 500 bhp, and the next-generation car (later launched as a 'Fiat concept car') would have been even more powerful. Unlike its obvious rivals, the Delta S4 had been a winner first time out, and it had *always* been a car which could win on any surface, in any conditions, anywhere.

But then, from Lancia, should we ever have expected anything else?

MG METRO 6R4

What's in a name? The MG Metro 6R4 was a product of the Austin-Rover competition department's programme, which had changed its name from BL Cars in 1982. The roots of this operation, however, lay with the famous BMC 'Comps' operation of the 1960s!

I must start, therefore, by recalling a bit of sporting history. BMC's competitions department had been set up at Abingdon in the 1950s, and achieved fame in the 1950s and 1960s, with Marcus Chambers and, later, Stuart Turner as its managers, and with the Austin-Healey 3000, and the Mini-Cooper S as the successful cars. Then came the takeover of BMC by Leyland, the unstoppable financial decline of the British Leyland combine and, with it, a loss of corporate interest in competitions.

In the mid-1970s, however, a revival was started, and for five seasons the re-born department, latterly led by John Davenport, struggled to make Triumph TR7s, and later Triumph TR7 V8s, competitive against the ubiquitous Ford Escorts, Fiat Abarth 131 Rallyes, and Lancia Stratos rally cars of the day. When the powerful but unwieldy TR7 V8s were withdrawn at the end of 1980, it looked as if the department would have to turn its back on rallies once again.

It was as early as 1981, however, that Davenport's department began to plan ahead for an exciting future, as several important events seemed to make a radical new project feasible. On the one hand, BL Cars (which became Austin-Rover in 1982) was in the middle of a huge new 'product-led recovery' programme, of which the front-wheel-drive Austin Metro was the first evidence, and on the other the Audi Quattro was just beginning to show that four-wheel-drive could be made to work on rallies. New rallying regulations were on the way, only 200 cars would need to be built to achieve Group B homologation, and it was thought that the company's marketing effort would benefit from a sucessful rally programme.

By coincidence, at this time BL were quite close to Williams Grand Prix Engineering in marketing and geographical terms, as the Ford-Cosworth-powered FW 07C F1 Williams Grand Prix cars were sponsored by Leyland Vehicles, and the race cars were designed and built at Didcot, which was only ten miles from BL's Motorsport headquarters at Cowley.

In a magazine interview, published in *Autosport* in 1984 on the occasion of the launch of the new car, John Davenport stated that: 'For sheer breadth of coverage in all the international markets in which we sell cars, you cannot beat rallying... Rallying would help boost the image, underline the viability of the company, and if it could be achieved with something that resembled a production machine, so much the better... We had a lot of ideas, but no instant answers, so it took time to decide what car it should be and then go back to explain what it

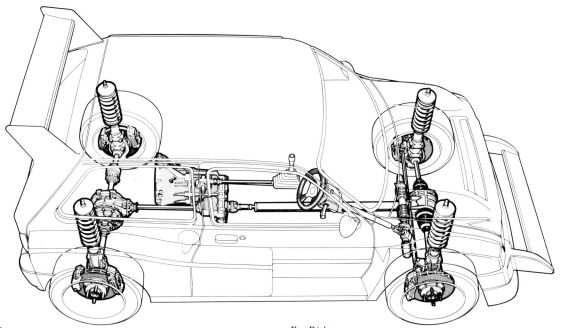

Above
This was the basic transmission layout of the Metro 6R4, as conceived for Austin-Rover by Williams Grand Prix Engineering.

Top Right
There was just enough space for the 90 degree vee-6 engine, and its vertically-mounted carburettors, in the rear of the Metro 6R4. This shot is taken from the extreme tail.
(Photo: Holmes)

Below
The original Metro 6R4s used a chopped-down Rover engine, and were much neater cars than they later became. This was one of the first three prototypes of 1983.
(Photo: Holmes)

Far Right
The 1983/84 breed of Metro 6R4 was recognisably derived from the Metro front-wheel-drive car, though the wheel arch extensions were clumsily profiled.

Centre Right
Features of the original prototype Metro 6R4 included the rear wheel arch extensions which also incorporated air scoops to the mid-engine bay, and quite a number of standard Metro body panels were retained.

Bottom Right
By the beginning of 1985, the development Metro 6R4s were carrying front and rear aerodynamic spoilers, and there were NACA ducts in the sides of the rear quarter windows.

would cost. We actually started with the traditional blank sheet of paper and an idea to build something based on the Metro, although our first concept was of a longitudinal engine in the front, with a gearbox at the rear, and rear wheel drive only.'

Those first moves, incidentally, were made in 1980, at about the time that the Triumph TR7 V8 programme was winding down, and at almost exactly the same time that Ford decided to produce the Escort RS 1700T on similar lines... but BL then abandoned the front engine/rear transaxle/rear wheel drive idea almost at once. In any case, there simply wasn't room at the front of the Metro's body shell to instal a more bulky engine than the transversely-positioned A-Series without major surgery to the bulkhead, and then the driver would have had to be moved a long way back from the nose, so far that he would not have been able to see the front corners of the car!

Davenport now takes up the story again: 'We had already made the decision to involve Williams Grand Prix Engineering because we did not then have the engineering staff on board that we have now. We wanted someone who was not only a competent structures engineer, but also a competent power-train engineer.

I went along to Patrick Head (technical design chief at WGPE), and explained that we didn't have any money, but that we would like him to design us a rally car. He laughed.'

Somehow or other, however, the initial amusement died down, a modicum of money was found from Motorsport's resources, and well before the end of 1981 a project team had been set up at Didcot to produce a prototype car for BL. Then, as later, it was always clear that the decision to use the Metro as the 'silhouette' for this new car was going to pose problems, but there was no lack of enthusiasm to get the job done. If Renault had been able to do a competitive job with the mid-engined 5 Turbo (this car had won the Monte Carlo rally in January 1981, which was exactly the right time to re-convince Davenport that he was making the right decision), then so could WGPE and BL's Motorsport division.

Patrick Head set up the team, and oversaw all the initial work, at Didcot, with Brian O'Rourke designing the structure, and John Piper taking responsibility for power train and suspensions. Even though Williams had lost its

Leyland Vehicles sponsorship at the end of 1981, during 1982 the various 'paper motor cars' were studied, and all but one layout was rejected before metal was cut. Patrick Head later admitted that 40 per cent of his time was spent on the Metro project in 1982 - and F1 enthusiasts will know that in the *following* year the fortunes of the Williams GP team took something of a tumble; there may be a connection between these sequences of events.

Williams concentrated its efforts on the Metro's package, although at one time the rather larger Maestro shell was considered as well. But, as Davenport recalled: 'We always reverted to the small car, as we were impressed by how well we could get everything into a small package. Small cars make small roads look big... certainly larger cars may have increased stability, but they also carry more weight. There was also an emotional attachment to the Metro itself, because it was the first Michael Edwards car which put us back on the road to profit and recovery.'

The team also looked at the front engine/-rear transaxle layout once again, but abandoned it, and at the same time the rallying establishment became more and more impressed with the performance of the Audis, in spite of their un-favourable weight distribution, and their cheap and cheerful four-wheel-drive installation. It was inevitable, therefore, that WGPE would produce a four-wheel-drive car.

The big decision for the project car - which was only meant to be a prototype, to get the show on the road - concerned its engine. The Peugeot, Lancia, Ford or Opel approach would have been to produce a turbocharged engine, but Davenport and WGPE between them chose the diametrically opposite solution. Instead of using a high-revving, high-boost competition engine, they opted for a larger-capacity, normally-aspirated, unit in which there would be no turbo lag, and no thermal problems. A larger-capacity engine, it was reasoned, would give smooth and instant positive (or negative) throttle response, would not be at all critical where high ambient temperatures were concerned, and would be considerably easier to drive. It would, in Rauno Aaltonen's now famous phrase, be a 'driver friendly' machine.

To get on terms with the turbocharged cars, therefore, the new Metro needed a larger-capacity engine than any of them. At BL, at the time, the light-alloy Rover vee-8 was an obvious choice, for it was an engine which had already proved itself in rallying (in the TR7 V8s) and in circuit racing (in the Rover 3500s). Unfortunately, and even though Patrick Head's team had already settled on a mid/rear-engined configuration for the 'silhouette' car, the vee-8 was just that important bit too bulky for the space, and the wheelbase, available, so the brave decision was taken to literally 'cut off' two of the Rover's cylinders, and evolve a rather shorter, 90 degree, vee-6 unit instead.

The 'lash-up' engine used in the first prototypes, therefore, was a 2,495 cc unit (which fitted neatly inside the 2.5-litre class limit), fitted with two triple-choke downdraught Weber carburettors, and tubular exhaust systems; it produced 240bhp at unstated rpm.

Although the structure looked rather like that of the Metro mass-production car (the most obvious differences being the large front and rear wheel-arch extensions and the large engine bay air intakes behind the line of the \ doors), there were very few carry-over panels \ only the standard roof, side panels, doors and   rear hatch back were retained. There was a   completely new steel floor pan strength-   ened

by two main longitudinal chassis members on either side of the transmission tunnel, and new front and rear suspension/power train subframes; the new car's wheelbase, in any case, was 5.0cm/2.0 in. longer than that of the standard front-wheel-drive car. Much of the Metro's shape was retained, but this was effectively (and - some say -clumsily) disguised by large front and rear wheelarch extensions which covered the wide tracks and the fat tyres and wheels, plus the wide plastic 'running boards' connecting those arch extensions and running under the doors. It was a car which BL's stylists could never have seen or approved of, before it was built, and it was a real contrast with the beautifully integrated alterations made to the Peugeot 205 to turn that car into the Turbo 16.

Those people, however, who didn't mind the *original* car's looks had to think again as rallying, testing, and development, proceeded in 1984 and 1985, for it became progressively more bizarre as time passed. In the next year or so the wheelbase would be stretched, the tracks widened, the suspension struts would need 'power bulges' in the bonnet, the air intakes would be

This was the definitive MG Metro 6R4, in 'International' tune, as revealed in May 1985. The wheelbase and the track had both been increased, compared with the 1983/84 original.

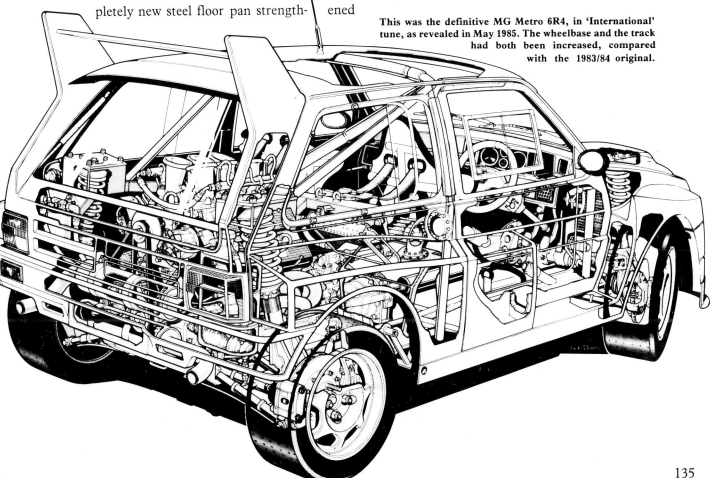

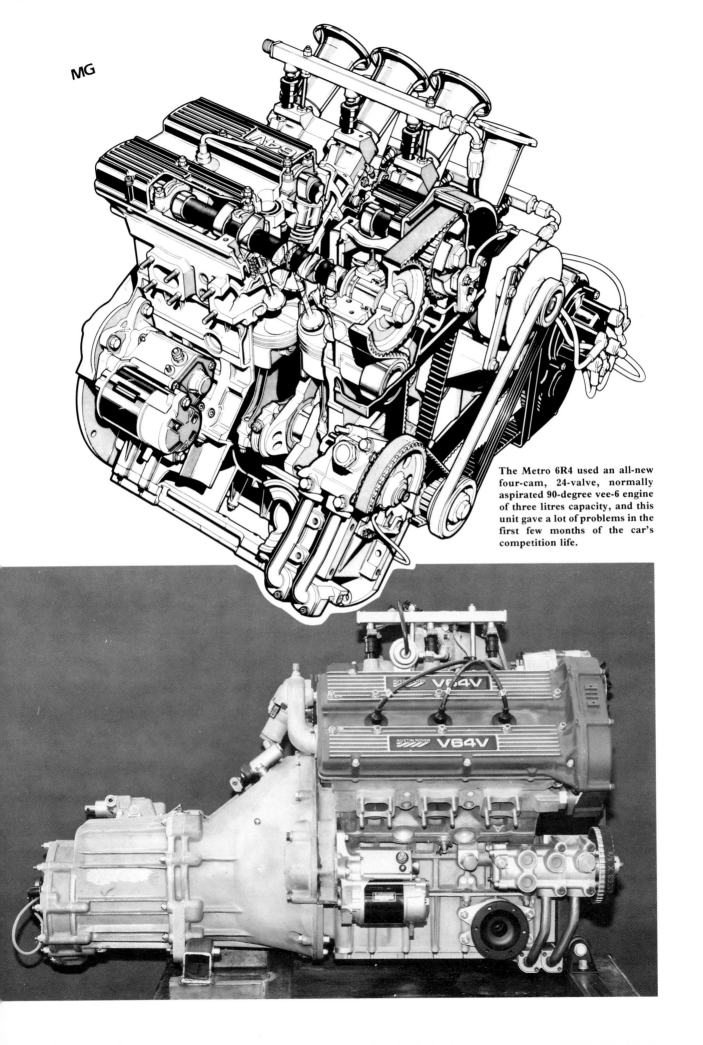

MG

The Metro 6R4 used an all-new
four-cam, 24-valve, normally
aspirated 90-degree vee-6 engine
of three litres capacity, and this
unit gave a lot of problems in the
first few months of the car's
competition life.

pushed forward along the side of the doors, and large aerofoil sections would be added at front and rear ....

The vee-6 engine was mounted as far back as possible, to allow space for the main transmission to be ahead of the power unit, between and below the seats, and to concentrate as much weight as possible over the rear wheels. The engine was mounted slightly to the left of the chassis centre line, along with the five-speed gearbox, which had been designed by Williams, but manufactured by one of their suppliers.

Ahead of the gearbox itself was a simple transfer box, to 'move' the drive to the right, where the centre FF-type differential and viscous coupling split the torque. An open propeller shaft led to the front differential, and a short quill shaft alongside the engine led to the rear diff whose housing was integrated into the engine sump casting. There was a short shaft running through the sump, to connect with the left side drive shaft. The entire transmission system was still being developed when the first cars were shown, so Austin-Rover were noticeably reticent about the internals. There was no provision for locking any of the differentials, nor for disconnecting drive to the front wheels.

Strut-type independent suspension, adjustable anti-roll bars at front and rear, four-wheel ventilated disc brakes (with a separate hand-brake caliper),

Above

The 6R4's engine, although a vee-6, had a 90-degree vee angle. This was the 'Clubman' tune, with 250bhp.

and rack and pinion steering were all absolutely conventional for an early-1980s rally car. The team had already signed up with Bilstein to help them finalise the suspension, and Michelin for tyres.

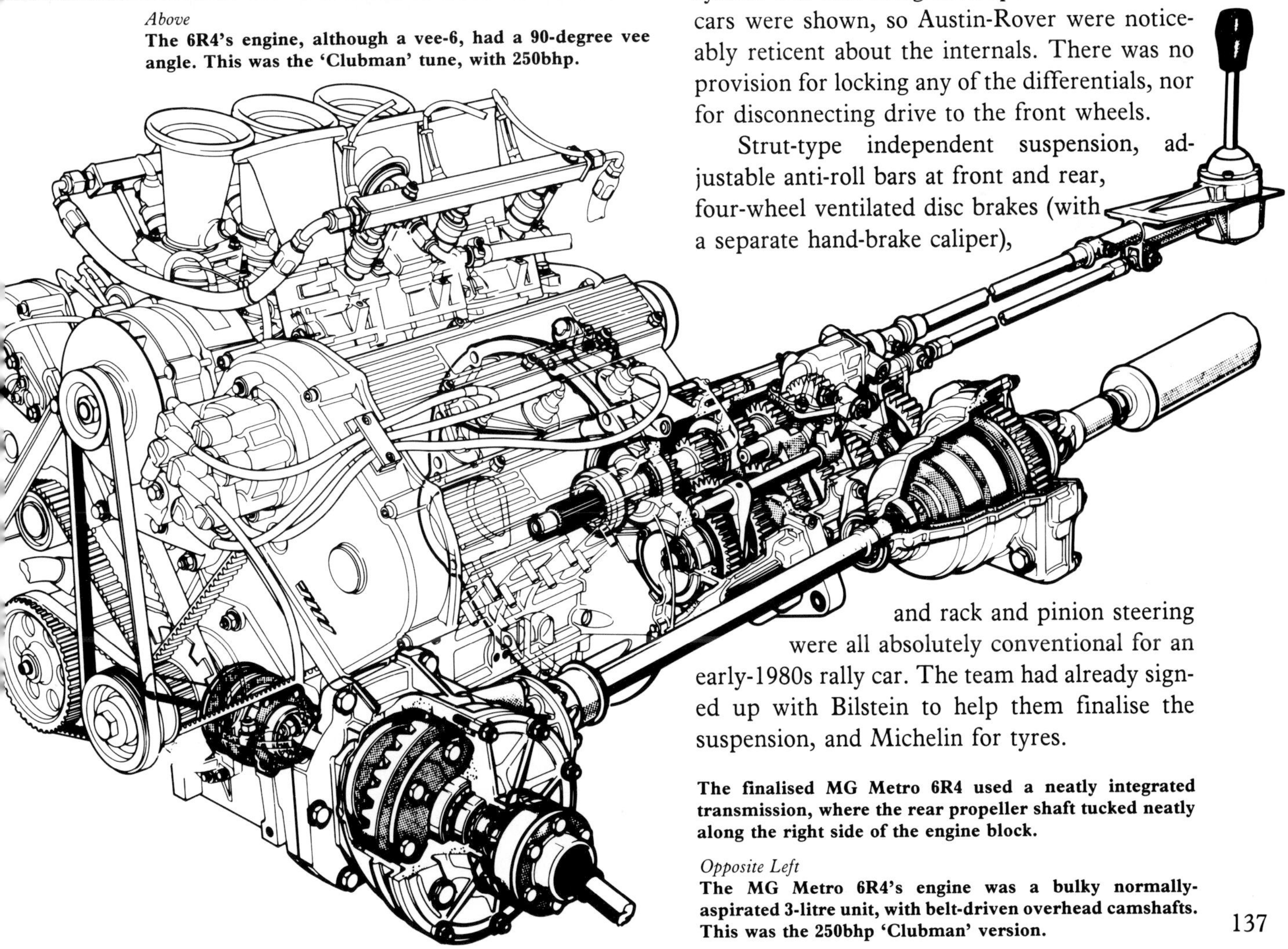

The finalised MG Metro 6R4 used a neatly integrated transmission, where the rear propeller shaft tucked neatly along the right side of the engine block.

Opposite Left

The MG Metro 6R4's engine was a bulky normally-aspirated 3-litre unit, with belt-driven overhead camshafts. This was the 250bhp 'Clubman' version.

137

Williams finished the project design in 1982, and the first prototype was delivered to Cowley, as a kit of parts, at the end of the year, along with two more body shells, and sets of mechanical equipment. The first car ran, for the first time, in February 1983, and Austin-Rover actually managed to keep their testing absolutely secret for another year, as the layout and styling was still a great surprise when it was unveiled to the press in February 1984. To emphasise their sporting image, Austin-Rover gave the car an 'MG' identity, and called it 6R4 (six cylinders, rally car, with four-wheel-drive). They also announced that a 'radically different, up to 320 bhp, all aluminium, V6 engine - again conventionally aspirated - is being designed and developed by Austin-Rover engineers.'

During 1984 Tony Pond drove the development cars on various events, not only to prove out the components, but to develop and finalise the transmission systems. In this period several different VC settings, and front/rear torque splits, were assessed. Right from the start, Austin-Rover thought they had a potential winner, because back-to-back tests of their 240 bhp Metro against one of David Sutton's 'long' Quattros were encouraging, and on its very first event (the snow-bound York National in March 1984) the car was leading the event until an electrical fire forced it to retire.

There were, however, two major problems in the first season - one was that the temporary engine was quite obviously not powerful enough (in spite of those encouraging test sessions), and the other was that the handling was still suspect due to chassis and aerodynamic deficiencies. The engine problem, of course, could not be solved until the new unit was ready, but by the end of the summer progress was being made with the handling. One move was to increase the tracks *and* the wheelbase, and another was to produce 'add-on' aerodynamic aids in the shape of aerofoil sections low down at the front, and at the top of the tailgate/hatchback.

By this time Austin-Rover had taken the decision to build 200 cars - but with a difference. Unlike Ford they planned to have their cars built 'in house', in a special facility at the Longbridge factory, and they were not proposing to build ready-to-rally competition cars, which would not have national Type Approval. This decision could only allow the 6R4s to be used on British roads if they were sold as incomplete 'kit cars', something which Austin-Rover were quite

Above
The Metro 6R4's four-cam just fitted into the rather cramped engine bay of the car, and clearly it was going to be very difficult to work on the cylinder heads without dropping the engine from the chassis.

Left
A Cowley competitions department shot, showing a complete 6R4 engine, gearbox and rear transmission ready to go into the car.

Below
The 'works' 6R4 evolution cars used an aerodynamic diffuser under the tail of the 6R4, which also doubled as a skid shield.

prepared to do in spite of some criticism of their methods.

(It was a ploy which worked well, up to a point, but when the banning of Group B rally cars was announced in mid-1986, Austin-Rover were left with a shed full of unsaleable cars which could not be converted for use on the roads ....)

The definitive MG Metro 6R4 'homologation car', with which Williams Grand Prix Engineering was no longer involved, was revealed in May 1985, when it was confidently stated that the 200 cars, along with 20 evolution cars, would be completed by 1st November 1985. It is to Austin-Rover's credit that this was achieved, and seen to be achieved, for the pictures of massed, be-winged, 6R4s distributed at the time were perfectly genuine. This car, however, was very different in many ways from the 1984 prototypes.

To improve the handling of the car, the wheelbase had been stretch by 90mm/3.5 in., while the tracks had also increased, such that the overall width of the car was up by 70mm/2.75 in. The road wheel diameter had also been increased (to 390 mm or 16 in. depending on the type of Michelin tyres used), and the net result was that the wheel arch extensions were much larger, and even more square in profile, than ever before.

Not only that, but chassis engineer Wynn Mitchell had developed longer front and rear suspension damper struts, which therefore required clearance bulges in the front panel ahead of the windscreen, while the front and rear aerofoil sections developed during the previous season had also been standardised. Getting enough fresh air into the engine bay was always a problem with such mid-engined cars, and to optimise it on the Metro 6R4 the intake 'pods' had been extended forward, half way along the side of the passenger doors.

Aerodynamic specialist Bernie Marcus had certainly done a very efficient job on the car, but the best that anyone, even an Austin-Rover spokesman, could say of the revised car was that it looked 'functional'. Some observers called it ugly, others called it appallingly ugly, and the writer even likened it to a Mothercare push-trolley. None of which would matter *if* it was fast enough, and strong enough, for World Championship rallies.

The car's future, therefore, depended on the

new vee-6 engine, which was a real surprise, when announced, for various rumours had been circulating in the previous year. The important thing was that Austin-Rover's competitions engineer, David Wood, had produced an all-new design, which was not compromised by having to use a Rover vee-8/vee-6 cylinder block, nor that of the vee-6 Honda engine which was known to be scheduled for use in the Rover 800 model of 1986. In view of Austin-Rover's well-known philosophy about engine torque and response, it was no surprise to see a normally-aspirated unit, with four valves per cylinder, and cogged-belt-driven twin-overhead camshafts per bank.

It may be no coincidence that David Wood worked at the Ford competitions centre at Boreham for some years, and was familiar with the work done by Cosworth to produce a four-cam 'GA' version of the Capri's vee-6 engine. Certainly, during the 6R4's development period, a Ford-Cosworth GA engine was acquired for study, and Cosworth were consulted over the design of the 'top-end' of the new design.

The design had progressed very rapidly, for detail drawing did not begin until early in 1984, and the first engines did not run until the begin-

ning of 1985. The engines were to be machined and assembled at an Austin-Rover factory in Coventry (one which had once produced transmissions for Standard-Triumph cars of the 1960s and 1970s), and where the six-cylinder in-line Rover engine was currently being produced.

Like the 'lash-up' Rover-based engine, the new V64V (vee-6, with four-valves per cylinder) engine was a 3.0-litre, 90 degree vee-6 unit - a layout which happened to fit into the Metro's engine bay very neatly indeed - which had a light-alloy cylinder block and heads. In 200-off 'Clubman' form it had a single-point Lucas fuel-injection system, and 250 bhp, while in fully-tuned 'International' form it had multi-point injection, and between 380 bhp and 410 bhp, depending on the state of tune.

The least altered part of the whole design, however, was the transmission. Jack Knight & Son had designed the main gearbox - synchromesh for the 200 cars, face-dog for the evolution versions - and an FF viscous coupling had been standardised in the centre differential; front and rear limited-slip mechanisms had not been standardised at the time of announcement.

Tony Pond had already won the Gwynedd (national permit) rally in a prototype 6R4, fitted

with the Rover-based vee-6 engine, and he went straight on to win a minor British event in the first of the four-cam cars. There was further success in the Audi National rally in October 1985, when Tony Pond won the event, with Marc Duez's sister car second, but everyone was waiting for the first World Championship appearances.

Before then, John Davenport had started to build his driving team for 1986, attracting

Malcolm Wilson from Ford to join Tony Pond, and eventually persuading drivers like Per Eklund, Jimmy McRae and David Llewellyn to use privately-prepared cars in major events in the U.K. and Europe. By this stage, the Metro design had been on the go for a long time - four-and-a-half years from concept to production - during which top-class rallying technology had moved ahead rapidly. The decision to concentrate on a torquey, normally-aspirated engine was already beginning to look mis-guided, not necessarily in terms of *immediate* competitiveness, but because when a second evolution car became necessary, there might not be any chance of increasing the power output.

The evolution car's first event was the Lombard-RAC of November 1985, an ideal start for PR and publicity purposes, as the media was interested in seeing the new, all-British, four-

The basic Metro 6R4 Group B car, as produced at Longbridge, had a free-standing aerofoil section down at the front, to trim the handling, slots and bulges everywhere, particularly on the front 'bonnet' panel to clear the extended strut top mounts.

Below
Side by side, here, are the basic 200-off Metro 6R4 'Clubman' car, and the fully-liveried, 410bhp 'International' specification evolution model which the 'works' team used right from the start in autumn 1985.

wheel-drive 'Metro' in action against rivals such as the Audi Quattro S1s, Peugeot 205 Turbo 16s, and Lancia Delta S4s. Austin-Rover, in addition, had cause for great jubilation, as they had achieved their promised homologation date, while the production timetable of the Ford RS200 had slipped behind! For this, their first major event, the cars ran with a 35/65 torque split, and with interesting 'aerodynamic' skirts under the car which also doubled as sump shields.

Pond and Wilson both set competitive times, right from the start of the event, but Wilson's car then broke its transmission during the first night, and it was Tony Pond, alone, who kept his Metro going to the end. Although the stubby, be-spoilered, car never actually led the event, it rose to second place at one time, and finally finished third overall, behind the two amazing new Lancia Deltas. In the process, Pond set nine fastest stage times, 14 second-fastests, and 15 third-fastest. Even allowing for Pond's great experience of British 'secret' stages, It was a splendid first showing, and everyone began to get excited about prospects for 1986, for which eight World Championship rounds were to be tackled.

As every British rally enthusiast now knows, the 'works' effort in the first half of 1986, before FISA put the brake on Group B development, was a complete failure. Fully-prepared Metro 6R4s started at Monte Carlo, Sweden, Portugal, and Corsica - and none of them reached the finish. The team elected to miss the Safari of 1986, which was probably wise, for in testing for the equally tough (but shorter) Acropolis rally, Malcolm Wilson's car broke its suspension, rolled off the side of a mountain, and was completely wrecked.

In the Monte Carlo rally, the two cars were said to have the full 410 bhp engines, and to weigh 980kg/2,160 lb. unladen. However, Pond's car crashed at an early stage, immediately after having his steering rack changed, and was rather unwisely withdrawn rather than disrupt tightly planned service schedules, while Malcolm Wilson's transmission failed after 11 stages, when he was lying eighth overall.

There was a brand-new 'works' car for Malcolm Wilson to drive in the snowy Swedish rally, together with Per Eklund starting in his Clarion-sponsored car, both cars being a little heavier, and better protected from damage, than

the Monte cars; this time a 45/55 torque split was chosen, after pre-event testing. But it did not help, with both Metros dropping out at an early stage, both (ominously enough) with engine failures.

Portugal, of course, was a complete wash-out for Austin-Rover, as it was for all the works teams which withdrew, but the team was looking for a good result in Corsica. For that very arduous tarmac event two new cars had been prepared for Pond and Wilson, while the French Driver Didier Auriol had his own 6R4. All were lighter than the previous 'rough-road' machines - but unhappily on arrival in Corsica it was found that the handling balance had been lost, and that the cars simply could not get on terms with their rivals.

There was worse to come. Auriol's car blew its engine on the very first stage, and had to retire, Wilson's car threw a cam timing belt (something which was very common to this engine), then the engine overheated, and finally caught fire, all within ten stages, and shortly afterwards Pond's Metro also threw a cam belt, and that was that.

Right
Every Metro 6R4 ever built had this sort of facia, and instrument panel display, for there was no such thing as a 'road car' - all the 220 Metros were meant to be rally cars.

Below
For 1986, ex-Toyota driver Per Eklund persuaded his sponsors, Clarion, to buy him an MG Metro 6R4. Dave Whittock was his co-driver.

Except for the inevitable teething troubles, the 6R4's chassis, and four-wheel-drive transmission, seemed to be right, and no-one who drove the car had any cause for complaint. Whether in the loose, in the snow, or on tarmac, the car was usually competitive - but there was the nagging doubt in everyone's mind that the engines would not last the distance in a World

Championship round.

In the U.K., and in Europe, the 6R4 began to notch up some successes, notably on events which were not too long to distress the engines too much. In the RAC Open Series, the first event, the National Breakdown, was almost wiped out by a blizzard, but David Llewellin's car so nearly beat Hannu Mikkola's Audi Sport Quattro (not the second evolution model, though), and Jimmy McRae's example took third place.

There was no mistake on the Circuit of Ireland, where Llewellin's car took the outright victory, after McRae led for a time, and was always competitive, until his car's front-suspension broke. In the Welsh, Mikkola's Audi won again, but Llewellin and McRae were always up there battling for the lead - until Llewellin indulged in a very high-speed, long-distance, roll which was captured on video by a spectator - and Jimmy McRae finished a mere 20

seconds behind the Audi.

Then came the Scottish, where a positive fleet of 6R4s - some 'works' or 'supported', some privately owned - took part, and where Malcolm Wilson was expected to mix it with McRae, Llewellin, and Per Eklund (whose car had been rebuilt after a high-speed suspension failure in a European event). Wilson, Llewellin and Eklund all used 45/55 torque splits in their transmission, the rest settling for the 'standard' 35/65 setting. This time there was to be no competition from Mikkola's Quattro, as Audi had abruptly withdrawn from competition following the Corsica tragedy.

It all started so well for Austin-Rover, whose main rivals were Lovell's Ford RS200, and Sundstrom's Peugeot 205 Turbo 16, for the 6R4s were all packed into the Top Ten, with Wilson leading from McRae, Sundstrom (Peugeot), Llewellin and Eklund - but then the engine troubles began to set in.

In the next few hours all the leading 6R4s blew up, as did Mike Stuart's, Ken Wood's and Harri Toivonen's engines - and only one car, that of David Gillanders (running with a near-Clubman's spec. engine) made it to the finish. Post-mortems, when the engines were stripped, seemed to indicate that inadequate inlet manifold filtration, against dust, had been a major factor.

By mid-1986, therefore, the Metro 6R4 programme was in disarray. Whereas the rivals, Ford, seemed to be getting their RS200 act together (and there would have been a stun-

Hidden by the wall of water is one of the very first 'works' Metro 6R4s.

ningly fast evolution car if the rule changes had not killed it off before arrival), the MG Metro 6R4s seemed to be stagnating, if not actually going backwards after that promising Lombard-RAC rally start.

Development work cured the dust ingestion problem, but the cam belt failures were never eliminated. Engine specialist David Wood abruptly left the company, thought to be as a scapegoat for the troubles.

Later in 1986 the 'works' team notched up respectable, if not outstanding results in the World Championship. Seventh, 8th and 10th places were achieved on the 1000 Lakes, fourth by Malcolm Wilson (behind three Delta S4s) at San Remo, and 6-7-8-9 in the Lombard-RAC. Didier Auriol's works-specification car won the French Championship, while in the British Open series, David Llewellin and Jimmy McRae finished third and fourth (behind an RS200 and an Opel Manta 400).

Austin-Rover then pulled out of top-level rallying completely, and sold off a mass of Metro 6R4 'homologation' cars at knock-down prices. These cars were still eligible for British National, though not Open, series events, and dominated the 1987 scene.

Early in 1987 Austin-Rover's Director of Motorsport, John Davenport, left the company at short notice, and the Fraud Squad moved in.

The definitive Group B Metro 6R4 differed from the earlier prototypes by having larger wheels, longer wheelbase, wider tracks, bulges at the front to clear the damper towers, air scoops brought forward along the doors, aerodynamic aids at front and rear, and the four-cam engine.

The Metro 6R4's first international outing was in the 1985 Lombard-RAC rally where this car, driven by Tony Pond, finished third overall.

OPEL KADETT 4X4

The most intriguing of all the four-wheel-drive rally cars surveyed in this book is the Opel-designed General Motors project. Not only was a front-engined layout chosen - and the design detailed in a way which impressed some rival engineers - but the car was specifically intended for the projected Group S category, which was due to come into force in 1988. It was all too late, of course, for although the car was unveiled in 1985, it was still not ready for serious rallying a year later, and by that time Group S had been abandoned. The smart Opel, therefore, goes down as a fascinating 'might-have-been' ....

According to its official policy, General Motors did not enter 'works' cars for competition, but by the 1970s it used the transparent excuse of encouraging a dealer-controlled 'Eurohandler Team' to get round this ruling, and to rally the 'works' Opels. ('Dealer Team Vauxhall' was a similar 'front' organisation for the British Vauxhall company to go rallying as well!). Although no less a driver than Walter Rohrl gave Opel its first World Championship rally success, the company's reliability record was most unsatisfactory for a time, and it was not until the British driver/team manager, Tony Fall, was drafted into Russelsheim, in West Germany, in 1977, that things began to improve.

Fall's first objective was to produce a category-winning Group 1 car (the Kadett GT/E), his second was to get a front-running Group 4 project under way

this became the Ascona 400 of 1979), and his third was to develop the more refined Manta 400 coupé from the Ascona's chassis. With the aid of Rothmans sponsorship in 1982 and 1983, his Asconas provided the right sort of rugged reliability for Walter Rohrl to become World Rally Champion in 1982, while the team itself finished second in the Makes series of 1982 (exclusively with Asconas), and third (behind Lancia and Audi, with Asconas and Mantas) in 1983. The Ascona 400 which Ari Vatanen used to win the Safari in 1983 was the last normally-aspirated car to win a World Championship rally.

Although GM Europe had decided to concentrate their rallying efforts with Opel from 1982 onwards, at the expense of Vauxhall, it was realised that the front-engined/rear-drive Manta 400 had only ever been a conventional compromise for Group B rallying. The car was a year late in becoming homologated (there was a long-running dispute between Opel and the authorities about numbers built, and the method of proving this ....), and by mid-1983, when Eurohandler first started using the cars, it was quite clearly no match for the four-wheel-drive Audi Quattro, except on tarmac/pace-note events. Tony Fall, however, could not immediately go back to his board of directors, admit that his front-line car was already out of date, and ask to be allowed to start again ....

At the end of 1983, therefore, Rothmans withdrew their sponsorship

Opel's early-1980s glory was with cars like this Group B Manta 400, as used by Phil Collins in British events.

In the meantime, Tony Fall had already sensed that there was no profit for Opel and General Motors, only potential honour and glory, in building a series of ultra-special 200-off four-wheel-drive machines. It was all very well for factory, favoured dealer teams, and rich private owners, to buy these machines, but what was to be done with the remaining 150 - 180 cars, which *had* to be built, but which might remain in store, unsold, unless rally car crashes began to 'use up' the remainder? Other manufacturers might choose to shrug off this overstocking problem (Austin-Rover, it seems, did precisely that with the MG Metro 6R4), but General Motors did not. They were in the business of building cars to sell, not building them to rot.

At the end of 1983, however, Fall sat down with his managers and engineers, one of whom was his Development Manager, Karl-Heinz Goldstein, to work out what Opel (and, indirectly, Vauxhall) *might* do for the future. Four-wheel-drive, for sure, was essential, but what else was needed and - in General Motors terms - what else was possible? The decision, to study various four-wheel-drive layouts, was made at first on an experimental basis, for at the time there seemed to be no chance of General Motors ever agreeing to a 200-off Group B project, whether built inside Opel, or outside, by a contractor. Nevertheless the first schemes postulated a new Group B car - the approval for such a car would have to come later. As Tony Fall said, two years later, when talking about the car:

'The one thing we couldn't do was sell an idea to management, until we had a concept, and that meant questions like "Where are you going to put the engine" '

Design work began in November 1983, but detailed design and construction did not get going until the first half of 1984. As with Ford, and the RS200, there was no compulsion for Goldstein and his colleagues to make their new rally car look like an Opel production car, but he could sense that this might be well received:

'We thought at the outset that Ford's idea had been good for the motorsport department.(The RS200 project was still supposed to be Most Secret at this stage - so who talked? - AAGR). A special car is not affected by changes in production models, for example. But in the end we decided on an existing Opel body.

(and moved on to sponsor a Porsche rallying programme, with some success at European and Middle East championship levels), which rather left Opel in the lurch - without a modern four-wheel-drive car, and without the external backing to support it!

For the time being, at least, Opel had to drop out of the rallying limelight, although their Mantas continued to win events, and Championships, all round the world. At a time when enthusiasts were expecting Opel to be developing a new four-wheel-drive rally car right away, Tony Fall's engineers were rather powerless to satisfy them. As a 'look-see' exercise they had already built a four-wheel-drive Opel Manta 400, using the usual type of FF Developments layout of transfer gearbox, exposed front and rear propeller shafts, but this had got no further than being photographed by journalists, and being demonstrated in Rothmans colours, by Ari Vatanen, in the snows of Sweden in February 1983. With its normally-aspirated engine, it would not even have been competitive with the Quattros, so there was little point in developing it further.

We reckoned a special car would not be so good for the company and they would be less likely to approve it. The Kadett was the obvious choice. It is planned to be in production until 1990 or 1991, and we reckoned that the Kadett was the smallest car into which we could fit the parts that our projected power outputs would demand. The Kadett is the right shape. The Corsa was just too small and the wheelbase too short.'

The new-style Kadett/Astra, incidentally, was not revealed until the autumn of 1984, although the Opel Sports Relations team knew that it was on the way. This explains, partly, why a strange 'one-off' front engine/rear-drive old-style Kadett was produced in the interim, and used in South African rallies, for Goldstein admits that the team was considering making this car their first four-wheel-drive prototype, but decided not to do so 'for budget reasons'.

The Germans, above all, are a logical race, always ready to listen to argument, and usually ready to react to truly expert opinion on any subject. Because of this, chief designer Goldstein was not necessarily swayed by the layout of other four-wheel-drive cars already revealed, but he *was* ready to listen to Rauno Aaltonen's opinions. Aaltonen, the vastly experienced Finnish driver who had been European rally champion as long ago as 1965, had been one of Tony Fall's driving team mates at BMC, briefly at Lancia, and later at Opel. He was known throughout the rallying industry as a compulsive designer, improver, and incisive thinker about a car's behaviour. Fall had hired Aaltonen, not only as the 'Old Fox' type of driver who could teach his young heroes a thing or two - but also to give him every opportunity of winning the Safari at last, something which had eluded the Finn for many years.

It was Aaltonen who had turned the Ascona 400 (and later the Manta 400) from a raw competition car, into a 'driver friendly' machine, easy and untiring to drive. It was Aaltonen, also, who convinced Fall and Goldstein that any new car which they developed should have a chassis with quite a large polar-moment-of-inertia.

How to describe polar moment? If a car has most of its weight concentrated near the centre of the chassis, is nervous in a straight line, and changes direction very eagerly indeed, it has a low polar moment - the Peugeot 205 Turbo 16 (and, from an earlier design period, the Lancia Stratos) was a perfect example. If a car has its weight well spread out in the chassis - engine at one end, fuel and oil tanks, maybe the transmission too, at the other - like the Ascona and Manta 400s of the 1980s, the Ford Escort RSs and Fiat 131 Abarths of the 1970s - this would have a high polar moment.

'When the mass centre is close to the centre of gravity of the car,' Tony Fall says, 'that's ideal for perfect cornering conditions like racing. A racing driver gets 100 shots at each corner, but a rally driver gets one shot only, so you need a more forgiving vehicle with a longer polar-moment-of-inertia chassis.'

Principally for that reason, but also because Goldstein became convinced that it would provide ideal packaging *and* ideal weight distribution, the new car, called Kadett 4 x 4, was schemed up around a front-mounted engine. However, it was neither like the transverse-engined Kadett production car from which the new prototype was derived, nor like the Audi Quattro whose engine was all the way up-front, ahead of the line of the front wheels.

The actual engine/transmission/propeller shaft layouts were actually made subservient to the car's suspension, where Opel was planning to have lengthy suspension links (so that the maximum of vertical wheel movement could be provided, without excessive camber change), and equal length front drive shafts. This meant that the front differential would have to be on

The cockpit of the Kadett 4x4 betrays the existence of a four-wheel-drive system because there are two transmission levers on top of the main tunnel. The alloy lever may be used by the driver to alter the front/rear torque split arrangements. *(Photo: Holmes)*

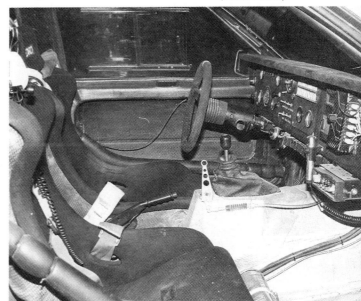

the centre line of the chassis, so the engine was arranged to be rather to the right of that centre line, aligned fore-and-aft with its clutch face towards the rear of the car, and its front face was just behind the line of the front wheels.

The 'corners' of the car were completely conventional by rally car standards, with combined coil spring/damper units, double wishbones, anti-roll bars, and adjustable *everything*. There were ventilated four-wheel disc brakes, and rack and pinion steering. Although prototype testing of this suspension was satisfactory, the entry of two cars in the 1986 Paris-Dakar 'raid' proved that the single spring/dampers were not good enough for a rough road car, and Karl-Heinz Goldstein was planning to use twin units (Ford RS200-style) on the fully-developed model.

Once the team had decided to use a (much-modified) second-generation Kadett body style, and a front-mounted, in-line engine, the rest of the mechanical package fell into place without too much aggravation. The clutch, main gearbox, and transfer box were behind the engine, effectively between the driver's and passenger's legs, the front propeller shaft lined up to the left side of the engine's crankshaft, meeting the front differential casing ahead of the timing gear cover, while the rear propeller shaft was slightly out of true 'north-south' alignment, picking up with a differential which was itself attached to a stout sub-frame under the rear of the floorpan.

Those pundits who did not stop to consider the logic of this layout immediately suggested that the design was misguided. No new Group B car, they announced, would ever again be competitive with a front-mounted engine. To get the weight distribution right, they insisted, the engine must be behind the seats.

Goldstein did not agree. Not only had he worked out the options, but he had discussed the matter of (heavy) engine location with Rauno Aaltonen, and Tony Fall himself, at some length. The new Opel, he said, was 'a sort of front-mid-engined layout'. Not only this, but:

'You have long stages on World Championship rallies where a driver must concentrate all the time. This demands a car which is easily driveable and we feel that a car with the engine behind the driver is too nervous. A driver will get much more tired in one of those cars. Remember we are designing cars to use 500 bhp, maybe even more. An engine behind the driver

is very good in predictable locations, like a race-track, but not on rallies where unexpected things happen just round the corner. And then on jumps a front-engined car is better. A car with a rear engine like a Porsche, or even a Peugeot or a Lancia, can be very dangerous. Sometimes the rear shoots up without warning, as it did in the Vatanen accident in Argentina.'

In any case, Goldstein's chosen layout gave a 51 per cent/49 per cent front/rear distribution when the car was at rest, and under hard acceleration more than half the weight was over the rear wheels.

In mid-1984 there were problems in choosing an engine, for Opel did not know if they would be allowed to go ahead with a 200-off Group B run, or merely have to use this car as a non-homologated machine. There was even a suggestion that the 'equivalency factor' might be changed from 1.4:1 to 1.7:1, which made forward planning very difficult indeed. By this time, the Group B 'going rate' was already 400/450 bhp, so Goldstein knew he had to plan for at least 500 bhp. The 2.4-litre Ascona 400/Manta 400 engine, being normally aspirated, was completely obsolete, and neither Opel, nor their British partners Vauxhall, had any experience of turbocharging.

Originally, a GM-Detroit Pontiac vee-6 engine was considered (there were 2.8-litre or 3.0-litre types in use at the time, the most powerful production unit being a normally-aspirated 140 bhp 2.8-litre, in the mid-engined Pontiac Fiero sports coupé), but this was soon abandoned in favour of a turbocharged version of the most modern GM-Europe engine, the single-overhead-cam 'Family 2' design. Developing this engine, was going to take time - when the car was first shown, in project form, in August 1985, it was suggested that the 'Family 2' size chosen would be 1,743 cc., but that nothing was then settled. In truth, the car had yet to run with that engine.

The very first prototype of 1984/85, in fact, was built up around a Ford-based Zakspeed racing unit, which might not have been politically acceptable, but which 'was easily available, approximately the size we were going to use anyway, and gave us an instant 500 bhp for testing.' That was the power unit used in the car sent out to Kenya for Safari-style testing in 1985 - but it was not the engine used when two cars were prepared for Paris-Dakar in 1986. Those, for all manner of practical reasons, were 250 bhp versions of the old Manta 400 unit!

I need only mention one word - Xtrac - to show that the transmission system chosen for the Kadett 4 x 4 was not a crude lash-up. This layout, although looking superficially like that of the original Jensen/Ferguson Formula installations, was completely different in detail. The only true likeness, in fact, was that there was a transfer gearbox, and centre differential, along with front and rear propeller shafts!

Before making its choice, the Opel team had also talked to Getrag, and FF Developments, but chose Xtrac as the most suitable for their purpose; it was the Xtrac's unique centre differential properties which attracted Opel to this company. Xtrac was the name given to a four-wheel-drive transmission system which Mike Endean had developed, after he had left the motor racing gear specialist, Hewland, to found his own business at the beginning of the 1980s. His earlier work had included the design of a transmission for Martin Schanche's now-famous four-wheel-drive Ford Escort rallycross car, and developments of this had already been seen on other one-off competition cars. The Opel contract, however, was his first link with a major manufacturer, and that seen in the Paris-Dakar cars was by no means identical to that which would have been used if the 4 x 4 project had finally gone ahead.

In the Xtrac system, for the Opel, Endean had designed a five-speed transmission, using Hewland racing gears; as a racing-orientated engineer Endean had never had to consider the use of strong reverse gears so those fitted were quite weak. This approach caused problems on Paris-Dakar in 1986.

As with other front engine/four-wheel-drive installations, the Opel's Xtrac transmission had its transfer gearbox and centre differential alongside the main gearbox, but the niceties included the ability to dismantle the gearbox and change gear wheels and other components without disturbing the transfer gear itself - and the very sophisticated nature of the centre diff. and its controls.

Like the FF viscous coupling differential, the Xtrac also used epicylic gearing to provide a primary front/rear torque split; in the Opel's case this was a surprisingly extreme 28 per cent front/72 per cent rear setting. But, as engineer Goldstein points out: 'The difference between

this and the Ferguson viscous coupling is how the torque split is locked and unlocked. The Ferguson simply locks up when the front and rear axles spin against each other at an excessive rate. The Xtrac allows other factors to be taken into account .... You must decide what factors you want - whether it is turbo boost, steering angle, side force, wheelspin and so on.'

There are internal secrets that Endean keeps to himself, and although the differential has plates (like the FF VC unit), its clutches are hydraulically controlled. A small pump, turned by an engine camshaft and using a mere 3 bhp, provides hydraulic pressure, and a compact electronic 'brain' monitors the needs of the unit. *That* is the complicated part of it all - the simple result is that front/rear torque supplies can therefore be altered, internally, up to a 50/50 figure, and the driver also has a secondary lever, alongside the main gear lever, to allow him to alter that split, instantaneously, in the middle of a stage.

It it sounds complicated, and something of a 'black art', then be reassured - that is precisely what it is at this stage, for Endean and Goldstein both agree that a great deal more remains to be learned. Tony Fall once told *Cars and Car Conversions* deputy editor that this system would 'enable his team to have sufficient transmission flexibility to last for the next 15 years'. (Is that being over-optimistic? Remember that 15 years *ago*, at the start of the 1970s, the most competitive rally car around was the rear-engined Alpine-Renault, or the cheap-and-cheerful front-engined Ford Escort ....)

There was nothing remotely as complex about the new Kadett's front and rear differentials, where FF-style VCs and ZF pawl-and-ramp types were both being tried. If the project had gone further ahead, though, Torsen Gleason and Xtrac systems would also have been tried.

When the car was finally ready to show to the press, this was still a single-prototype programme, and the 4 x 4 was so beautifully finished, and liveried, that some cynics were convinced that it was a mock-up. It was, of course, a running car, even though Opel were not then ready to reveal that it was using Ford-Zakspeed power to get development under way. In the first place, the Eurohandler team had taken the traditional rallyman's way out, by adding sturdy wing bulges to accommodate larger tyres and a great wheel movement, but Opel's stylists had then taken one look at it, discovered that they could find time (or make time!) to do a complete styling job, and fired up their computer drafting machines to re-shape the sides of the car as necessary.

The result was a squat, big-wheeled, prototype, which sat lower than the ordinary Kadett, but with broader shoulders, and a very close family resemblance to the mass-production machine. It looked much closer to standard than - say - the Delta S4, it was as pretty and impressive as the Peugeot 205 Turbo 16, and it made the MG Metro 6R4 look like a backyard special.

The whole basis of the structure was the standard monocoque, though Matter, near Hockenheim (the West German equivalent of Safety Devices), had to graft in a completely new floor, while the skin and non-stress-bearing panels were all in Kevlar. Fall's philosophy was that he wanted these cars to be used by many other drivers, if the project got the go-ahead, so he wanted to keep it as simple as possible:

'We want to be able to recycle these cars, and would like to think that we can not only have our own team running them; we've got 13 national dealer teams to think about as well, and they can't all afford carbon-fibre/Kevlar things, it has to be reasonably affordable ....'

By the time the car was on the way to completion, a projected new formula, Group S, had arrived on the scene at FISA. At a stroke, this gave Opel a chance to plan ahead, and to get back into World Championship rallying, without having to lay down 200 cars first. Although Group S's engine capacity, and other limits, were not then settled, it was clear that FISA was proposing to authorise a limited-power 'Formula 1' type of rally category, where only ten cars of each type would have to be built. Clearly this meant that any sizeable competitions operation (Opel/Eurohandler could handle it, for sure) could prepare ten special cars, and go rallying on near-equal terms with the big-spending teams once again. Tony Fall was delighted; in mid-1984 he had hoped to get approval for the Kadett 4 x 4 as a Group B project, but now he was certain that he could build ten Group S machines instead. Morale at Russelsheim rose perceptibly.

After launching the project, Eurohandler then took a car to Kenya, for a concentrated session of high-speed, rough-road, hot-weather testing, using their two Safari specialists, Rauno Aaltonen, and Erwin Weber, as drivers. Right away the car proved that it was a lot faster than the Ascona 400/Manta 400 cars had been on the same sort of going, but there were many development problems to be solved, notably the way that the car seemed to have an appetite for bending, or even breaking, Bilstein dampers.

Nothing daunted, the team then returned to Russelsheim, to get on with building two special Kadett 4 x 4s, to be entered in the gruelling Paris-Dakar event in January 1986. Opel already had experience, good and bad, of Paris-Dakar. In 1984 Guy Colsoul had finished fourth overall in a rear-drive Manta 400, the first non-four-wheel-drive car to finish. In 1985, the same car/driver combination was actually leading the entire event, 13,000 km into a 15,500 km event, when it was caught in a sandstorm; not even Opel's carefully-developed precautions could keep the sand out of the engine, which was completely ruined. In 1984, by the way, Cosworth were asked to rebuild the fourth-place car's engine afterwards, and announced that nothing, but nothing, was worth using again!

For Paris-Dakar in 1986, therefore, the two 4 x 4s were equipped with individually prepared and modified Manta 400 engines, the rear differential was a modified Opel Monza assembly, complete with ZF limited-slip differential, front and rear wheel movements of 305 mm and 350 mm (that's 12.0 in. and 13.7 inches - which explains Fall's quip that 'at Opel we measure wheel travel in feet!'), and bag tanks totalling 300 litres/66 gallons in capacity. It was no wonder that the 'dry' car weighed 1,040 kgs., but that its fully-charged, all-up, weight, with the crew on board, was 1,550kgs/3,415 lbs.

The Paris-Dakar entries were driven by Guy Colsoul and Erwin Weber, carrying Bastos (cigarettes) and Texaco sponsorship. The results show that the two cars finished, well down, in 37th and 40th places, but what this cannot show was how fast, and basically how strong, these 250 bhp Kadetts actually were.

In spite of some early shock absorber overheating problems, the two Kadetts were lying fifth and sixth as they left the Tamanrasset halt, right in the middle of the Sahara desert, but separate incidents then caused them to drop back. While carrying a full load, Erwin Weber's car got stuck in soft sand, the driver used reverse gear to power his way out, snapped off a tooth,

and damaged the internals. He had to wait for a service truck to arrive, see the sand tunneled out under the car to allow a gearbox change, and eventually lost ten hours. Mike Endean took note of a rally driver's occasional need to go backwards as hard as possible, and sat down to modify the design; in any case, a six-speed transmission was already under consideration for the definitive Group S Kadett 4 x 4.

Guy Colsoul, the Paris-Dakar veteran, had his own personal misfortune, between Dirkou and Agadem. Climbing one soft dune, scrabbling all the time for grip, he quite suddenly discovered that there was a sheer drop of about 16 feet on the other side of the brow. The consequent, unavoidable, nose dive, meant instant immobilisation, a long wait for the service truck, and a repair which added up to another 10 hour time loss.

Top
A prototype Opel Kadett 4x4 was taken to Kenya for rough road testing in a hot climate, during 1985. At this point it used a Ford-based Zakspeed four-cylinder engine, but Opel didn't tell GM too much about that! *(Photo: Holmes)*

Centre
The entire nose of the Kadett 4x4 could be removed for servicing and rebuilds. *(Photo: Holmes)*

Below
Opel entered two cars for the Paris-Dakar marathon of January 1986. Both finished, but there were serious delays, not due to the transmission itself. Incidentally, although Paris-Dakar crosses the Sahara desert, that is snow at the side of the (French) road!

In most World Championship rallies, a few
seconds lost due to a spin is considered a
tragedy, in the Safari penalties are measured in
minutes, but on Paris-Dakar it's the hours that
count.

Back in West Germany, Opel cleaned out
the cars, and looked for damage and deteriora-
tion. Apart from the obvious scrapes and scrat-
ches (and the result of Colsoul's nose-dive), there
weren't any. Tony Fall, Karl-Heinz Goldstein,
and the ever-present Rauno Aaltonen already
knew what had to be done to make their new
Group S car competitive - if, that is, the
authorities ever settled on an engine formula
which everyone would agree with.

The 1987 Kadett 4 x 4, it seemed, would
have the six-speed transmission, the new turbocharged 'Family 2' engine, the double coil spr-
ing/damper installation at every corner - and an
even more sophisticated Xtrac transmission, and

its hydraulic-cum-electronic control systems.

However, just when the 4x4's specification
was settling down, Henri Toivonen's Tour de
Corse crash caused FISA to scrap the proposed
Group S category.

The British arm of this European-wide
team, GM dealer Sport, had almost completed
its first car, to be called the Astra 4S, but after
this shock it was demonstrated to GM dealers,
then used once on a British event where it took
fourth place behind two 'works' Ford RS200s
and an MG Metro 6R4.

In spite of vigorous lobbying by Opel,
Peugeot and Lancia, who were all interested in
promoting a new category for 10-off, limited-
horsepower, specials (and for which the Kadett
4x4 could have been ideal), nothing was achieved, and the GM four-wheel-drive project was
abandoned.

In 1987 the British car was sold off to

Hopes dashed! Russell Brookes (left) and Mike Broad were
ready to swap their old Manta 400 for the Vauxhall version
of the Kadett 4x4, but this car never started an event.

rallycross expert John Welch, and it was fully
competitive, and winning races by the spring of
1988.

PEUGEOT 205 TURBO 16

Just as one can credit the birth of the Ford RS200 project to Stuart Turner, and that of the Lancia Delta S4 to Cesare Fiorio, the powerful personality behind the French Peugeot 205 Turbo 16 was Jean Todt. No other individual, perhaps, could have persuaded Peugeot, whose previous rallying experience had been with solid, durable, but essentialy unexciting 504s and 504 V6s, that they should go ahead and produce a mere 200 Group B four-wheel-drive 'homologation specials', then attack the rallying 'establishment', head-on.

Perhaps it is the name - Peugeot - which is slightly misleading here, for the company was no longer on its own in the French industry, and there were elements of Citroen, and even Talbot (née Chrysler-Europe) influence in the new car.

As ever, I must delve back a few years, to detail the corporate links and rallying events which led to this project ever getting started. For many years Peugeot itself was an independent family-owned concern, one of the great pioneers of the French motor industry, and it was not until the 1960s that any tentative co-operative links (actually with Citroen) were made. In spite of moves to produce common engines and other components with Renault and Volvo in the early 1970s, the big commercial tie-up came in 1974, when Peugeot joined hands with Citroen, and soon took it over completely. The final link was made in 1978, when Chrysler sold their European subsidiaries to Peugeot as well, this meaning that the British firm which some people still knew as the British 'Rootes Group' became a Peugeot company. In 1968 a 'works' Hillman Hunter had won the original London - Sydney marathon, and in the 1970s, Chrysler-U.K. had supported a small competitions operation, managed by Des O'Dell. This department had limited success with the Avengers, but from 1978 it began to develop what O'Dell called 'a better Escort', the 16-valve 2.2-litre engined Chrysler Sunbeam-Lotus hatchback. The Chrysler marque name was dropped in favour of 'Talbot' in 1979, and so it was the Talbot Sunbeam-Lotus cars which became more and more successful in World Championship rallying.

The Sunbeam-Lotus's first success was fourth overall in the San Remo rally of 1979, its first World Championship victory coming in the Lombard-RAC rally of 1980, and then in 1981 the 'works' team won the World Championship for makes. In 1979 Jean Todt acted as Jean-Pierre Nicolas's co-driver, while in 1980 and 1981 he co-drove for Guy Frequelin. It was towards the end of that World Championship year that he also took over the management of Peugeot-Talbot Sport, in Paris. Whereas Des O'Dell's programme had been organised from Coventry, Todt was determined to shift PTS's main effort back to France.

Peugeot itself had won many long-distance endurance rallies in the 1970s, with its very strong, but essentially standard, 504s, but it had completely opted out of European-style 'sprint' events, where a Group 4 homologation special was needed to be competitive. In 1981, however, Todt could see that the whole face of rallying was about to change, and because he not only had a forceful personality, but also had a great reputation in the 'corridors of power' at Peugeot, he persuaded Peugeot that they should get directly involved. Not only did he win approval to develop a new Group B car, but he received *carte blanche* to do whatever was necessary to produce an outright winner. Peugeot's directors, however, insisted on one other thing - that the new car should look, superficially at least, like one of the company's mass-production machines.

known as the Peugeot 205 Turbo 16, broke new ground in several technical respects, and it was the first successful example of the second generation of four-wheel-drive rally cars. Whereas the all-conquering Audi Quattro of 1981 - 1984 was a production car first, and a competition car second, the new Peugeot was to be designed as an out-and-out rally car, in which function came ahead of all other considerations.

Except, perhaps, style - for as it turned out, the 205 Turbo 16 was also a very pretty little car which, in road-going '200-off' trim, was also a very pleasant and flexible Supercar to use on the road.

Although it must have been a pleasure for the design engineers to work on such a single-purpose project, it must also have been a little

Immediately after the Talbot Sunbeam-Lotus team had won the 1981 World Championship, Todt held a press conference at which he made several promises: Peugeot was starting to design a new four-wheel-drive car, it would be unveiled in 1983, and it would start rallying in 1984. The object, no less, was to field a full team in 1985, and win the World Championship for Makes. These were bold predictions, and we now know that every single one of them was fulfilled. Not only that, but the car started winning events, consistently and without luck, in the autumn of 1984.

The new car, which eventually became

frustrating for them to have to fit everything into the modified silhouette of the mass-production 205. This small/medium-sized hatchback was still a secret project when development of the rally car started, and from an early stage it became clear that there would be an enormous publicity spin-off if the mass-production car and the rally car could both be launched at the same time. This hope, like all the others, was achieved, for both met their public in February/March 1983.

The basic statistics of the front-engined, front-wheel-drive, 205 mass-production car included a wheelbase of 7 ft. 11.3 in., and an

overall width of 5 ft. 1.5 in., yet the 200-off rally car's wheelbase was 8 ft. 4 in., and its width was 5 ft. 6 in. If the car's were viewed separately, they looked remarkably similar (except, of course, that the rally car had a large hot air outlet above the front-mounted radiator, and air scoops ahead of the rear wheels); it was only when they were inspected side by side that the stretching, in length *and* width, became clear.

Nevertheless, the decision to use the basic silhouette, and proportions, of the new 205 model *may* have compromised the layout of the rally car to some extent. Peugeot would never admit this, but other eminent engineers have raised their eyebrows at the location of some components, especially at the basic location of the engine, which was across the car, and well to

Above
The Talbot Sunbeam-Lotus was a successful front-engine/rear-drive car in 1980 and 1981, but team chief Jean Todt wanted a better prospect for the 1980s.
(Photo: Hugh Bishop)

Top Right
Talbot won the World Championship for Makes in 1981 with the Sunbeam-Lotus, and future Peugeot team chief Jean Todt was Guy Frequelin's co-driver. *(Photo: Holmes)*

Left
Peugeot had to make a complete change in their thinking about rally cars for the 1980s, as their previous successes had been gained with models like this 504.

one side of the centre of gravity.

It was the layout of the engine, gearbox and drive line which was the most interesting to the engineers, for the steering, suspension, and braking installations were all straightforward enough, and a significant proportion of the body shell was retained from the three-door mass-production 205 model.

Todt's team knew that Audi were already claiming more than 300 bhp for their 'works' Quattros, so they reckoned on needing at least 155

350 bhp from the start, for their new Peugeot, and more than 400 bhp as soon as the next series of evolution cars was produced. None of the group's normally aspirated engines had that sort of potential, so it was decided to produce a turbocharged engine and, because of attractive minimum weight-limits which were offered, to aim for the equivalent of a 2.5-litre unit. That, by definition, meant that the engine's actual swept volume would have to be just less than 1,786 cc., and the block would have to be sturdy enough to accommodate this, and the greatly increased pressures of turbocharger boost.

If Peugeot/Citroen had not already been developing a new range of engines - the XU series - for its next generation of cars, at the time the 205 T16 was being designed, the car's chief project designer, Bernard Perron, along with his associate Jean-Claude Vaucard, would then have been faced with very difficult choices. The front-wheel-drive, transversely-mounted, Peugeot 104-type engine (which was to be used in the Citroen 1000 Pistes Group B car, already described), was too small, and its configuration was all wrong; the rest of the company's engines was an uninspiring bunch.

The new XU family of four-cylinder engines, however, was not only in exactly the right size range - typical swept volumes were 1.6-litres and 1.9-litres - but had a light alloy cylinder block, and a five-bearing crankshaft. There was also to be a 1.9-litre diesel version,

Des O'Dell's British Talbot department commissioned Lotus to build this mid-engined, rear-drive, Horizon model in 1981, but nothing came of it. It would never have been a Quattro-beater.

with a very sturdy cylinder block and bottom end, with a bore of 83 mm and a stroke of 88 mm, and this looked like a very good place from which to start. For the Group B Peugeot, this basic bottom end was to provide the basis of the new rally engine - and thus it was that XU8T was born.

With the basic dimensions of the engine known, the transmission and drive lines could now be laid out. At this point, Jean Todt consulted his old 'boss' at the British Talbot factory,

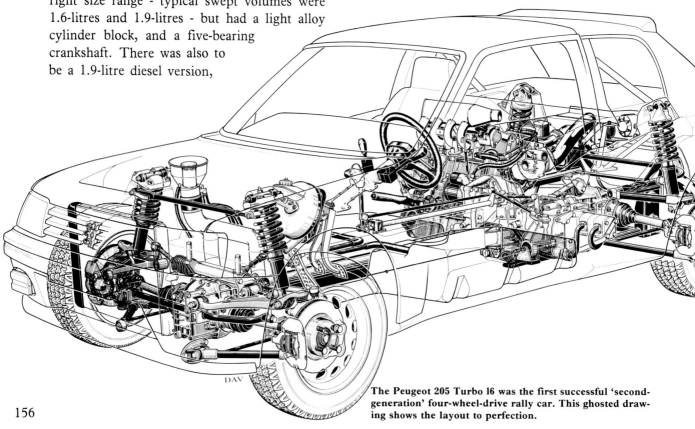

The Peugeot 205 Turbo 16 was the first successful 'second-generation' four-wheel-drive rally car. This ghosted drawing shows the layout to perfection.

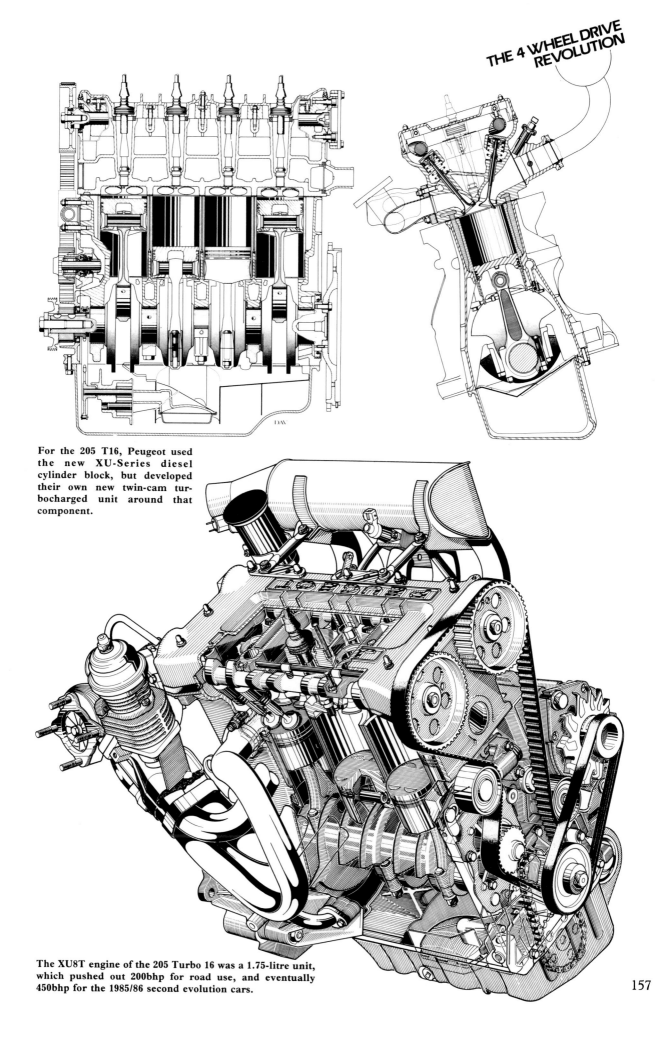

For the 205 T16, Peugeot used the new XU-Series diesel cylinder block, but developed their own new twin-cam turbocharged unit around that component.

The XU8T engine of the 205 Turbo 16 was a 1.75-litre unit, which pushed out 200bhp for road use, and eventually 450bhp for the 1985/86 second evolution cars.

157

Des O'Dell, concerning the practicality of various layouts, and indeed he asked O'Dell to work in France during 1982 while the first car was taking shape. Although there was never any doubt that the car would have four-wheel-drive (Jean Todt had promised as much, after all, at his press conference in 1981), and little doubt that the engine would be placed behind the seats, but ahead of the line of the rear wheels, the actual layout chosen was unique. One reason for this, I am sure, is that it allowed an existing main gearbox to be used.

Rather than in line with the chassis, the engine and main gearbox assemblies were placed transversely, across the car, approximately where the rear seats would have been on a normal four-seater Peugeot 205, and therefore behind the vertical bulkhead placed immediately behind the two passengers' seats. The engine was totally to the right side of the car (behind the left-hand-drive co-driver's seat), while the main gearbox was all on the left side of the car (behind the driver's seat).

As Jean Todt and Jean-Louis Moncet have written in their own personal study of the 205 T16 project (*Peugeot 205 - The Story of a Challenge* - which is also published by Haynes):

'The first design of the M24-Rally (this was the internal code-name for the car) showed the engine in a central, longitudinal position.

You don't win World Championships in the mid-1980s with three men and a dog. This was Peugeot's massive 1984/85 'works' effort. Jean Todt is in the front line, towards the left of the shot, with his 1985 team drivers to his immediate left.

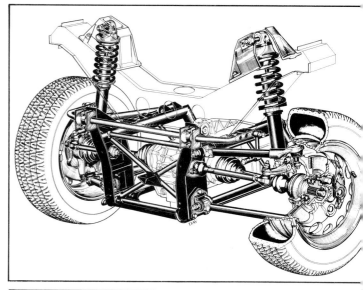

Above Top
The 205 Turbo 16's rear suspension was sturdy, and simple to adjust, to meet the drivers' wishes.

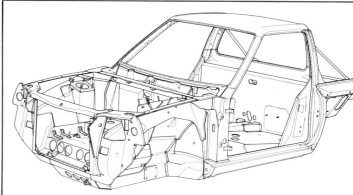

Above
This was the structure of the original 205 Turbo 16, which used the 205 road-cars shell as the basis for its centre section, but there were many new sections at front and rear.

Another design showed it to the right at the back, off-centre, Des O'Dell offered a strong argument for the second possibility. In a rally car there is one part of the engine that cannot be altered: the side on which all the transmission belts (distribution, alternator, pumps) are mounted. This side must, without question, remain accessible. Right, at the back, would be an ideal spot .... In March 1982 the engine design defined itself as a central rear transverse, offset to the right, with access to the transmission belts via a quickly removable body panel in front of the right rear wheel ....' - the translation from the French is a little quaint, but the logic is crystal clear.

The five-speed, two-shaft, all-indirect gearbox, though mounted in a strange position, was a very familiar design, and is recognised by all motoring enthusiasts as the front-wheel-drive Citroen SM unit. However, it is worth recalling that the SM box evolved from that of the front-wheel-drive Citroen DS19 of the 1950s, that it was also used in the Maserati Merak and Lotus Esprit/Esprit Turbo sports cars and the Citroen C35 commercial vehicle - and that it was soon to find a home in the Citroen BX 4TC four-wheel-

Drive from the engine, therefore, came in to the top, primary, shaft, and left the gearbox below that level by the secondary shaft. Then, on the centre line of the car, the drive was turned through 90 degrees by a simple pair of gears. with propeller shafts leading to the front, and rear differentials and final drives.

The 'centre' differential (which was actually placed behind the line of the engine/gearbox, but just ahead of the rear final drive) was an FF Developments epicyclic gear design with a viscous coupling. This, like all VCs of this nature, could be swopped for another component with a different torque split, and when Peugeot announced the car in February 1983 they advertised extremes of 25/75, and 45/55 -and several other ratios were under development.

Although they were housed in separate light alloy castings, the engine, main gearbox, 90-degree turn of drive, centre differential, and rear final drive assemblies were all bolted together in a single assembly, and when the car was announced, there was a conventional ZF bevel gear limited slip rear differential.

This bulky block of machinery was con-

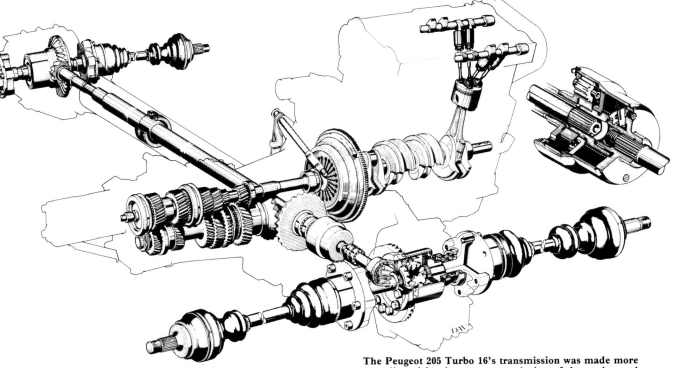

The Peugeot 205 Turbo 16's transmission was made more complicated by the transverse placing of the engine and main gearbox. The torque splitting centre differential, and viscous coupling, is behind the line of the engine/gearbox. All four drive shafts are identical components.

drive Group B car. Above all, it was a strong gearbox, but it was quite a versatile piece of kit as well, as these very different applications prove.

nected to the front differential/final drive by a large diameter torque tube, this front diff either

The main casing of the 205 T16's transmission laid out for inspection. The 'SM' gearbox, facing sideways, is in the centre of the assembly.

not having a limited slip device at all, or a ZF-type at first.

Once the basis of the engine had been chosen, the rally car 'conversion' was soon produced. PTS's designers produced a completely new light-alloy cylinder head, with twin belt-driven overhead camshafts, and four valves per cylinder, narrowly opposed to each other. While retaining the same cylinder bore as the other XU family of engines, the T16's engine had a shorter, 82 mm, stroke, which brought the capacity down to 1,775 cc (or 2,485 cc with the 'equivalency factor' applied).

For packaging reasons, the engine block leaned backwards by 20 degrees. The exhaust side of the head was to the rear of the engine (as installed in the car), as was the KKK turbocharger, while the Bosch fuel injection and inlet manifolding were towards the front, with the manifolding swept high and towards the centre line (clutch end) of the car. The air-to-air intercooler in the inlet side of the engine was well over to the left of the engine bay, close to one of the fresh air intakes, while the cooling radiator was up front, behind the car's front grille, and the oil cooler was in the tail. The fuel tanks were mounted low, near the centre of the wheelbase,

under the passenger seats.

It was an interesting, well-packaged, and ruthlessly logical layout of components, let down only by the fact that there must, inevitably, be a preponderance of weight on the right side of the car, and particularly the right rear wheel. Nevertheless, when the road car was eventually announced, Peugeot claimed an unladen weight (with full fuel tanks) of 1,145kg/2,525 lb., with just 54 per cent of that weight over the rear wheels.

When they were first shown the car, the lovers of graceful machinery were also delighted by its looks, for the Peugeot stylists had done a truly remarkable job in keeping the graceful shape of the original, even though the wheels had been pushed out towards the corners, and larger diameter wheels with larger wheel arch cut outs were also specified. When the MG Metro 6R4 was finalised, the comparison was stark, indeed.

There were three distinct sections to the monocoque of the new car. The centre section was largely that of the standard car's steel monocoque, while at the front there were much modified, or totally new, steel cross-members above and behind the main engine/transmission assemblies, and tubular sub-frames to stiffen it all up.

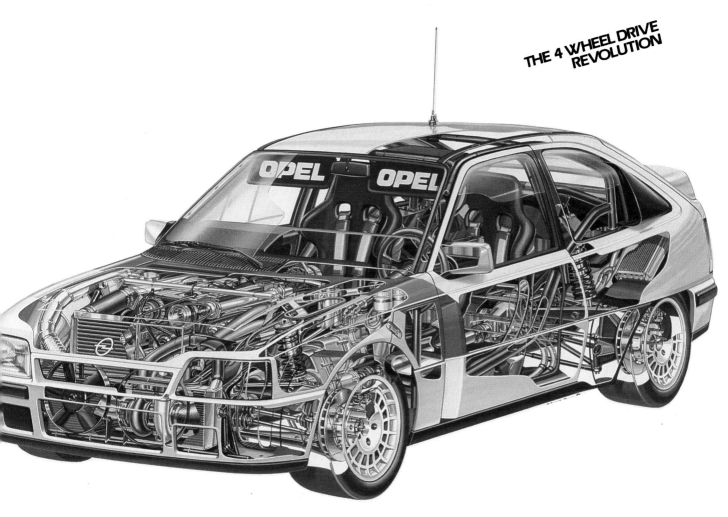

Opel's Kadett 4 x 4 was the first major user of the Xtrac
transmission system and was really a 'front/mid engined'
machine.

The prototype Kadett 4x4, a front/mid-engined car built
with Group S in mind, was unveiled in August 1985.

(Photo: Holmes)

The front of the car looked remarkably standard, with the grille and headlights of the normal 205, though the large hot air outlet in the bonnet behind the water radiator was unmistakeable. At the rear there were large air intake scoops ahead of the broad-shouldered rear wheel arches, to feed fresh air into the crowded engine bay, and the whole of the rear body work, which was a glass-fibre moulding, was arranged to hinge upwards and forwards around pivots on the roof panel immediately behind the passengers' heads. Naturally, a full roll cage was

built into the structure, and a nice touch on the road car which followed was that the hatchback window glass was also arranged to open, independently of the big rear section, so that a *very* small piece of luggage, which didn't mind getting hot, could be extracted from the lid above the engine bay. At this early stage, Peugeot knew little about the dynamic aerodynamics of their little rally car (though mock-ups had already been in a wind-tunnel to check out the efficiency of the various scoops, grilles, and slots), so the only 'add-on' aerodynamic aid was a small, full-

Above
The 205 Turbo 16 road cars had a very civilised, completely equipped, two-seater passenger compartment. Apart from internal noise, this was a very pleasant car to drive fast on the road.

Top Left
The 205 T16's engine was installed behind the seats, towards the right of the car, with all its drive belts and pulleys behind a removable body panel, and easy to service.

Bottom Left
This was the 200-off 205 Turbo 16 road car, which was much more civilised, and considerably prettier, than most of its rivals.

width, spoiler at the rear top edge of the roof.

Des O'Dell's main, and very important, contribution to this very French programme was to keep insisting on practicality, of design, of construction, and of maintenance. It was O'Dell's experience which led to the wheel nuts and the suspension retaining nuts being of the same size, to all four drive shafts being the same, and to the wishbone pivots all being fixed by the same bolts. It was also O'Dell who demonstrated the speed at which a complete transmission could be changed on one of the old front-engined Sunbeam-Lotus team cars - if his mechanics could do the job in 15 minutes, O'Dell said, then the new Turbo 16 transmission should be capable of similar rebuilds.

By the beginning of 1983, however, O'Dell's job was done - or so Todt insisted, anyway - and by the time the first car was ready to run, at the Peugeot (née Chrysler-France) private testing ground at Mortfontaine, north of Paris, the French were totally in command. On 16th February, less than a year after the general layout had been agreed, and only 14 months after Jean Todt had stated publicly what his policy would be, the very first prototype ran, for the very first time. Veteran Jean-Pierre Nicolas

was at the wheel. That machine was in 'road car' trim, for the evolution machine had not been completed. The original goal, of unveiling the rally car at the same time as the new mass-production 205, had been achieved.

There was, however, quite a lot wrong with the car at that stage, and a lot of development work, some strengthening of the structure, and some re-design, was needed to tame the turbo engine, and to get the handling right. The first 'works' specification evolution car, finished in August 1983, also needed much attention to make it competitive. Even so, the team's target, of getting the cars on to the start line of the Tour de Corse in May 1984, looked possible.

At the beginning of 1984, however, it all began to come right. Production of the 200 homologation cars was ready to begin at the Poissy factory, Andre de Cortanze joined the team from Renault as the team's Technical Director, Jean-Pierre Nicolas extended his testing contract - and the 1981 World Rally Champion Ari Vatanen agreed to move from Opel, to become the team's star driver. So, if the car could be homologated in time, Jean Todt was ready. Not only were the 200 bhp gun-metal homologation cars built before 1st April 1984, when the new car was homologated, but they were all lined up for inspection, and for counting by FISA observers, with photographs taken to prove this well-organised feat. At the same time, the 20 evolution cars (which would later, retrospectively, become known as 'Evolution One') were also finished off - and Peugeot were ready to go rallying.

Todt did not expect to win Corsica, first time out - he was too much of an experienced old hand for that - but the French press who flocked to the island to watch *their* car, on *their* event, thought otherwise. His 335bhp cars were too new, Todt thought, to make it to the end.

For such a 'raw' car, therefore, the result was astonishing. Bettega's Lancia Rally 037 led for the first seven stages before going off the road, in the fog, whereupon Vatanen took over the lead, and went even faster until he crashed after spinning in a pool of water. 'Jumbo' Nicolas, on the other hand, kept everything together, and took fourth place, in the car's debut event. In the Acropolis event, it was the same sort of story - both cars were fast, Vatanen led for a short period - and then both cars were forced out with mechanical problems.

163

The Peugeot 205 Turbo 16's first World Championship rally victory was in the 1000 Lakes of 1984. Ari Vatanen was the driver.

No doubt how many wheels are driving here, as the Peugeot 205 Turbo 16 scrabbles for grip on this gravelly corner!

This 'Evolution 2' Peugeot has come perilously close to side-swiping a spectator's car as it slides in to the left-hand hairpin! Note the aerodynamic 'add-ons'.
(Photo: Hugh Bishop)

Then came the Finnish 1000 Lakes, a début win for Vatanen, and the start of an amazing sequence of successes for the Peugeot Talbot Sport team. Ari, co-driven by his British partner, Terry Harryman, won the 1000 Lakes by a couple of minutes from Alen's Lancia Rally 037, won San Remo by more than five minutes from Bettega's Lancia Rally 037, and won the Lombard-RAC by a couple of minutes from Hannu Mikkola's A2 Quattro (and even found time to indulge in a rollover accident, on the last night!). Quite suddenly, and as secretly predicted by Todt many months earlier, the Quattros were on the run.

With such a record, achieved so comfortably, one might have expected Peugeot to stick to a proven specification. But Todt was not easily satisfied. In spite of the thousands of headlines already achieved, and the 'knock-on' factor of 205 Turbo 16 success already being felt in normal 205 sales, Todt was not satisfied. For 1985 he wanted a better car, and even more talented drivers.

Jean-Pierre Nicolas, having done his development job, and back-up driver job, finally retired, to run the Sports Promotion department. Ari Vatanen, naturally, stayed on as team leader, while Todt made offers to several leading drivers - including Markku Alen, Walter Rohrl, and Henri Toivonen - before finally settling on

Timo Salonen, and (for events where his team

could support three cars) Bruno Saby. Salonen was a rather laconic Finn whose talents had been wasting away at Nissan for several years, while Saby, the Frenchman, was something of a tarmac-and-pace-notes specialist.

At the team's pre-season conference, Todt announced that a second evolution model was already being developed, and that this type would be ready for use in Corsica, just a year after the *original* type had been homologated. The original evolution Turbo 16 might be an outright winner as far as the world was concerned, but in Todt's and de Cortanze's eyes it was already obsolete!

Left
By San Remo in October 1984, the 205 T16 had already won its first World Championship event; the Italian spectators are clearly very impressed by the pace of Nicolas's car.
(Photo: Hugh Bishop)

Below
For once, this first-evolution Peugeot 205 T16 is jumping straight and square - it was more often seen with its tail up! Jean-Pierre Nicolas, driving here, did an invaluable development job on the car in 1983 and 1984.

The original car, indeed, had several shortcomings. apart from its rather limited power output (by Sport Quattro and - reputedly - Lancia and Ford standards), and a weight bias towards the right rear corner, it was a car which 'flew' rather awkwardly over big jumps, and there was a big rotating mass across the car to screw up the gyroscopic stability of the machine at such times. As its critics had often predicted, it tended to kick its tail very high over certain jumps, and 'wriggle' awkwardly if the throttle was suddenly snapped shut at that moment.

While the original car, therefore, went on to complete an amazing sequence of wins - for Vatanen won at Monte Carlo with Salonen third, the same 1-3 finish was achieved in Sweden, while Timo Salonen won in Portugal after Vatanen broke his car's suspension - which made it six wins in six starts, the 205 Evolution 2 cars were taking shape. Not even humiliation in the next event - Safari, where the Peugeots were outclassed by conventional front engine/-

Timo Salonen's 'Evolution 2' Peugeot 205 T16 in a
hurry during the 1985 San Remo rally. It was spectator enthusiasm - and foolishness - like this, which
led to the upheavals of 1986... *(Photo: Hugh Bishop)*   169

The second-evolution 205 Turbo 16 had a different chassis rear end, entirely tubular, with Kevlar inner wheel arches.
(Photo: Holmes)

rear drive cars - could obscure that unique showing.

The second evolution 205 Turbo 16, however, might have looked similar to the original, but was a very different car indeed, for there were major improvements to the engine, the structure, the weight distribution, the brakes and the steering. It was an even more formidable competition car than the original car had been.

With a lot of work to the engine's breathing, turbocharger, and injection system (water injection was successfully tested), peak power was

pushed right up. In Corsica in 1984 335 bhp had been available, but for the same event a year later that peak had rocketed up to 424bhp. Maximum torque was now no less than 362 lb.ft., and this would reach 383 lb.ft. for the 1000 Lakes cars.

The transmission, with a central VC, and conventional ZF units at front and rear, was unchanged - and even the awkwardly disposed gear selector linkage stayed where it was, and seemed to work adequately.

The structure behind the cabin was completely reworked, with the box section 'chassis' extensions discarded in favour of a new tubular structure. At the same time there was a relocation of the various cooling radiators and intercoolers around the car, to produce more equal weight distribution. The result was that right-rear bias was reduced, but not eliminated (it is actually 20kg/44lb) - and the cars still needed spring platforms slightly raised at that corner to make the cars ride level...

Surprisingly, manual steering was retained for a time, and it was not until the autumn of the year that power-assistance was first made available. Similarly, the rather marginal braking, and damping installations had to be retained (homologation rules!), though Peugeot developed a steam cooling system for the dampers to keep them in one piece on more arduous events.

As far as the spectator was concerned, the second evolution Peugeot's most obvious

This very smart studio shot of the second-evolution Peugeot 205 Turbo 16 shows the large, extra, aerodynamic aids at the front corners, and on the roof panel. They trimmed the 'flying' characteristics very well indeed.

characteristic was its new aerofoil sections. At the front corners there were 'splash guards' which also acted as trim tabs to produce downforce, while a large aerofoil section was fitted to the top rear corner of the car (and fixed to the lift-up rear section of the body), to help it fly more straight and level on events like the 1000 Lakes. Peugeot had wanted to fit more ambitious aerodynamic aids, but these were refused by FISA.

For the rest of 1985 the Peugeot was as competitive as ever, in spite of a charge from Audi's latest E2 Sport Quattro, and the arrival of the Lancia Delta S4, but the season was marred by a bad crash in Argentina, where Vatanen's car bucked high over a bump, rolled end over end, and injured the driver severely. Happily, the popular Finn has recovered well.

That accident was almost certainly due to the habitual tail-kicking characteristic for which this car had become known, and it was one for which Peugeot had no obvious answer.

The rest of the season, in any case, was dominated by Timo Salonen, who had already won in Portugal, then won in the Acropolis, New Zealand, Argentina *and* the 1000 Lakes, with second in San Remo. Naturally Peugeot and Salonen became World Champions for 1985. In the meantime Kalle Grundel won the German National Championship in an 'E1' derivative.

For 1986, with Vatanen still recovering, Jean Todt had to reshuffle his team, so Salonen and Saby were joined by Juha Kankunnen (who had already won the Safari and Ivory Coast, in 1985, for Toyota). Michele Mouton was lured from Audi to attack the German Championship.

Although there was stronger competition than ever before, the Peugeots were still rally-winning cars, and during a very full season the team cars won in Sweden, Corsica, Acropolis, New Zealand, 1000 Lakes and the Lombard-RAC rallies. Peugeot also led San Remo at three-quarter distance, and were then disqualified by the stewards for running 'illegal aerodynamic devices'. This decision was later thrown out by FISA, and the rally's results annulled.

At the end of the year, Peugeot and Juha Kankkunen (three victories) won their respective World Rally Championships. The only real disappointment was in the Safari, where the T16s could not get on terms with unique conditions.

Even though his team had achieved so much in three years, Jean Todt was angry at FISA's sudden ban on Group B cars. He had every reason, for without the T16, and no competitive Group A Car on the horizon, Peugeot would effectively be out of business.

The result was that Peugeot sued FISA, and pursued its case for damages through the French courts (the case dragging on into 1988), and then turned to long-distance 'Raid' events. Modified longer-wheelbase 205 T16s won Paris-Dakar in 1987 and 1988 (Ari Vatanen and Juha Kankunnen respectively), but in 1988 the 405 version of the 205 T16 was robbed of victory when Vatanen's car was actually stolen from an overnight park in deepest Africa!

To summarise the Group B period, one has to say that although Audi recorded most wins, Peugeot mounted the most ruthlessly successful operation. If only the competition had carried on, unfettered, into 1987 and 1988, there might have been some magnificent confrontations between Peugeot, Lancia and Ford.

Peugeot took the second-evolution 205 T16 to Kenya for the Safari in 1986, but could not get on terms with the local conditions, and had no success. Note the large rear-of-roof spoiler.   *(Photo: Holmes)*

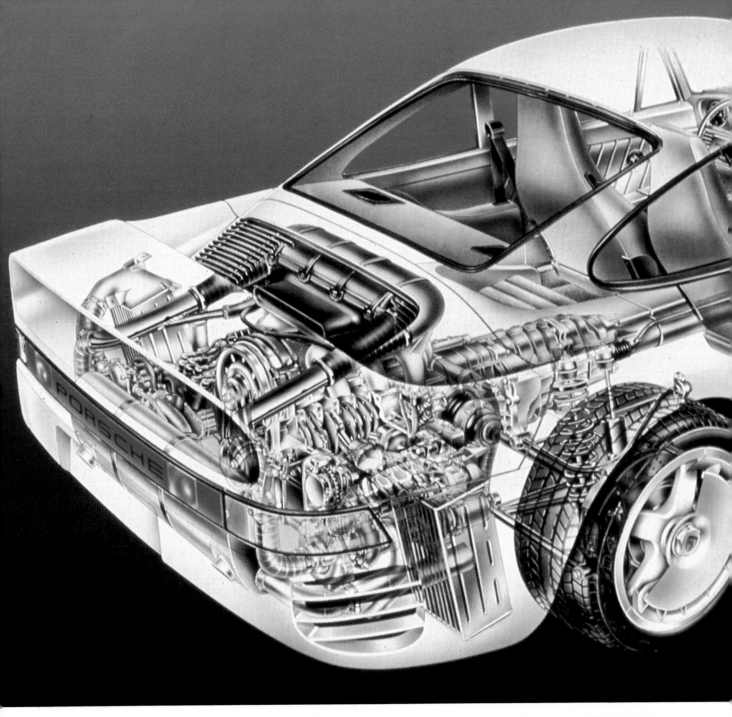

You would expect nothing less than a rear engine, and air cooling from a Porsche, even a 4 x 4! The 959 had the most sophisticated of all early-1980s four-wheel-drive competition cars.

Bottom Left
It can be very lonely in the Sahara desert - one of the Porsche 959s in Paris-Dakar.

Below
For Paris-Dakar, the Porsche 959 was given phenomenal ground clearance. Porsche 4 x 4s won this marathon in 1984 and 1986.

Above

Four-wheel-drive Porsches won Paris-Dakar in 1984 and 1986. On the second occasion full-specification 959s were used - this was Jacky Ickx's car, which finished second overall. The reason for snowy conditions is that this was the 'Prologue' test in France itself.

Right

For 1985, Porsche entered Paris-Dakar with a team of prototype 959s which, however, did not have all the electronically-controlled transmission items fitted.

(Photo: Holmes)

PORSCHE 959

Ever since the Second World War, Porsche has gone its own way. When the world of motoring produced cars with water-cooled engines, Porsche chose air-cooling. When everyone else used front-engined cars, Porsche put its motors in the tail. When everyone had become so used to the rear-engined air-cooled Porsche ethic, the West German company stood its own little world on its head - and produced front-engined cars with water cooling!

So, when the time came for Porsche to produce its first four-wheel-drive car, no-one quite knew what to expect. Would it be a completely new chassis? Would it be based on the 928S? Or would it be based on the evergreen 911? All we *did* know (and then not for sure) was that Porsche would justify the chosen layout in its own way, and according to its own logic. As it happens, the first Porsche 4 x 4, the 959 Coupé, was broadly based on the layout and proportions of the 911, but with a lot of racing 956/962 technology built in as well.

The story really begins, way back, with the 911 of the early 1960s. Before then, Porsche had built a whole series of road cars with flat-four engines, and a good deal of VW chassis ancestry. The 911, although sticking close to the air-cooled, rear-engine, spooky-handling ethic that everyone recognised, and understood, was completely new; at the heart of its design was a flat-six, single overhead camshaft, engine.

In the next two decades Porsche carried out a whole series of improvements to the 911 design, a period in which the engine was gradually enlarged from 2.0-litres to 2.2-litres, turbocharged versions were introduced, and road-car horsepower moved all the way up, from 110 bhp for the 911T, to an utterly reliable 300 bhp for the 3.3-litre Turbo.

Porsche was always much more interested in motor racing than rallying, and although it produced a series of specially-tuned 911s, some of which certainly qualified as 'homologation specials', these were usually intended for circuit racing. From time to time, however, it also dabbled in rallying at the highest level, and a 911 was just as competitive on tarmac, or in the snow, at the end of the 1970s as it had been fifteen years earlier.

The Porsche 911, in fact, was always an under-estimated rally car, rarely backed by a dedicated 'works' programme. Yet it won Monte Carlo rallies (several times), Swedish rallies, rough, fast, or endurance events all round the world - yet it narrowly failed to win the Safari, and never shone in the 1000 Lakes or the RAC rallies. Even in the early 1980s, though, a 911 SC RS model was good enough, in the interim, to attract Henri Toivonen to sign up with Rothmans, and it could certainly have won the European Rally Championship if the driver had not suffered a back injury part way through the season.

When the Audi Quattro ushered in the four-

wheel-drive revolution, however, and especially when Peugeot unveiled its exciting 205 Turbo 16, Porsche seemed to have been left behind, and for a time showed no interest in joining in. The company caused a considerable surprise at the Frankfurt show of 1981, therefore, by showing an intriguing prototype; this was a 911 Convertible, with the 3.3-litre Turbo engine and four-speed all-synchromesh gearbox, four-wheel-drive, with an almost empty 924 transaxle (usually found at the rear of that car) providing the means of driving the front wheels. There was a lockable free wheel in the system, which allowed the car to be used in rear-drive only, but no other sophistication. Porsche were irritatingly vague about the meaning of this car, why they had produced it, or what would happen next, although chief executive Peter Schutz later claimed (just as Audi was doing with the Quattro road car), that four-wheel-drive was actually more efficient than 'dragging two big undriven tyres around.'

He also claimed that Porsche's rear-engined layout was the optimum for four-wheel-drive, and that such a chassis worked best with a rear weight bias. But then, as one notorious young lady once said in a juicy vice case: 'Well, he would say that, wouldn't he?'

Nothing more was seen of that project (although the fully-convertible style was eventually offered on rear-drive Porsches from the spring of 1983), and perhaps we all thought that Porsche had lost interest in four-wheel-drive, when Porsche suddenly startled the pundits, at the Frankfurt Show of 1983, by exhibiting an exotic design study called Gruppe B. The implication was obvious. Here was a newly-conceived, perfectly stunning four-wheel-drive car, developed around the 911's monocoque and running gear which *might* (if Porsche willed it to be so) become a front-running competition car.

The new design, however, was strictly one-off at that point, and was by no means fully-developed, or ready for sale. Porsche talked about a drag coefficient of 0.32, which was

creditable enough (and a *lot* better than the ordinary 911), of a 400 bhp engine, which everyone believed, implicitly, and a provisional price tag, fully-prepared, of £160,000! It was not for some time that Porsche would drop the rather vague 'Gruppe B' title, and revert to their usual project number practice. This Porsche was, and always had been, the 959. The feeling persisted, however, that the car had been shown well before Porsche was ready to put it on sale - and, in fact, promised delivery dates went back steadily - from mid 1985, to late 1985, then to mid-1986 - and at the time of writing no private customer had yet taken delivery of a four-wheel-drive Porsche.

It was a car which looked rather like the ever-successful 911, but was different in so many ways. Indeed, if Porsche had not thought it desirable (for image purposes) to keep a similarity going, the engineers might have done a quicker, light, and more efficient job by starting from scratch. Honour, however, was preserved for here was a technologically advanced Supercar which remained faithful to the Porsche 911's image - with a rear engine, and with an air-cooled engine.

But only just. As ex-Grand Prix driver John Miles, writing about the definitive car when assessing it for *Autocar*, put it:

'To recap, the 959 uses a 911 body shell (galvanised, of course) with a heavily modified floorpan, engine bay and front end cell.... In fact few components owe much to previous production cars. The aluminium doors and front lid remain, but most of the additional body panels are polyurethane, Kevlar, Aramid and glass-fibre-reinforced RRIM or autoclave mouldings.'

It was, in fact, a very different car indeed, in all but the very basic layout, and originally-derived style. Like the 911, it had a flat-six cylinder engine in the tail, well behind the line of the rear wheels, and it had the usual 2+2 seating, but almost everything else was changed, or new. Neither the engine, the transmission, the suspension, the brakes, nor the aerodynamic aids had ever before been seen in a Porsche road car. The engine had a racing heritage all of its own. Although the racing flat sixes of the 1960s had used much of the standard single-overhead-cam unit's components, by the late 1970s they became more and more specialised, until only elements of the cylinder blocks, and the crankcase, remained unchanged.

Opposite
Ford's RS200 was just reaching maturity when FISA banned further Group B car development. Stig Blomqvist was leading the Acropolis rally when this picture was taken - a few minutes later he went off the road!
(Photo: Hugh Bishop)

177

Even so, there were limits to the power outputs which could be developed if the two-valve, single-cam head layout was retained. Logically, therefore, the designers had to consider four valves per cylinder, and twin overhead camshafts, but they could not do this at the same time as retaining air cooling. Accordingly, for 1978 (and the amazing 935/78 race car, affectionately known as 'Moby Dick') a new turbocharged 3.2-litre version of the flat-six was developed, still with air-cooled cylinder barrels, but with *water-cooled* cylinder heads, four-valve heads, and twin cams. A Japanese firm, for sure, would have lost face with this move, but Porsche faced their critics with a brave smile, and pointed out just how much of an improvement had been achieved.

After that, Porsche began to develop a

Above
This was the Porsche 959's transmission, ready to be offered up to a car. The clutch face is closest to camera. Note the torque tube connecting front and rear ends.
(Photo: Holmes)

Left
The 959/961's independent front suspension included twin coil spring/damper units. *(Photo: Holmes)*

Below
The Porsche 959 evolution car is more properly known as the 961. This car, seen under preparation at the Silverstone workshops of the Rothmans rally team, competed in, and won, the 1985 Pharaohs rally. *(Photo: Holmes)*

2.65-litre version of this engine for the Interscope team to use at Indianapolis (but the Indy organisers then changed the turbo boost rules, which made the new engine uncompetitive before it could race!), and for 1982 the design was modified yet again, in 2.65-litre form, for use in the new 956 Endurance Championship racing sports car.

Still with me? Good - for it was a de-tuned

version of the 956's engine which found a home in the tail of the new four-wheel-drive Porsche. For 'road car' use, Porsche planned to use the 2,850 cc unit in 400 bhp form (this was later raised to 450 bhp before production was ready to start), and everyone knew that 700 bhp, and maybe more, was available for out-and-out motorsport. At a time when Audi's best Quattros were producing about 320/330 bhp, and Peugeot's 205 Turbo 16 was planning to offer 200 bhp in standard form, and 'only' 350 bhp for the 'works' rally cars, this gave everyone cause to think! And if Porsche could keep this engine adequately cooled in the 956, there would surely be no problems in the 959?

In 1983, when 'Gruppe B' was first shown, there was still a great deal of secrecy about the details of its transmission, though the general layout was always known. Between the rear wheels was a gearbox/transaxle casing of the same *general* type as the 911 always used, except that it had six forward speeds. The front differential, and casing, was different from that originally seen under the 1981 project car, and front was rigidly connected to rear by a stout torque tube, with the propeller shaft running inside it. Torque tubes, of course, were already an established part of the Porsche scene - the 924, 944 and 928 front-engined models all had them, connecting their front engines to the rear transmissions - so when Porsche engineer John Wheeler joined Ford to develop the Escort RS1700T, it was no wonder that a torque tube figured in that car's transmission layout!

According to Porsche, the use of a torque tube: 'is essential in maintaining the accurate running of the drive line, and also helps the car withstand front impact.'

The gearbox itself was a six-speed unit (which Audi would also use in the final derivative of the Sport Quattro S1 rally car), which in itself was quite conventional. The expected Porsche technical wizardry, however, surfaced in the control, and graduation, of the torque split, which could be varied - electronically, or by direct intervention from the driver -between 100 per cent torque to the rear wheels, or even 100 per cent to the fronts, with the ability to lock everything up for a 50/50 split also built in to what was a very advanced system.

When 'Gruppe B' was announced in 1983, Porsche would say no more than that there was a secret torque proportioning device, electronical-ly monitored, which would decide how much of the torque should be fed to the front wheels. They also pointed out the fourth control stalk on the steering column, which would allow the drive to vary the split to suit different conditions - an extra dial on the facia indicated these modes: S-bends of tight radius, accelerating from a bend, running straight, and entering a larger radius bend. Helmuth Bott at least had the grace to admit that this item was under development -and, surely, even a Superstar would have been too busy with the rest of the car to swop the torque-split settings at such moments of stress?

Even now, years after the 959 was first put on show, Porsche is somewhat reticent about the actual mechanism of the torque split, though the driver-controlled settings were changed to indicate dry, wet, ice-snow, or traction conditions, which was a lot more sensible, and predictable, than before.

There was originally a viscous coupling centre differential, but later there was a different variable control of torque fed to the front wheels of the 959. As Porsche told John Miles, when he drove the finalised car, front-to-rear torque is monitored, and split, by a continuously operating hydraulically filled sintered steel/plain steel multi-plate clutch, with a similar device taking the place of a conventional limited-slip unit within the rear differential. Both are hydraulically clamped up to a maximum of 20 kgs. The principle of this, in fact, sounds similar to the Xtrac transmission used in the Opel Kadette 4 x 4.

Electronic control came from the sensing of throttle position, engine speed (the combination of the two indicating the torque to the electronic 'brain'), while the ABS brake sensors also told their own story about wheel speeds, or accelerations. Porsche, it seemed, had thought of everything - for instance drive torque was reduced to the front wheels on closed throttle to assist the turn in to corners, while the torque split automatically reverted to 50/50 whenever the brake pedal was operated.

It was, in other words, the most sophisticated four-wheel-drive system ever seen on a road-going car, yet one has to ask if it would all have been needed if Porsche had not decided to stick with a tail-heavy rear-engined layout?

Perhaps they could not afford to abandon *everything* which they had held so dear, for so long. The suspension of the 959, for instance, was completely different from that of the 911 itself. Whereas the 911 used torsion bars and struts at the front, with transverse torsion bars and trailing arms at the rear - and had that well-known set of cornering characteristics which could lead an over-driven 911 to spin viciously - the 959 was provided with double wishbone 956-type suspension all round, along with coil springs and twin dampers at each corner. Not only that, but the huge performance was to be kept in check by the use of 956 disc brakes as well. The 959 was, in other words, much more of a pure racing car than the very best 911 Turbo could possibly be.

Then, of course, there was the body style. When the original Porsche 911 had been developed, aerodynamic efficiency was not thought to be as important as style, so its relatively high drag coefficient (about 0.45 by the time the various spoilers and wheel arch extensions of the Turbo had been grafted on) was considered quite acceptable.

Porsche went to a great deal of trouble to reduce that figure for the 959 (which suggests, perhaps, that they were more interested in using it on the race track, where a high top speed is usually important, rather than on rallies where acceleration and consistent aerodynamic downforce take priority), not only producing a very slippery body style, but one which, in its 'un-sponsored' form, was also stunningly attractive.

The nose had been smoothed out on 'Gruppe B', with flushed headlamp profiles, and no protruding bumpers, there were massive, but delicately profiled, wheel arch extensions at front and rear, broad 'running boards'/sills under the doors to connect those arches, and a neatly integrated, full width, slotted spoiler across the tail.

The difference between the 959 and any previous Porsche 911-family car was that *this* example, for the first time, looked as if the whole shape had been considered by the whole team; at times, with cars like the 911 Carreras and Turbos, it looked as if one stylist had been let loose at the front, and another at the tail ....

The 1983 Frankfurt show car was a functional mock-up, and the complex transmission system was by no means fully-developed, so it was a real surprise when Porsche then entered three special four-wheel-drive 911s for the Paris-Dakar rally of January 1984, with sponsorship

from Rothmans, who were already the main supports for Porsche's Endurance racing effort. Jacky Ickx, already famous as a Porsche racing driver, and who had won the 1983 Paris-Dakar in a four-wheel-drive Mercedes-Benz G-Wagen, led the team, along with 1982-winner Rene Metge, and with two Porsche-Weissach technicians (Roland Kussmaul and Eric Lerner), in the third car to act as a 'flying service crew' for the professionals.

For this event the engine and four-wheel-system was greatly simplified, compared with the projected 959, for there was a 225 bhp normally-aspirated air-cooled 3.0-litre flat six engine, a production-type five-speed gearbox, and a simple mechanical centre differential lock. Reliability, and simplicity, was thought to be more important than performance on this occasion.

After three weeks, in what is now recognised to be the most gruelling rally in the world, all three Porsches made it to the finish, in Dakar. Ickx's car, which had led, suffered a wiring loom fire which the 'flying mechanics' had to rebuild; after dropping to 139th place, he stormed back to finish sixth. The mechanics, apart from doing their double duties, also indulged in a high-speed roll, but still finished 26th. The best news of all was that Metge kept it all together, and won the event outright.

Porsche then showed a finalised version of the 959, in the autumn of 1984, which had visual changes. There were new style 17in. diameter road wheels, with flush nave plate covers (and pressure sensors to indicate to the driver if wheel, or tyre, failures, was occurring!) while there were extra intakes to improve the flow of cooling air to the water radiator, in the front corner of the body apron, and scoops at the top of the rear wheel arch, and exit grilles in the rear corners (for the cooling of the twin KKK turbochargers).

Porsche, like most other makers of putative 200-off Group B cars, then found that it was more difficult to *make* the cars than to talk about making them. In 1983 they had planned to start building cars before the end of 1984, so that 959s could start their competitions career in 1985. At this point, chief executive Peter Schutz decided to make the engine comply with all known exhaust emission requirements (and especially those which applied, so severely, in California), without destroying the performance of the

Jacky Ickx and his film star co-driver Claude Brasseur have tried to win Paris-Dakar, in a Porsche, on three occasions, but failed narrowly. In 1986, in this 959 model, they were second overall.

engine. This effectively put the programme back by a year, while a late decision to standardise power-assisted rack-and-pinion steering added more months to the development programme. Porsche's engineers are *always* thorough, but cannot be rushed. And all the time this was going, the unladen weight was creeping up, and up. The 200-off 'customer' cars would weigh about 1,450kg/3,200 lb, whereas the fully-prepared evolution car, for competition, might get down to 1,100kg/2,425 lb.

In the meantime, there was another Paris-Dakar entry in January 1985, this time with Jacky Ickx, René Metge, and ex-F1 driver Jochen Mass in the three prototype 959s, while engineer Kussmaul drove a Mercedes-Benz G-Wagen as part of the service back up, and there were two huge MAN trucks to take part in the event, and carry all the spares.

The 1985 cars were described as 'prototype 959s', for they had full 959-style coachwork, including the smooth front and rear styling, and the massive wheel arches, along with a truly phenomenal static ground clearance of nearly 12 inches. Compared with the 1984 cars, the new machines used 230 bhp 3.2-litre engines, the 959's new six-speed gearbox, but a simple mechanical torque splitter was retained, 16 in. wheels were used, and the unladen weight was 1,190kg/2,625 lb.

On this occasion, however, there was no success, for, Mass's car retired at an early stage after

an accident, Ickx's car was badly damaged when he hit rocks hidden by the sand, and Metge's car broke its engine oil pump and had to retire. Ickx had got his car up to second place before the disaster occurred, but none of the 959s had led the event at any stage.

The only way to avenge such a defeat was by going out and winning another event, but this had to wait until October 1985. Not only did Porsche then send two fully-equipped, all-electronic-transmission cars to the Pharaohs rally, but they were the intended 'evolution' models, which carried the Porsche project code of 961. If you understand me, therefore, the 959 *rally* car wasn't a 959 at all, but a 961 ....!

Two cars were prepared for the Pharaohs - one was a new car, prepared at Stuttgart, for Jacky Ickx to drive, the second being prepared by the Rothmans Rally team at Silverstone, being the repaired and re-built Jochen Mass 1985 Paris-Dakar machine, which had been given a completely new front end, ahead of the doors, and was now fully up-dated with the finalised transmission control equipment, and to be driven by Saeed Al Hajri. This second entry was something of a sop for the British team, for David Richards had set it up in 1984, with Charles Reynolds as his team manager, specifically to get a grip on the new four-wheel-drive Porsche. Henri Toivonen had agreed to drive for him, too, with that in mind - but then there had been delays, delays, and more delays.

For the Pharaohs rally (ten days, and 4,000 km of desert rallying in Egypt, which suited the car's design perfectly), the evolution '961s' had a 40 per cent front/60 per cent rear weight distribution, while the engines had been de-tuned to a mere 370 bhp, in order to be able to use the 85 octane fuel which was available in Egypt. If the right sort of fuel was available, Porsche said, their turbocharged 2.85-litre engine (which was equal to 4.0-litres after the 'equivalency factor' was applied) could produce 650 to 700 bhp!

Another important innovation for the 961s, which was not at all obvious when looking at the car from the outside, was that the car's wheelbase had been increased by about 20mm/0.8 in., and that the rear suspension geometry was different. The wheelbase change had been achieved by moving the rear wheels slightly backwards, relative to the body shell (and the drive shafts were re-angled to suit),

181

while the rear suspension had much longer wishbone arms (and a different set of mountings under the shell), to allow for even more rear wheel movement than usual.

Even though the Pharaohs cars weighed about 1,400kg/3,085 lb (the fully stripped-out evolution 961s were likely to be 250kg/550 lb lighter than this) they were quite definitely the fastest and most competitive four-wheel-drive Porsches ever built. Not that Jacky Ickx had much chance to find out, as his 961 was burnt out, after a fire, on the very first stage. Al Hajri, on the other hand , won the event outright against rather meagre opposition, which pleased his sponsors - especially as they were also sponsoring the rally as well!

The Pharaohs success, however, was really just a side-show, and to properly prove the worth of the cars it was decided to enter three new 961s for Paris-Dakar in January 1986. Although the production run of 959s had been confirmed, yet again, and would now be for 250 cars, there was still no accurate date for this to start, and Group B homologation was not likely to be achieved until the end of 1986.

The 1986 Paris-Dakar cars were logical improvements of those built, and run, during 1985. This time, however, they had a complete 959/961 specification, complete with 2.85-litre engines having water-cooled cylinder heads and four valves per cylinder, and probably about 400 bhp because of the need to reduce total boost from 2.0 Bar to 1.5 Bar. The electronically controlled transmission was installed, complete, and as ever there were no fewer than four different transmission modes for the driver to play with.

The team was back to its successful 1984 format, with Jacky Ickx and René Metge driving the front-running cars, technical Roland Kussmaul driving the 'flying mechanics' machine, a Porsche 928-engined Mercedes-Benz G-Wagen, and two MAN trucks also being involved to service the cars at every night halt. Ickx, as usual, was partnered by the French film star Claude Brasseur.

As usual, the 'works' Porsches started gently, so by the time the cavalcade reached In Salah, on the northern edge of the 'real' Sahara desert, the best 961 was lying fourth (Metge) with Ickx seventh. By Niamey in Niger, through the Sahara, and well on the way down into Equatorial Africa, Metge's car was in the lead, and Ickx had moved up to fourth place. Even so,

there had been drama for the Belgian, who had to swerve to avoid a motorcyclist who fell off in front of his 961, holed the car's radiator, and had to wait for Kussmaul's 'service' 961 to arrive, complete with spare radiator, to get him back on the road again. Metge, too, had stuck fast in soft sand at one point, only to be pulled out by teammate René Metge.

Towards the end of the event, a pall was cast over the entire event when the event's creator, Thierry Sabine, was killed in a helicopter crash while following the event, at which point the Porsche's were leading (Metge), second (Ickx) and fourth (Kussmaul). Before the finish, on the Atlantic coast in Dakar, Porsche had been hoping to make this a crushing 1-2-3 result, but misfortune at a late stage made Roland Kussmaul have to cruise, and drop down to sixth place.

Nevertheless, the three Rothmans-Porsches arrived on the beach in line-astern, with the marathon won for the third time by 44-year-old René Metge, with Jacky Ickx second, and Mussmaul sixth. A look down the finishing order shows that every other machine in the top ten was a rugged off-road 4 x 4 - a Mitsubishi, Lada, Toyota, or Range Rover.

Porsche, therefore, needed no further proof that their 959/961 was not only the most sophisticated, but the most durable, four-wheel-drive competition car in the world. It was an appropriate moment for a company spokesman to announce that there would be no more 'works' 959/961 rally cars, and that further competition would be left up to the customers.

There was probably more to this announcement than meets the eye. It was made immediately after the crash had turned the Portugal rally into a nightmare, and it was also made when the pace of the latest 'Formula 1' style Group B rally cars had become apparent. Even Porsche could see that their 961 would have to battle hard to keep on terms with the latest four-wheel-drive lightweights - and Porsche were not in the business of finishing second, or being graceful losers.

On the other hand, the 961 might be a very good IMSA, or Le Mans racing car, and a car was therefore prepared for the 1986 Le Mans 24 Hours race. But that's another story ....

GROUP A-
New regulations for safer rallying

For 1987, FISA wiped the slate clean and imposed a new set of rules for all major rallies. In an effort to reduce the pace of the cars, Group B cars were banned from the end of 1986, and a Group A formula took its place. Whereas Group B had only required 200 identical cars to be built in a year, Group A required 5,000 cars instead.

That much was logical, but the supplementary rulings were not. FISA also took the view that no rally car should have more than 300 bhp (they could not be convinced, incidentally, that a maximum power/weight ratio was more valid - after all a heavy 300 bhp car was likely to be a lot slower than a lightweight 300 bhp car!), and produced a short 'black list' of Group A cars which could not be used in rallies.

At the same time FISA also ruled that 'evolution cars' could no longer be used in rallies, which meant that a manufacturer had to get it right in the first place - or build *another* 5,000 cars of the modified type.

Although several good two-wheel-drive Group A cars were being produced (the fastest, and most powerful, being the BMW M3 and the Ford Sierra RS Cosworth), everyone seemed to agree that four-wheel-drive was still needed to win rallies at World Championship level.

Right away this upset the balance of power:

Peugeot, which had been 'top team' in 1985 and 1986, had no four-wheel-drive car of any type, and was forced onto the sidelines. Jean Todt's team turned to Paris-Dakar instead.

Ford could choose between two types of Sierra, but the four-wheel-drive Sierra XR4x4 was too heavy, and was handicapped by an ancient and untunable vee-6 engine.

The lack of a four-wheel-drive car, and scandals over financial mismanagement led **Austin-Rover's** rallying effort to be wound down completely.

Opel's Group S Kadett was killed off, so the 'works' team turned instead to front-drive Kadetts of reduced performance.

Audi saw an opening for its less-specialised, but useful, four-wheel-drive Quattro models, and came back into the sport which it had abandoned only months earlier.

Toyota had been working away at a new four-wheel-drive Group B (or Group S) car in 1986, but this was abandoned.

Mazda now found itself with a chance to develop the 323 4WD Turbo hatchback.

Lancia - guess who! - were able to develop a newly announced mass-production four-wheel-drive Delta, the HF 4WD.

The pundits looked at the new line-up, and decided that Lancia, once again, were favourites for victory in 1987 and beyond, that Mazda *might* just match them,

Gary Smith's Ford Sierra XR4x4 was driven in New Zealand, in 1987, by 'works' driver Stig Blomqvist. As on other occasions, the chassis behaved well, but the engine was short of horsepower.

Mazda on the other hand, struggled with fragile engines and transmissions in its 1987 four-wheel-drive cars, then suffered humiliation when the homologation of an improved 323 was rescinded in November 1987.

Looking ahead to 1989 and 1990, would Ford eventually marry the 300 bhp of the Sierra Cosworth engine to the four-wheel-drive transmission of the XR4x4? Would Audi produce ultra-powerful Group A Quattros? Would Peugeot's forthcoming four-wheel-drive 405 model be competitive? It was an intriguing prospect.

Mazda's four-wheel-drive car was rejuvenated for 1988, but was still beaten by three Lancias in the Rally of Portugal.

(Ralph Hardwick)

Miki Biaison's Landia Delta HF 4WD, driving hard through all four wheels, on a 1987 San Remo special stage.

(Ralph Hardwick)

if their cars were reliable, but that no other team would get a look-in until a new generation of four-wheel-drive machines were developed for the late-1980s. This, on the other hand, was going to take much longer than it had in Group B days, as the building of 5,000 identical cars meant facing up to a full-blown design, development *and* manufacturing programme.

The pundits were right. In 1987 Lancia not only dominated the World Championship scene, but the team's engineers also found time to evolve a better version of the four-wheel-drive Delta, called the Integrale, which made a flying start to its career in March 1988.

AUDI 200 QUATTRO AND COUPE QUATTRO-
Group A cars

and braking components could be fitted, and the 2,144 c.c. engine could be tuned to produce around 300 bhp, which was all that FISA was prepared to accept in a Group A car at this time. The 200 Quattro used the Torsen torque-sensing centre differential, along with a robust new six-speed gearbox. The wheelarches were also large enough for 16 in. wheels to be matched to the Michelin tyres.

Audi knew, of course, that this was not an ideal car for the job (especially in the face of yet another fine rally car - the Delta HF4WD - from Lancia), so the company decided to pick and choose its events. The drivers, though extremely well paid, resigned themselves to a rather sparse season.

First time out, in the Monte Carlo rally of 1987, Walter Rohrl did extremely well to force the 200 Quattro into third place behind two Lancia Deltas, but it was clear that the power-weight ratio was unfavourable for 'sprint-type' events.

In Kenya, however, the big Audi was an admirable 'battle cruiser' for such an arduous event. Two cars started, two cars finished - and back at the finish in Nairobi they occupied first and second positions! Hannu Mikkola won outright (having done virtually no competitive motoring since mid-1986), while a sulky and unhappy Rohrl finished second.

Two cars also started the Greek Acropolis rally in May,

Almost as soon as it had withdrawn from World-class rallying, Audi began to suffer withdrawal symptoms. Not only was success in motorsport useful from the marketing aspect, but Audi still kept open its experienced motorsport department, and it still had excellent drivers like Hannu Mikkola and Walter Rohrl under contract. When FIA announced a full-blown Group A World Championship for 1987 Audi made a swift comeback.

After launching the original Quattro in 1980, Audi had gradually applied the same basic four-wheel-drive installation to every other car in its range. By the end of 1986 there were four-wheel-drive Audis as various as the new-style 112 bhp 200 Quattro saloon. All were being built in sufficient quantities to make Group A recognition a formality.

Although private and national teams chose to use the Coupé Quattro models - which were effectively non-turbocharged versions of the famous Turbo Quattros of earlier years, and could produce about 210bhp - the 'works' team put all its effort behind the mighty 200 Quattro saloon car, which was large (4.80 metres/15 ft. 9 in. long, with four passenger doors) and heavy 1,410 kg/3,110 lb).

That was the bad news. The good news was that it used virtually the same chassis as the Turbo Quattro, so all the well-proven competition transmission, suspension

and this time it was Mikkola's turn to finish third, while Rohrl's car broke on the very last test. Thereafter Audi decided that the 200 was not good enough after all, and as changes to FISA homologation rules were pending for 1988 (which would mean that they would have to use a smaller intercooler, and the engine would be even less powerful) the team was quietly broken up. Rohrl was retained for 1988, but Hannu Mikkola moved to Mazda.

The Coupé Quattro won several minor events (David Llewellin won the Scottish rally, for instance), and took some good 'top ten' places in World Championship rallies, but was not nearly fast enough to challenge the latest Lancias. Until and unless Audi produced a more powerful, lightweight, Group A car, the company was not likely to be on the winner's rostrum very often.

In 1987 there was one outstanding performance by the old Sport Quattro S1 car. As in previous years the 'works' team mounted an attack on the Pikes Peak hill climb in the USA - this time with a 700 bhp 'sprint' version of the car which had even more extraordinary aerodynamic devices at front and rear. In a stunning and ruthlessly efficient performance Walter Rohrl not only won the event, but pulverised the outright record time for the hill. The patriotic North Americans were not amused ....

Audi's moment of glory in 1987 came when the big 200 Quattros finished first and second in the gruelling Safari rally. Hannu Mikkola won the event; this is Walter Rohrl's car on its way to second place.

(Martin Holmes)

The ultimate statement of Audi's Group B Quattro project was this 700bhp monster, used by Walter Rohrl to dominate the Pike's Peak hill climb in 1987.

Above

In the UK, David Llewellin spent the first part of 1988 trying to get the bulky Audi 200 Quattro to the finish of an event. Although it was much larger and heavier than the outlawed Group B cars, it was surprisingly competitive.

Left

David Llewellin's UK 'works' Audi 200 Quattro three-wheeling its way around Northern Ireland in April 1988, just before its 275bhp engine let go.

Below

The Group A Audi Quattro used the same chassis and transmission as the old Group B Quattro, but its non-turbocharged engine could only produce about 210bhp, and it was no longer competitive. The handling, and the reliability, were as good as ever.

The anatomy of the 1988 Lancia Delta Integrale, better than the 1987 model because of its more powerful engine, its larger intercooler, its fatter wheels and its bigger brakes. It was the standard-setter for all other Group A cars to match.

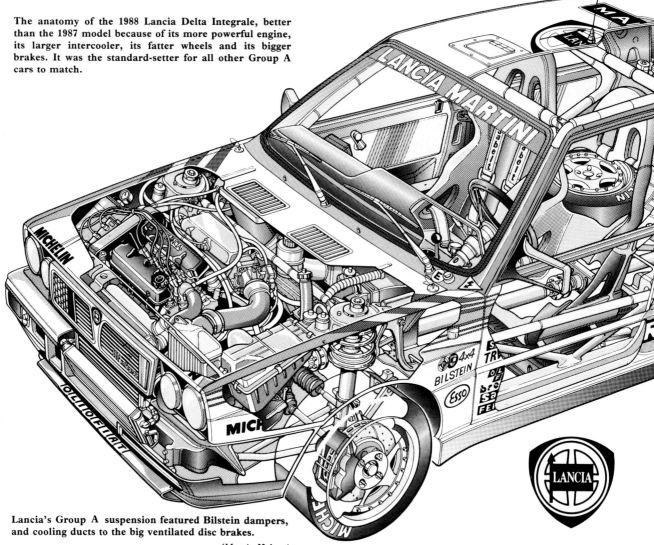

Lancia's Group A suspension featured Bilstein dampers, and cooling ducts to the big ventilated disc brakes.

(Martin Holmes)

The engine bay of the Delta HF 4WD was well-filled, especially when the optional large turbo intercooler and trunking was fitted.   *(Martin Holmes)*

For fast tarmac rallies, Lancia fitted these Kevlar brake cooling discs to their Delta HF 4WD cars.   *(Martin Holmes)*

LANCIA DELTA HF 4WD, AND INTEGRALE

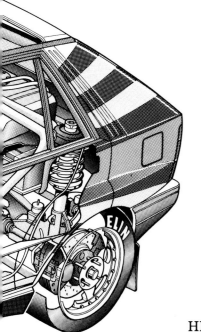

The arrival if the Group A Delta HF 4WD car was timely for Lancia. The new car was launched in the same month that saw Henri Toivonen killed in a Delta S4 crash, and when FISA decided to kill off Group B completely. For 1987 the World Rally Championship was organised for Group A cars - and the Delta HF 4WD was homologated on 1 January 1987.

Lucky? Certainly not. Lancia had been preparing the HF 4WD for a long time, and had always intended it for use in Group A - if not by the 'works' team then by the private owners. As one show business personality once retorted, when he was accused of being lucky: 'It's amazing, the harder I work, the luckier I get!'.

I should make one thing crystal clear, right from the start. The Group A Delta HF 4WD was a completely different car from the Group B Delta S4. Except that the styling of the S4 had purposely been arranged to resemble that of the road car, there was no conceivable link.

Ing Lombardi, the Abarth engineer who headed the design team responsible for the Delta S4, and for development work on the HF 4WD, confirms that when the Delta HF 4WD was launched in May 1986, no work had then been done to develop it as a rally car. A Group A 'package' was produced in double-quick time, at the same time as full-scale competition continued with the Group B Delta S4.

It is now a matter of record that the Delta HF 4WD only *just* achieved Group A homologation in time to compete in the Monte Carlo rally of January 1987. Lancia persuaded FISA inspectors that the necessary 5,000 cars had been produced by 31 December 1986, though it was admitted that two types of turbocharger - Garrett and KKK - were being fitted. Lancia were given a short period of grace, but told that a full 5,000 cars would have to be fitted with Garrett turbos before homologation could be confirmed. This was done by February, and (almost) everyone was happy.

As we shall see, Mazda Rally Team's boss, Achim Warmbold, was convinced that Lancia's interpretation of the regulations was wrong, and protested the cars in the Monte, but was rebuffed. There was never any doubt that a full 5,000 cars had been built - the Delta HF 4WD was a much more genuine Group A car than some earlier-generation Group B cars had been.

In the beginning the Lancia Delta project had evolved as a smart but essentially conventional family of transverse-engined, front-wheel-drive, hatchbacks which used mainly Fiat Strada running gear. Later the Delta was joined by the Prisma saloon, which was a booted version of the same design.

Fiat-Lancia then began to develop four-wheel-drive versions of its existing cars, and in April 1986 the first medium-sized car, the Prisma 4x4, was launched. This car, having the same basic 'chassis' as the Delta, could be said to blaze a trail for the Delta as well. In the case of the Prisma, however, the engine was normally-aspirated 2.0-litre twin-cam unit.

The Delta HF 4WD was revealed a few weeks later, when Abarth's thinking on the design became clear. Although it had the same basic layout as the Prisma, the Delta was fitted with a 1,995 c.c. eight-valve twin-cam, a Garrett T3 turbocharger, and an intercooler; the peak power output was 165bhp, vastly more than the 115bhp of the Prisma 4x4. The engine was the latest of a long running family, and used twin counter-rotating balancer shafts, to cancel vibrations which are endemic with four-cylinder engines.

As with the Mazda 323, and other transverse engined four-wheel-drive cars, the Delta's transmission was really a conversion of the normal front-drive layout. Drive to the front wheels was by a free-floating differential, the output shaft to the rear drove a Ferguson viscous coupling torque-splitting centre differential, and a Torsen torque sensing rear differential was between the rear wheels. The Ferguson VC was set to split the torque, 56 per cent to the front wheels, and 44 per cent to the rear.

Naturally the Delta had all-independent suspension by MacPherson struts, power-assisted steering, and four-wheel disc brakes. Compared with ordinary front-wheel-drive Deltas the only styling changes were to the nose, and by fitting special alloy road wheels.

Right away, Abarth's engineers saw that there were two important problems. One was that the standard car only had 185/60 14in. wheels, and rather restricted wheel arches, the other was that there was distinct need for more air flow in the engine bay.

Group A development went ahead rapidly in the autumn of 1986, and the definitive 'works' car was shown to the press in October 1986. By that time Ing. Lombardi had specified 15in. wheels, with a maximum tyre section of 205mm, which was a good deal less than FISA's Group A Regulations allowed. The problem, however, was that it was not permissible for tyres to protrude outside the wheelarches ....

Compared with the Delta S4's phenomenal power outputs, about which Lancia regularly boasted, claims for the HF 4WD were very

The Lancia Delta Integrale made a fine début in Portugal in March 1988. The wider wheels and the extra engine bay cooling arrangements are obvious in this shot.

(Ralph Hardwick)

In the 1000 Lakes, as in so many other events in 1987, Lancia reigned supreme. This was Markku Alen's car, jumping its way towards victory.

(Ralph Hardwick)

modest indeed. The first 'works' cars were said to develop only 230bhp, then 240bhp was claimed for the 1987 Monte cars. These figures were always greeted with suspicion by Lancia's rivals. Perhaps there was an element of verbal 'detuning' here by Lancia, to keep FISA's legislators happy? FISA wanted to see all cars running with less than 300bhp, so Lancia wanted to be seen to be well under that limit. The evidence of Lancia's performance in 1987, however, convinced the pundits that there was a lot more power on tap, or that Italian horses were *much* more brawny than ever they had been in the past.

Development work already completed included a choice of torque split percentages for the centre differential - 56/44, 50/50, 45/55 and 40/60 - and the inclusion of a pair of large holes in the front apron, which were certain to improve air flow in the engine bay area.

With massive support from Martini, and from the Pirelli tyre company, Lancia's 1987 driving team included Markku Alen, 'Miki' Biaison and Juha Kankkunen. Team chief Cesare Fiorio was so confident that he limited each of his top men to seven World Championship events, and would let them fight it out for the Drivers' crown.

The easy way to sum up the Delta's 1987 season is to use one word - Domination! The 'works' cars won eight World Championship events, with Franz Wittman's ex-works example winning once (in New Zealand), and also recorded an overwhelming number of second and third places too; such performances were only ever spoilt when the management decided to apply 'team orders'. Not only that, but Dario Cerrato used a Delta HF 4WD to win the European Rally Championship, scoring twice the points of his nearest rival.

The first victory, at Monte Carlo, not only saw Juha Kankunnen 'pulled' to finish behind Miki Biasion, but it saw Mazda's Achim Warmbold protest the winning Lancia on several counts. This protest was thrown out by the

The Lancia Delta HF 4WD never seemed to lose its poise - this was Miki Biasion's car on its way to third place in the Tour de Corse of 1987.

(Ralph Hardwick)

organisers, and no more grumbling was heard against Lancia for the rest of the season.

Mazda beat Lancia, fair and square, in Sweden, but Lancia won in Portugal. Lancia then missed the Safari, and were beaten by Bernard Beguin's BMW M3 in Corsica (though Loubet's Lancia was close). The Lancia 'steamroller' then rumbled on, with a 1-2 finish in the Acropolis, 1-2-3 in the Olympus, first in New Zealand, 1-2 in Argentina, first in the 1000 Lakes, first at San Remo, and first in the Lombard-RAC.

Along the way the Delta won the manufacturer's Championship at a canter, but the Drivers' series was not settled until the Lombard-RAC rally, where Alen rolled his car twice, Kankkunen picked up his second victory of the year, and won the title for the second year in succession.

During the year the car was progressively improved, and refined. Power was progressively lifted to an 'official' 260bhp, though some say that the quoted figure was less than the truth. The transmission became stronger, to cope with the above, but the choice of limited-slip mechanisms changed more than once. At one time the 'works' cars had extractor vents in the roof, but these were later withdrawn after rivals protested that they might also encourage aerodynamic downforce ....

Lancia also started the 1988 season in the same emphatic way, this time with the help of Michelin tyres. Bruno Saby won at Monte Carlo and Markku Alen in Sweden. Was there really any need to make any changes before 1989?

Lancia's 'works' team thought so. Even in 1986, Cesare Fiorio, Ing. Lombardi and Lancia's celebrated test driver Giorio Pianta were well aware of the Delta HF 4WD's shortcomings, and speedily asked management to approve a second-generation version of the car. The result was that an evolutionary version, the Delta HF Integrale, was unveiled in October of 1987. Production had already begun, the full 5,000 cars were produced in the next four months, and the Integrale was duly homologated on 1 March 1988.

The word 'Integrale' was used to denote a car which was now completely developed and optimised around its four-wheel-drive system, and was a better car in many respects. Although Fiorio had not been granted everything for which he asked (the 16-valve cylinder head, which would fit, and which had been used on the Rally 037 and, before that, on the Fiat Abarth 131 Rallye, was not specified), many of the *original* car's shortcomings had been overcome.

The Integrale had flared wheel arches, used 195/55-15in. tyres in standard form, and could use 16in. wheels in rally trim. This, and the fact that the car could therefore use even larger brakes than before, sorted out the chassis problems for the foreseeable future. A six-speed gearbox was to be homologated, but would not be rally-ready until the spring of 1988.

At the front of the car the apron seemed to be more hole than metal. This allowed much more air to enter the engine bay, and because larger intercooler, water cooling and oil cooling radiators were also fitted, peak power was raised to 185bhp at 5,300 rpm, and to at least 265 bhp in Group A Rally trim.

For the Integrale, Lancia had engineered the competition car first, then evolved the road car from it. Accordingly, the five-speed version went into its first event - the Portugese rally of 1988 - with confidence, and this was not misplaced. Although Mikael Ericsson's car broke its transmission, as did Markku Alen's car in front of the TV and film cameras on the very first stage, Miki Biasion's car was never headed, and won from two 1987-style Delta HF 4WDs. The best 'other make' was Hannu Mikkola's Mazda, a full 10 minutes adrift.

Although Ing. Lombardi had already commented that the team was now 'working on cars which we did not design in the first place' -which made one think that he was not too happy about the original situation, the Integrale was clearly to everyone's liking. Not only that, but a stronger six-speed gearbox was on the way. No-one was really surprised when Lancia took the new Integrale to the Safari rally - and won the event outright.

Even though Ford's rear-drive Sierra RS

Top Left

Lancia's Group A four-wheel-car, the Delta HF 4WD, took over successfully from the Delta S4 'Supercar' in 1987. It was not as successful on tarmac as in the loose, mainly because the wheel rims and tyres were not wide enough. Bruny Saby's car retired from the Tour de Corse after setting two fastest stage times.

(Martin Holmes)

Opposite

Lancia started its Group A programme with a bang - Miki Biasion's car winning the Monte Carlo rally from his teammate Juha Kankkunen.

Cosworth defeated them on the serpentine tar-mac roads of Corsica, no-one was prepared to forecast the next time that a 'works' Delta would be beaten. In 1988, as in so many previous years, it seemed that Lancia was *the* team to beat - the standard-setter for everyone else to match!

The 1988 Lancia Delta Integrale on test before starting its first event. Compared with the original Delta HF 4WD model, there were more, and larger, air intakes in the front panel, which helped cool a larger intercooler and the more powerful transverse engine. The wheelarches, too, were flared to allow fatter wheels and larger tyres to be fitted.

MAZDA 323 TURBO 4X4

Like the Lancia with which it was to compete for rally successes, the Mazda 323 Turbo 4WD was the 'flag-ship' of a very large range of family cars, which included three-door and five-door hatchbacks and five-door estate cars. The 'base' model in the 323 Familia was a 1.3-litre machine, with 74 bhp and front-wheel-drive, introduced in January 1985. The much more specialised four-wheel-drive hatchback followed in October 1985.

The new Mazda was similar in layout, size, and weight, to the Lancia, being 13ft. 1in./ 399cm long, and weighing about 2,450lb/1,110 kg. Its engine was at the front, and transversely-mounted, with the main gearbox (a five-speed all-synchromesh unit) mounted 'end on' to the crankshaft.

The engine itself was a 1,598cc four-cylinder unit. In the mass-market 323s it used a single-overhead camshaft with two valves per cylinder. For the four-wheel-drive car (and also, incidentally, for the 323 GT, which retained front-wheel-drive only) it was equipped with a twin-cam, four-valves per cylinder, head. Camshaft drive was by an internally toothed belt, and the bucket tappets enclosed hydraulic lifters.

This deep-breathing engine also had an IHI turbocharger, an air-to-air intercooler, and Nippondenso electronic fuel injection, the result being that in standard form it produced 148bhp (DIN) at 6,000 rpm. There must, however, have been aerodynamic limits to the cylinder head or turbocharger breathing, for the rally cars were never claimed to have more than 240 or 250bhp.

Like other transverse front-engined four-wheel-drive cars, that fitted to the Mazda was very simple - in effect it was a front-drive transmission with rear drive 'tapped' off the final drive at the front. Torque split was fixed at 50%/50%, and the entre differential was lockable via a dashboard-mounted switch. A limited-slip differential was not standard at the rear, but was optional for motorsport purposes.

One did not have to be a qualified transmission engineer to realise that the Mazda had a very simple (if not actually 'cheap and cheerful') four-wheel-drive system, which was not at all sophisticated by Group B standards. Mazda's European rally team, Mazda Rally Team (Europe), run by Achim Warmbold from West Germany, would have to live with is frailties until 1988.

The 323 4WD car was sold with 5.5in. rim wheels as standard, and with four-wheel disc brakes, but although it had twin 'cosmetic' spoilers above and below the rear window (which *might* - but probably did not - gave better balanced handling at high speeds), it did not have very capacious wheel arches, and was by no means an 'homologation special'. The Lancia Delta HF 4WD and the two-wheel-drive

BMW M3 and Ford Sierra RS Cosworth cars were able to take full advantage of FISA Group A rules, whereas the Mazda was not.

The 4WD Mazda went on sale in the autumn of 1985, and was homologated into Group A in July 1986. MRT (Europe) had already been using front-wheel-drive 323s before this date, and gave the 4WD Turbo model its World Championship début in the 1000 Lakes rally of Sepember 1986. On that event one Group A car blew its engine after two stages, and another broke its transmission, so it was a relief for Peter Geitel to win Group N in a privately-prepared example.

MRT (Europe) continued to have trouble with the car's transmission later in the year, but Ingvar Carlsson's Group A car, and David Maslen's privately-prepared Group N car won their category in the Lombard-RAC rally, while Rod Millen's USA-built car won Group A in the Olympus event in December.

In 1986 Mazda's rallying impact had been limited, but for 1987 there was to be a much more ambitious programme. Not only was Mazda likely to be fighting for outright victories, rather than for category wins, but MRT (Europe) also signed up Timo Salonen to lead the team.

Achim Warmbold soon homed in on the major problems. One was that the Mazda's main gearbox, frankly, was not capable of dealing with 250bhp where wheel grip was high. On ice and snow, perhaps, the car could be reliable, but on grippy gravel or tarmac it would not last the pace of a World Championship event. The other was that engines which produced 250bhp on the test bed often only produced 220bhp when installed in the chassis; this was mainly due to restricted engine bay air flow which raised air temperatures far too much.

At Monte Carlo, Salonen's car retired (of all things with persistent turbo pipe failures), while Ingvar Carlsson's car suffered similar problems but finished fourth (fifth until Stig Blomqvist's Ford Sierra MR4x4 was excluded), 10 minutes off the Lancia winning pace.

Three weeks later, in Sweden, Mikael Sundstrom's privately-prepared 323 led the rally until he rolled out of the event, after which Timo Salonen's 'works' car took over the lead, which he never lost. Ingvar Carlsson's sister car finished fourth overall.

Then the troubles started in earnest. Two

Mazda's 323 4WD car in action in the Rally of Portugal, where its lack of power was a big disadvantage against the Lancias.

Like other transverse engined cars, Mazda's 323 Turbo 4WD machine had a well-filled engine bay. The 16-valve engine is well-advertised!

(Martin Holmes)

On the Group A Mazda, the front skid shield not only protected the engine and transmission casings, but it also helped to extract hot air from the engine bay. It was that sort of attention to detail which made Group A cars so competitive, so quickly.

(Martin Holmes)

Mazda's 1987 1000 Lakes effort was a failure, but this shot clearly shows the compact lines of the transverse engined four-wheel-drive car.

(Ralph Hardwick)

323s started the Rally of Portugal, but Salonen's car broke a drive shaft, then its main transmission, at an early stage, while Carlsson's car repeated the same trick a few hours later.

After that debacle, MRT withdrew from rallying until mid-summer, and concentrated on the development and homologation of a new version of the car. Notable among that car's features were much enlarged air intakes in the nose, for the engine bay, which were intended to improve the efficiency of the intercooler and improve the cooling of the turbocharged engine.

The British Xtrac concern was contracted to produce a new six-speed gearbox, front and centre differentials; this would allow a variation in torque split between front and rear axles. Xtrac later began work on a new rear differential. These, as homologated options, were specified for the new version of the car, which was homologated from 1 July 1987 and duly made its first apperance in the Argentine rally in August 1987.

Nevertheless, the rest of the season was still a disaster, for Carlsson's car broke its transmission in Argentina, two engines blew up in the 1000 Lakes, and the team then failed to start the Lombard-RAC rally. The reason, quite starkly, was that FISA demanded proof that 5,000 of the revised car had actually been produced, and when permission to consult sales records at the Japanese factory was refused, the new car's homologation was rescinded.

Mazda, however, was determined to stay in world-class rallying, so for 1988 they paid FISA a hefty fine (reputed to be $250,000), rejigged

their options around the old-type 4WD car (whose homologation had not been rescinded) - which meant that MRT (E) could henceforth use the Xtrac transmission in the old-type car. Hannu Mikkola was persuaded to leave Audi after six successful years, and joined Timo Salonen and Ingvar Carlsson in what was clearly going to be a big effort. The team looked forward to better things in a new season.

Unhappily, time and other teams' development had marched on while MRT (E) was out of action, so at the start of the season the rejuvenated 323 was no nearer winning than it had been in mid-1987.

At Monte Carlo, the Xtrac transmission was still set at 50%/50%, and the Belgian-built engines produced about 220bhp. Early in the event Hannu Mikkola's car was forced out when it was discovered that there was diesel fuel in the petrol tank, while Carlsson crashed his example. Timo Salonen's car also suffered the diesel fuel problem, lost a lot of time, and later sustained a turbocharger failure, but eventually stormed back through the field to finish fifth overall.

Two cars were sent to Sweden for Mikkola and Salonen, but the 1000 Lakes problem repeated itself - both cars blew cylinder head gaskets after the first few hours. The same two cars then tackled the Portugese rally in March 1988, but Ingvar Carlsson's mount broke its   197

suspension after a brush with a non-competing car, while Hannu Mikkola's 323 finished fourth overall, behind three Lancia Deltas, but ten minutes behind the winner. Money already seemed to be a problem, even at that early stage of the season, and the four-wheel-drive 323 was faced with an uphill task for the rest of the season.

There was also the very Japanese problem of 'face' being lost, and no-one was prepared to forecast how long the company would put up with failure.

Even four-wheel-drive cars lift wheels sometimes - this was the 1988 Mazda, Hannu Mikkola at the wheel, on the 1988 Rally of Portugal.

(Ralph Hardwick)

The 1988 version of the Mazda 323 Turbo, still with 1987 styling, but now with a stronger transmission. Timo Salonen trying hard on the first, all-tarmac, stage.

AND NOT FORGETTING....
Other four-wheel-drive rally cars

The first four-wheel-drive machine to start a rally was almost certainly a Jeep, or a Land-Rover, but the first relatively modern attempt to produce a total-traction competition car was the BMC Twinni-Mini of 1963, where the normal front engine/front wheel drive pack in that stubby little 10 ft. saloon car was joined by another one in the tail, driving the rear wheels. F1 constructor John Cooper nearly lost his life in one of these cars, when it crashed inexplicably on the Kingston by-pass, near London, and another such car was driven by Paul Frère, without success, in the 1963 Targa Florio.

Then there was a lull, and it was not until the end of the 1960s that a trio of Ford Capri 4WD cars were produced. These had 3-litre vee-6 engines, the earlier, crude, type of Ferguson Formula transmission, and according to one of their drivers, Roger Clark, were real pigs to drive. Even so, they were good enough to win the U.K. Rallycross series of 1970/71 before being discarded.

There was still no place for four-wheel-drive in world-class rallying, so the occasional British appearances of Land-Rovers and Range Rovers were confined to events where there was a prototype, or special four-wheel-drive category, for them to contest. There *was*, however, one early win in a major event, where Gene Henderson's Jeep Wagoneer 4 x 4 won the USA's Championship Qualifier, the Press-on-Regardless rally of 1972.

When the use of

four-wheel-drive was authorised, cars like the Range Rover and Subaru were the first to take part, but the one was too large and bulky to be truly competitive, while the other (and its descendants, like the Leone of the mid-1980s) was under-powered, and not specifically developed for rallying.

The rush began in the 1980s when the Audi Quattro made its astonishing début. Not everyone, incidentally, remembers that the same four-wheel-drive system was used in every other Audi 80, 90, 100, and 200 of the early-1980s range. At one stage it was thought that the Audi 80 Quattro would be a very useful Group A, or even Group N, car, but Audi never found the time (or, to be honest, the enthusiasm) to develop this concept much further, though Stig Blomqvist drove an early (Group B) example into second place overall, in the 1983 Swedish rally, behind team-mate Mikkola's *real* Quattro!

The point has also been well-made that for World Championship Group A rallying, the turbocharged Audi 200 Turbo Quattro could be a very effective machine indeed. And don't think that the factory, and their drivers, have missed this possibility ....

Before the flood of purpose-built four-wheel-drive competition cars arrived in rallying, there was time for the American Chrysler Corporation to make their one-off, one-event, point. For the 1981 Safari, a team of four massive 5.9-litre vee-8 engined Dodge Ramchargers

were entered, two of them driven by no less notable drivers than Sandro Munari, and Robin Ulyate. These Range-Rover size, two-ton American machines, were quite outclassed, and both the European drivers had to retire with transmission problems, but the two American drivers, Malcolm Smith, and Rodney Hall, finished ninth and tenth respectively. That doyen of world rallying, Martin Holmes, later wrote that their arrival in Nairobi 'was greeted with a mixture of scepticism and humour', but they performed well for a first attempt. They were never seen again on a World Championship round.

In 1982 Opel spent a lot of time on a four-wheel-drive conversion of one of their still-unhomologated Manta 400s, the work on the Opel Manta 400 4 x 4 being carried out in the U.K. by FF Developments, in much the same way that this company had modified scores of Rekords, Commodores, Ford Granadas and the like. Even so, this was only a one-off prototype, which was never used in competition, as Opel was still committed to getting the rear-drive Manta 400 into World Championship rallying - and this was taking a great deal of time.

Another project with a very similar history to the Opel was the Mitsubishi Colt Starion 4 x 4 which was not built in Japan, but entrusted to Allan Wilkinson's British Ralliart concern in 1983 and 1984. Wilkinson had been Ford-Borehams chief engineer in the 1977-1980 period (when the Escort Mk II was at the height of its fame), and had a great deal of practical experience.

The 4 x 4 layout was similar to that of the Opel, in that an exposed front propeller shaft was taken up one side of the engine's cylinder block, and it seems that some components from the Pajero 4WD off-road vehicle (which regularly does so well in events like Paris-Dakar) were used. Unfortunately, by the time the car was adjudged rally-ready (it had competed, with some success, in the 1000 Pistes rally of 1984), it was clear that it had been overtaken by cars like the Peugeot 205 T16, so the project was cancelled. Mitsubishi, therefore, lost a little face, rather than a lot if they had homologated an obsolete car!

There was a lot of 4 x 4 activity in West Germany at this time. Porsche, having shown a 911 4 x 4 project car in 1981, allowed Walter Rohrl to test-drive it in 1982. More seriously, the VW

201

Below
Looking in to the engine bay of Rod Millen's Mazda RX7 4 × 4, showing the engine set well back behind the line of the front wheels, and the front differential over to the far (left) side of the bay, very close to the steering column U/J.
(Photo: Holmes)

Above
Rod Millen's four-wheel-drive Mazda RX7 was an intriguing one-off, financed by the Mazda factory. Here he is seen competing in the Michigan International, in the USA, in 1983.
(Photo: Holmes)

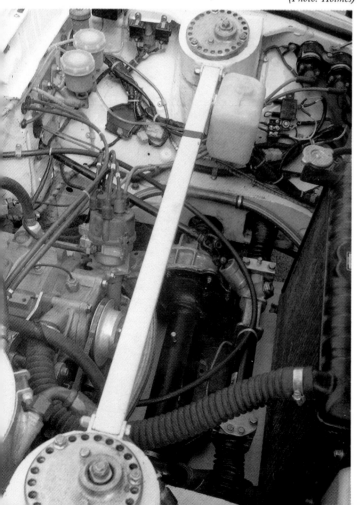

Above
The four-wheel-drive Mazda RX7 has the familiar FF-type of transmission layout, with a transfer gearbox behind the main gearbox, and a front propeller shaft leading up the left side of the rotary's engine's sump. *(Photo: Holmes)*

Top Right
The four-wheel-drive Subarus all use flat-four, overhead cam engines, which at least gives the scrutineers a fresh view on things when looking at competing cars.
(Photo: Holmes)

Centre Right
Subaru make many tens of thousands of four-wheel-drive cars every year, and such cars are entered in the Safari every year. This was one of the Fuji Heavy Industries 'works' entry of 1986. *(Photo: Holmes)*

Bottom Right
Mitsubishi rather half-heartedly carried out a 4 × 4 development programme in the U.K., on the basis of a turbocharged Starion coupé. Lasse Lampi drove it, successfully, in the 1000 Pistes event of 1984, to win the experimental cars category but the 200 homologation cars were never built.
(Photo: Holmes)

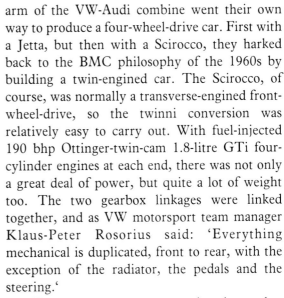

arm of the VW-Audi combine went their own way to produce a four-wheel-drive car. First with a Jetta, but then with a Scirocco, they harked back to the BMC philosophy of the 1960s by building a twin-engined car. The Scirocco, of course, was normally a transverse-engined front-wheel-drive, so the twinni conversion was relatively easy to carry out. With fuel-injected 190 bhp Ottinger-twin-cam 1.8-litre GTi four-cylinder engines at each end, there was not only a great deal of power, but quite a lot of weight too. The two gearbox linkages were linked together, and as VW motorsport team manager Klaus-Peter Rosorius said: 'Everything mechanical is duplicated, front to rear, with the exception of the radiator, the pedals and the steering.'

There was never any suggestion that such a car could be built in numbers, and homologated, so VW was eventually reduced to using it in events where homologation was not required. A twin-engined VW Golf GTi later raced up Pikes Peak considerably faster than the Americans had ever expected it could but by this time VW had adopted an entirely different, single-engined, 'Synchro' system for four-wheel-drive cars, and the twin-engined project has faded away.

Rod Millen's Mazda RX7 4×4, which was rallied exclusively in the USA, where FISA homologation was not required, was built at about the same time, and achieved several outright wins in competition with John Buffum's homologated Audi Quattro A1 model. The RX7 (which was superseded by a new-style RX7 4×4 in 1986) was the only rotary-engined four-wheel-drive car in top-class rallying at this time, and had a very similar front-engine/central transmission/FF-type 4×4 layout as several other such prototypes. Incidentally, this car was usually taken off the start line in rear-drive only.

One of the most significant new cars of 1983 was European Rallycross Champion Martin Schanche's Ford Escort Mk III 4×4. Ford, as a factory, had not been involved, for this was a private-enterprise effort, but in the seasons which followed this car did as much for Ford's competition reputation as any other model in their range.

Schanche, who had dominated rallycross in old-style rear-drive Escort Mk IIs, wanted to use a new-shape Escort Mk III, but wanted it to have four-wheel-drive in order to beat the Audi Quattros, and the specially-built Porsche 911

4×4s which were flooding into his sport.

The new car, therefore, was conceived in the U.K. by Schanche, David Bignold of Gartrac (whose company was used to building *rear*-drive conversions of front-wheel-drive Escorts), and Mike Endean (whose Xtrac-Hewland transmissions were very new). The result, first seen in the autumn of 1983, had a 500 bhp Zakspeed-Ford BDT turbocharged engine up front, installed in an in-line position, with a central gearbox and Xtrac hydraulic torque-splitter, and exposed propeller shafts to front and rear differentials. This was the car which blooded, and proved, the unique Endean/Xtrac system, with its continuously variable front/rear torque split facility, which has already been fully described in the Opel Kadett 4×4 chapter. Schanche won 22 rallycross events during 1984, to win the European Rallycross Championship against cars sometimes with 200 bhp more than the nimble Ford.

Replicas of that car were later built, notably for British rallycross expert John Welch, but another Ford Escort 4×4 found in rallycross, for which Ford-Boreham provided advice and some hardware, saw the transverse engine and end-on transmission retained, and four-wheel-drive taken to the rear wheels by an arrangement similar to that of the Citroen Visa 1000 Pistes.

There were two other interesting one-offs in 1984. The British tuning-shop, Rally Engineering Developments, produced the *RED 4T*, which used a much-modified rear-drive Ford XR4i, complete with turbocharged 2-litre BDA engine, in UK national events during 1984, and in 1985 they modified this to four-wheel-drive, using many FF Developments components (and some help from Ford Motor Co.), when in Willie Rutherford's hands it won two national events outright, and finished second in the National Championship.

Ford, itself, was not interested in this project, nor was it interested in the Ford Escort 4 x 4 produced by Welshman Alun Edwards. This was an astonishing cheap-and-cheerful one-off

Above
Alun Edwards's fierce Ford Escort 4 × 4 used a 3.4 litre four-camshaft Cosworth GA vee-6 engine, set well back in the engine bay, with some Ford Fiesta components in the front end .... *(Photo: Holmes)*

Opposite
This was the 'business-end' of the RED 4 × 4 one-off of 1985, with a specially cast engine sump also housing the front differential and drive shaft arrangements. *(Photo: Holmes)*

Top Left
One of the most successful 'home-brewed' 4 × 4 'specials' built in the mid-1980s was Martin Schanche's Ford Escort, which was originally dominant in rallycross, but which also competed in the USA, at the Pikes Peak hill climb, in 1984. *(Photo: Holmes)*

Centre Left
The Schanche Ford Escort had a Ford-based Zakspeed engine (producing about 500 bhp) up front, with an Xtrac transmission driving all four wheels. *(Photo: Holmes)*

Far Left
.... the front diff. casing being entirely separated from the sump pan. *(Photo: Holmes)*

Top Right
The enterprising British company, Rally Engineering Developments, rallied a turbocharged BDA-engined Ford Sierra XR4i in 1984, then converted it to four-wheel-drive in 1985. *(Photo: Holmes)*

Bottom Left
The rear end of Martin Schanche's Escort 4 × 4 shows just how far from the *original* front-drive Escort this chassis had been developed, for that is an 'Atlas' live axle, with radius arm location. *(Photo: Holmes)*

205

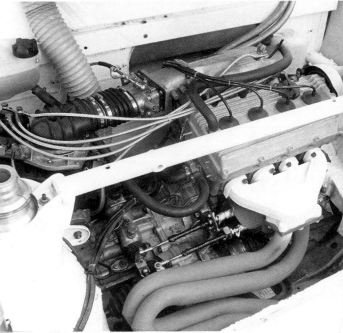

Above
The twin-engined VW Golf used 190 bhp 1.8 litre engines with Ottinger DOHC 16-valve cylinder head conversions. This particular view is of the rear unit ....

(Photo: Holmes)

Left
Jochi Kleint, ex-Opel team driver, was the brave young West German who drove the twin-engined VW Golf GTi at Pikes Peak in 1985.

(Photo: Holmes)

rally car, combining some Gartrac/Xtrac ideas with a brutally powerful Ford-Cosworth GA engine, a 1970s vintage 3.0-litre vee-6 of about 400 bhp *without* turbocharging, and (as one jealous competitor remarked) '£50 and a bag of welding wire'!

An in-line engine position was naturally chosen, while the front differential and drive shafts were derived from Ford's Fiesta Group 2 specification. This was always an exciting car to inspect, and to watch in action, but it was not very reliable. The second car, with even wider track and fatter wheels than before, was even more fearsome than the first.

Ford, in any case, were going into the four-wheel-drive mass-production business, for the Ford Sierra XR 4 x 4 was launched in the spring of 1985. This car was never intended to be a competition model, for it combined a well-equipped five-door hatchback body shell with the old push-rod 150 bhp fuel-injected 2.8-litre vee-6 and five speed gearbox of the Sierra XR4i/Capri 2.8i, with a slightly-modified FF Developments four-wheel-drive installation which included viscous coupling limited-slip differentials at the centre and the rear (but a free front differential), and a 34/66 front-to-rear fixed torque split.

The engine was known not to be very

Above
.... and there is clearly plenty of space compared with some 4 x 4 rally cars.
(Photo: Holmes)

Top Left
VW made a succession of twin-engined cars, thus achieving four-wheel-drive, in the early 1980s. This was the 1985 derivative, whose 1.8 GTi engines produced a total of 390 bhp.

tuneable, so Ford did not bother too much with it. Nevertheless, in truly Arctic conditions, the car was so sure footed that it started to win European Championship rallies outright, notably Boucles de Spa early in 1986. For the late 1980s, with a newly-designed vee-6 engine, the XR 4 x 4 *could* be a competitive Group A car ....

One project which was purely a 'spare time only' job was the twin-engined Lancia Trevi of 1984, which Lancia's chief engineer Giorgio Pianta built. This, incidentally, took shape at the same time as the Lancia Delta S4 was being finalised, and had a similar layout to all those other twinnis - BMC Mini-Cooper, Citroen Visa, and VW Jetta/Scirocco/Golf - of earlier years. Just for laughs - wasn't it?

The last project I must mention here has not appeared in public, and may never do so, now that FISA has changed the rules. Team Toyota Europe had used a series of front-engine/rear-drive Celicas with great honour, and a lot of success, particularly on 'endurance' rallies, from the early 1970s. In the early 1980s, faced with a change from Group 4 to Group B, and with the arrival of the Audi Quattros, TTE asked their Japanese masters for a new rally car. The result, announced early in 1983, was the conventional (though turbocharged with 320 bhp) Celica Twin Cam Turbo. As team chief Ove Andersson commented to the press, at the time: 'I asked for a four-wheel-drive car - and I got this!'

Nevertheless, the team won several World Championship events in 1984 and 1985, but a four-wheel-drive project was inevitable. By the end of 1984, not only had Toyota announced a new mid-transverse engined MR2 sports car, but similar new Celicas, and even four-wheel-drive Celicas, were on the way. In 1986, TTE were busily designing and developing a new four-wheel-drive Toyota Group S project - until FISA abruptly cancelled Group S proposals.

The Toyota may now never be seen, along with other exciting projects being considered for Group B, and Group S, in the late 1980s.

Four-wheel-drive came a long way, in rallying, in six years, but there were so many technical developments still to appear. With transmissions as complex as those used in the Porsche 959, and as versatile as those produced by Xtrac designer Mike Endean, still in their infancy, the prospects were enthralling.

Will rallying ever see a period like this again?

APPENDIX:
World championship rally successes by four-wheel-drive cars, 1981–1986 –1988

Four-wheel-drive rally cars took time to become established, but from 1983 there was no doubt that they would soon dominate most major events. By 1983, it was only the brilliance of the mid-engine/rear-drive Lancia 037 which was keeping the Audi Quattros at bay, and from 1984 on, two-wheel-drive cars were only 'winners' on events where durability was equally as important as four-wheel-drive traction.

Because of their cost and complication, it took time for four-wheel-drive cars to be taken up by competitors at European Championship level, and for that reason this Appendix concentrates on the World Championship scene. This is how World Championship rallying has changed in six short years:

1981: 12 qualifying events (for Makes *and* Drivers), 3 victories, 1 third place, 2 fourth places - all by Audi Quattros.

1982: 12 qualifying events (Makes *and* Drivers), 7 victories, 4 second places, 1 third place - all by Audi Quattros.

1983: 12 qualifying events (Makes *and* Drivers), 5 victories, 3 second places, 5 third places - all by Audi Quattros, of which one second was by 80 Quattro saloon.

1984: 12 qualifying events (Makes *and* Drivers), 10 victories, 6 second places, 5 third places - 7 wins by Audi Quattro, 3 by Peugeot 205 Turbo 16.

1985: 12 qualifying events (Makes *and* Drivers), 9 victories, 9 second places, 6 third places - 7 wins by Peugeot 205 Turbo 16, one by Audi Quattro (SI), one by Lancia Delta S4.

1986 : 13 qualifying events (Makes *and* Drivers) *including* San Remo, later annulled by FISA. All 'works' cars withdrew from Portugal after accidents to spectators; 10 victories, 9 second places, 9 thirds. Six wins by Peugeot 205T16, four by Lancia Delta S4.

_____

1987 : New Group A regulations applied. 13 qualifying events (Makes *and* Drivers). 11 victories, 8 seconds, 6 third places - a record 9 wins by Lancia Delta HF 4WD, one each by Mazda 323 4WD Turbo and Audi 200 Turbo.

1988 : (To May 1988, following the Tour de Corse) 5 qualifying events. 4 victories, 4 second places, 3 third places. All four victories to the Lancia Delta 4WD.